CHINA

THE RULERS OF CHINA

HISTORY, PHILOSOPHY, ECONOMICS

CHINA: HISTORY, PHILOSOPHY, ECONOMICS

I	The Chinese Economy	*Adler*
II	A Documentary History of Chinese Communism	*Brandt et al*
III	China's Economic System	*Donnithorne*
IV	A History of China	*Eberhard*
V	The Spirit of Chinese Philosophy	*Fung*
VI	Chuang Tzŭ	*Giles*
VII	People's War	*Girling*
VIII	China's Regional Development	*Goodman*
IX	Health Care and Traditional Medicine in China	*Hillier & Jewell*
X	The Political Philosophy of Confucianism	*Hsü*
XI	Religion in China	*Hughes & Hughes*
XII	Ta T'ung Shu	*K'ang*
XIII	China's Foreign Relations since 1949	*Lawrance*
XIV	Confucian China and its Modern Fate V1	*Levenson*
XV	Confucian China and its Modern Fate V2	*Levenson*
XVI	Confucian China and its Modern Fate V3	*Levenson*
XVII	Crisis and Conflict in Han China	*Loewe*
XVIII	The Performing Arts in Contemporary China	*Mackerras*
XIX	The Rulers of China	*Moule*
XX	The Fading of the Maoist Vision	*Murphey*
XXI	The Grand Titration	*Needham*
XXII	Within the Four Seas	*Needham*
XXIII	Education in Modern China	*Price*
XXIV	Sino-Russian Relations	*Quested*
XXV	Contest for the South China Sea	*Samuels*
XXVI	The Classical Theatre of China	*Scott*
XXVII	Macartney at Kashgar	*Skrine & Nightingale*
XXVIII	The Analects of Confucius	*Waley*
XXIX	Ballads and Stories from Tun-Huang	*Waley*
XXX	The Book of Songs	*Waley*
XXXI	Chinese Poems	*Waley*
XXXII	The Life and Times of Po Chü-i	*Waley*
XXXIII	The Opium War Through Chinese Eyes	*Waley*
XXXIV	The Real Tripitaka	*Waley*
XXXV	The Secret History of the Mongols	*Waley*
XXXVI	Three Ways of Thought in Ancient China	*Waley*
XXXVII	The Way and its Power	*Waley*
XXXVIII	Yuan Mei	*Waley*
XXXIX	Confucius and Confucianism	*Wilhelm*
XL	Sociology and Socialism in Contemporary China	*Wong*

THE RULERS OF CHINA

221 BC - AD 1949

A C MOULE

Routledge
Taylor & Francis Group
LONDON AND NEW YORK

First published 1957 by Routledge

2 Park Square, Milton Park, Abingdon, Oxon OX14 4RN
711 Third Avenue, New York, NY 10017, USA

Routledge is an imprint of the Taylor & Francis Group, an informa business

First issued in paperback 2016

British Library Cataloguing in Publication Data
A CIP catalogue record for this book
is available from the British Library

The Rulers of China
ISBN 978-0-415-36163-7 (hbk)
ISBN 978-1-138-99366-2 (pbk)

China: History, Philosophy, Economics

THE RULERS OF CHINA

221 B.C.—A.D. 1949

Chronological Tables
compiled by

A. C. MOULE

With an Introductory Section
on the Earlier Rulers c. 2100–249 B.C.

by

W. PERCEVAL YETTS

ROUTLEDGE AND KEGAN PAUL
London

Preface

In 1933, when Chinese research became for a time part of my duty, I asked Paul Pelliot if he could recommend me any useful piece of work to do which would not be beyond my powers, of which he better than anyone else knew the limitations. He said that I had already printed Tables of two dynasties which gave more detailed dates and other information than do the Tables commonly employed, and that he thought it would be really useful if I would make similar, but even more detailed, Tables of all the dynasties. I set to work at once, but had only done the Ch'in dynasty when my unexpected collaboration with Pelliot himself in his work on Marco Polo began to fill all my spare time. The dynasties were put away till the war brought unwelcome leisure and in a Norfolk rectory amid the incessant din of English, American, and sometimes German aeroplanes I was able at last to finish a rough draft of all the dynasties; nor did I dream that Pelliot would not live to see and criticize the work which he had encouraged me to begin.

To the end of the Ming dynasty the Tables were based at first on the 二十四史 Erh shih ssŭ shih (ed. 集成圖書公司, Shanghai, 1908), without access to other sources for correction or corroboration. I had by me also the handbooks, M. Tchang Synchronismes chinois, 1905; P. Hoang Concordance des Chronologies néoméniques.., 1910; 中國人名大辭典 Chung kuo jên ming ta tzŭ tien, 3rd ed., 1923; 中國文學家大辭典 Chung kuo wên hsüeh chia ta tzŭ tien, 1934; 姜亮夫 Chiang Liang-fu 歷代名人年里碑傳總表 Li tai ming jên nien li pei chuan tsung piao, 1937; and 胡正支 Hu Chêng-chih 中國帝號標題一覽 Chung kuo ti hao piao t'i i lan, 1939.

While I was in Norfolk and after my return to Cambridge the inexhaustible kindness & learning of the late Professor Gustav Haloun added very greatly to the value of the Tables for at least two dynasties, Liao and Wu Yüeh; and I have myself been able, still under his guidance at first and later with the help of Mr H.C. Chang, to take some further details from the 會要 Hui yao of the 唐 T'ang, 五代 Wu tai, and 宋 Sung, from the 明實錄 Ming shih lu, and from some other sources.

The very great majority of the dates given are the best available, but unfortunately that does not mean that they are certainly right, for if the Chinese have had a most laudable passion for recording exact dates they seem to have had an almost equal passion for misprinting them. Thus in the "New China Review", 1912, p. 452, after giving the dates of some of Matteo Ricci's movements, I wrote, "The Chinese history is inaccurate in every date"; and in Christians in China, 1930, p. 221, there is a list of 37 extant decrees referring to Christians in the Mongol dynasty, and then, "It is curious that the dates do *not agree exactly with the dates of any of the decrees referring to Christians which are recorded in the Yüan shih or Yüan tien chang".*

Professor Yetts's contribution of his original chronology of the Three Dynasties adds greatly to the value and completeness of the book. To him; to Sir Percival David whose generosity has made the transcription of my Tables possible; to Mr H. C. Chang (張心滄), who has not only copied half my untidy draft but has corrected mistakes, checked references, and found new sources for me; to Miss M. I. Scott for very kind and expert help in the University Library; to Mr Rawlings and other friends there; to the memory of Paul Pelliot and of Gustav Haloun, I owe a debt of most special gratitude.

A. C. M.

Cambridge

Contents

CONTENTS

The Cycle

1. 甲子 *chia-tzŭ*	2. 乙丑 *i-ch'ou*	3. 丙寅 *ping-yin*	4. 丁卯 *ting-mao*	5. 戊辰 *mou-ch'ên*	6. 己巳 *chi-ssŭ*	7. 庚午 *kêng-wu*	8. 辛未 *hsin-wei*	9. 壬申 *jên-shên*	10. 癸酉 *kuei-yu*
11. 甲戌 *chia-hsü*	12. 乙亥 *i-hai*	13. 丙子 *ping-tzŭ*	14. 丁丑 *ting-ch'ou*	15. 戊寅 *mou-yin*	16. 己卯 *chi-mao*	17. 庚辰 *kêng-ch'ên*	18. 辛巳 *hsin-ssŭ*	19. 壬午 *jên-wu*	20. 癸未 *kuei-wei*
21. 甲申 *chia-shên*	22. 乙酉 *i-yu*	23. 丙戌 *ping-hsü*	24. 丁亥 *ting-hai*	25. 戊子 *mou-tzŭ*	26. 己丑 *chi-ch'ou*	27. 庚寅 *kêng-yin*	28. 辛卯 *hsin-mao*	29. 壬辰 *jên-ch'ên*	30. 癸巳 *kuei-ssŭ*
31. 甲午 *chia-wu*	32. 乙未 *i-wei*	33. 丙申 *ping-shên*	34. 丁酉 *ting-yu*	35. 戊戌 *mou-hsü*	36. 己亥 *chi-hai*	37. 庚子 *kêng-tzŭ*	38. 辛丑 *hsin-ch'ou*	39. 壬寅 *jên-yin*	40. 癸卯 *kuei-mao*
41. 甲辰 *chia-ch'ên*	42. 乙巳 *i-ssŭ*	43. 丙午 *ping-wu*	44. 丁未 *ting-wei*	45. 戊申 *mou-shên*	46. 己酉 *chi-yu*	47. 庚戌 *kêng-hsü*	48. 辛亥 *hsin-hai*	49. 壬子 *jên-tzŭ*	50. 癸丑 *kuei-ch'ou*
51. 甲寅 *chia-yin*	52. 乙卯 *i-mao*	53. 丙辰 *ping-ch'ên*	54. 丁巳 *ting-ssŭ*	55. 戊午 *mou-wu*	56. 己未 *chi-wei*	57. 庚申 *kêng-shên*	58. 辛酉 *hsin-yu*	59. 壬戌 *jên-hsü*	60. 癸亥 *kuei-hai*

CHRONOLOGICAL TABLES
OF
THE THREE DYNASTIES
三 代

C. 2100 — 249 B.C.

Compiled by
W. PERCEVAL YETTS

HSIA DYNASTY

夏代 CLAN: SSŬ 姒 c. 2100 – c. 1600 B.C.

① Yü 禹. Reigned 45 yrs. (Formerly Po Hsia 伯夏 Wên Ming 文命) [Yü]

② Ch'i 啟. Hui 會. Reigned 39 yrs. Died aged 78. (Ch'i) [Ch'i. Chien 建. Yü Tê 余德. Reigned 9 yrs. Died aged over 80.]

③ Ta K'ang 大康 (T'ai 太 K'ang) [T'ai K'ang Reigned 29 yrs] ④ (Chung K'ang 仲(or 中)康) [ditto]

⑤ Hsiang 相. His 7th. yr. mentioned. (Hsiang) [Hsiang. Hsiang An 相安]

⑥ Shao K'ang 少康 (Shao K'ang) [Shao K'ang]

⑦ Chu 宁 or 杼. (Chu 宁 or 予) [Chu 杼, 宁, or 予. Kung-sun Man 公孫曼. Reigned 17 yrs.]

⑧ Fên 芬. Reigned 44 yrs. (Hui 槐) [Fên. Hui. Tsu Wu 祖武. Reigned 26 yrs.]

⑨ Huang 荒. Wang, Huang, or Mang 芒 Accession in 58th yr. (Huang etc.) [ditto & Ho 和]

⑩ Hsieh 世. His 21st. yr. mentioned. (Hsieh) [Hsieh. Shih 世. Hsieh Tsung 泄宗. Reigned 16 yrs.]

⑪ Pu Chiang 不降. Reigned 69 yrs. (Pu Chiang) [Pu Chiang. Chiang 降. Pei Ch'êng 北成]

⑫ Chiung 扃. (Chiung) [Chiung. Yü 禺 Kao Yang 高陽. Reigned 21 yrs.]

⑭ (K'ung Chia 孔甲) [K'ung Chia]

⑬ Chin 廑. Yin Chia 胤甲. (Chin) [Hsü 頊 Tung Chiang 董江. Reigned 20 yrs.]

⑮ Kao or Hao 昊. Reigned 3 yrs. (Kao 皐) [Kao 皋. Kao Kou 皋苟]

⑯ Fa 發. Ching 敬. (Fa) [Fa]

⑰ Chieh 桀 (Chieh Li Kuei 履癸) [Chieh]

This Table is compiled from the *Bamboo Annals*, the *Shih Chi*, and the *Ti wang shih chi*. Items from the two latter are written within curved and squared brackets, respectively, to distinguish them. The *Annals* say: "From Yü to Chieh the reigns of 17 kings, together with the period without a king, lasted 471 years." The interregnum was when Prince I 羿 seized the power and afterwards his henchman Han Cho 寒浞 murdered and succeeded him. In the *Ti wang shih chi* these two usurpers appear between Hsiang and Shao K'ang in the list of 19 Hsia kings. Evidently their years of rule are not counted in the 432 which Huang-fu Mi assigns to the dynasty, since the term by which this figure falls short of the other is about the same as that of the usurpation. Besides the listed 19 kings Huang-fu Mi mentions Ti Ch'iao 帝喬, brother of Pu Chiang, and Ti Kuang 帝廣, son of Ti Ch'iao. The alternative name Pei Ch'êng, attributed to Pu Chiang, is written 北城 in the *Shih pên* (IV, 12). Chang Chu 張澍 in his A.D. 1821 reconstruction of that book declares "Pei Ch'êng" a mistake, and he cites from two different sources either "Chiang Ch'êng 江成" or "Chiang Wu 江武" as being more likely.

SHANG-YIN DYNASTY

商殷代 CLAN: TZŬ 子 c.1600 – c.1050 B.C.

① Ta I 大乙. T'ang 唐. (T'ien I 天乙. Ch'êng T'ang 成湯. T'ang 湯) = Pi Ping 丙

Ta Ting 大丁 (T'ai 太 Ting) = Pi Mou 妣戊 ② Pu Ping 卜丙 (Wai Ping 外丙 Shêng 勝) ③ Nan Jên 南壬 (Chung Jên 中(or 仲)壬, T'ai Tsung 太宗)

④ Ta Chia 大甲 (T'ai 太 Chia) = Pi Hsin 妣辛

⑤ ? Tsu Ting □ 祖丁 (Wu Ting 沃丁. Hsüan 絢) ⑥ Ta Kêng 大庚 (T'ai 太 Kêng. Hsiao 小 Kêng Pien 辨) = Pi Jên 妣壬

⑦ Hsiao Chia 小甲 (Hsiao Chia Kao 高) ⑧ ? (Yung Chi 雍己. Chou 伷) ⑨ Ta Mou 大戊 (T'ai 太 Mou. Chung Tsung 中宗) = Pi Jên 妣壬

⑩ Chung Ting 仲丁 (Chung Ting) = Pi Chi 妣己, Pi Kuei 妣癸 ⑪ Pu Jên 卜壬 (Wai Jên 外壬) ⑫ ? Chia □ 甲 (Ho Tan Chia 河亶甲. Chêng 整)

⑬ Tsu I 祖乙 (Tsu I. T'êng 滕) = Pi Chi 妣己, Pi Kêng 妣庚

⑭ Tsu Hsin 祖辛 (Tsu Hsin) = Pi Chia 妣甲, Pi Kêng 妣庚 ⑮ Ch'iang Chia 羌甲 (Wu Chia 沃甲. Ti K'ai Chia Yü 帝開甲踰)

⑯ Tsu Ting 祖丁 (Tsu Ting) = Pi Chia 妣甲, Pi Mou 妣戊, Pi Chi 妣己, Pi Kêng 妣庚, Pi Kuei 妣癸 ⑰ Nan Kêng 南庚 (Nan Kêng. Kêng 更)

⑱ ? Chia □ 甲 (Yang Chia 陽甲) ⑲ P'an Kêng 般庚 (P'an Kêng 盤庚 Hsün 旬) c.1325 B.C. ⑳ Hsiao Hsin 小辛 (Hsiao Hsin. Sung 頌) ㉑ Hsiao I 小乙 (Hsiao I. Han 斂) = Pi Kêng 妣庚

㉒ Wu Ting 武丁 (Wu Ting. Kao Tsung 高宗) = Pi Mou 妣戊, Pi Hsin 妣辛, Pi Kuei 妣癸 c.1230 B.C.

㉓ Tsu Kêng 祖庚 (Tsu Kêng. Yao 曜) c.1171 B.C. ㉔ Tsu Chia 祖甲 (Tsu Chia. Ti Chia 帝甲. Tsai 載) c.1164 B.C. = Pi Mou 戊, Pi Chi 己

㉕ Hsiung Hsin 兄辛 (Lin Hsin 廩辛. Fêng Hsin Hsien 馮辛先) c.1131 B.C. ㉖ K'ang Ting 康丁 (Kêng Ting 庚丁) c.1127 B.C. = Pi Hsin 妣辛

㉗ Wu I 武乙. Wu Tsu 武祖 I (Wu I) = Pi Mou 妣戊 c.1123 B.C.

㉘ Wên Wu Ting 文武丁 (T'ai Ting 太丁. Ta Ting 大丁. Wên Ting 文丁) c.1088 B.C.

㉙ Fu I 父乙 (Ti I 帝乙. I 乙) c.1077 B.C.

㉚ □□ (Ti Hsin 帝辛. Chou 紂. Shou 受. Ti Hsin Shou 帝辛受) c.1075 B.C.

SHANG-YIN DYNASTY

(continued)

The Oracular Sentences provide our primary entries of names and the archaic script in which they are written. Within brackets are the traditional names as preserved in the 3rd and 13th chapters of the Shih chi and the 20th chapter of the Ch'ien Han shu. Ta Ting, second on the list, is without a serial number because he is said not to have reigned, having died before his father. Dates are few for lack of credible information; what there are will be justified presently.

The chief estimate of the dynasty's duration comes from the Bamboo Annals in these words: "From T'ang's extinguishing of the Hsia until Shou 受 there were 29 kings [whose reigns] covered 496 years. Presumably the reckoning ends at the accession of the last king. Mencius's utterance that "from T'ang until King Wên there were 500 years and more" may amount to only a slight increase (Chinese Classics, II 502). The sayings of a philosopher named Yü Hsiung 鬻熊 in the 3rd century B.C. were collected in the T'ang period and reconstituted at the end of the 19th century in a small book entitled Yü tzŭ. In it the reigns are counted as 27 and the years as 567 stretching from T'ang's seizure of the throne to the last king. According to the Tso chuan, 600 years were assigned to the dynasty by King Ting's envoy answering in 606 B.C. a Ch'u prince's sneers at the decline of Chou power (Chinese Classics, V 293). All considered, about 550 years seem a fair compromise that warrants our date c. 1600 B.C. for the start of the dynasty.

More is known about chronology after the capital was removed to An-yang. A comprehensive measure of this later period comes from the Bamboo Annals in the following entry: "During the 273 years which elapsed between P'an Kêng's move to Yin and the downfall of Chou 紂 there was no further transfer of the capital." Actually the number of years varies in different quotations, one giving 773, another 275. Commentators agree that "773" is a misprint for "273". Denial of any further transfer conflicts with the tradition, repeated in the Ti wang shih chi, that Ti I 帝乙 removed the capital to Chao-kê 朝歌, a tradition which archaeology confirms. It is a warning against blind acceptance of everything stated in the Bamboo Annals.

KING	YEARS	AUTHORITY
P'an Kêng	95 (P'an Kêng, Hsiao Hsin, Hsiao I)	
Hsiao Hsin		
Hsiao I		
Wu Ting	59	Wu i 無逸 of the Shu ching
Tsu Kêng	7	Shih chi as quoted in T'ai p'ing yü lan
Tsu Chia	33	Wu i of the Shu ching
Hsiung Hsin	4	
K'ang Ting	4	
Wu I	35	Bamboo Annals
Wên Wu Ting	11	"
Ti I	2	"
Ti Hsin	25	Inscription on the Tsai Ch'ü chio 宰椃角

The above list is tentatively devised on the assumption that the last 12 reigns covered approximately 275 years from 1325 to 1050 B.C. Reliable information is

SHANG-YIN DYNASTY
(*continued*)

lacking about lengths of reigns beyond 1325 B.C. Accession dates which are
in the Table accord with the above list, and they are highly speculative as may
be judged from the following observations. In respect of only 7 of these 12
kings are there definite clues to the length of time each occupied the throne.
Moreover, only the reigns of Wu Ting and Tsu Chia are completely accounted
for; the others are given minimum figures derived from mention of a certain
year in each reign. Mention in the *Bamboo Annals* of the 35th year
of Wu I conflicts with a generalization in the *Shu ching* that comes after figures
for the reigns of Wu Ting (called Kao Tsung) and Tsu Chia quoted in the above list.
It says: "The kings who arose after these enjoyed ease all their lives.... They sought
after excessive pleasures so that not one could attain longevity: some [were on the
throne] 10 years, some 7 or 8 years, some 5 or 6 years, and some 3 or 4 years"
(*Cf. Chinese Classics* III 468). On the strength of this passage we guess the years
reigned by Hsiung Hsin and K'ang Ting to have been 4 in each case. Cause
to assign a minimum of 25 years to Ti Hsin may be recognized in the well-known
inscription on the *Tsai Ch'ü chio* (*Yin wên ts'un*, 殷文存, 下, 23). It tells how
Tsai Ch'ü cast the vessel to commemorate a royal gift of 5 strings of cowries
he received when in attendance on the king at a place called Lan 闌 in the
25th year. Tung Tso-pin gives reasons for his belief that Tsai Ch'ü was a son of
the King Wên Wu Ting whom he identifies with the Fu Ting 父丁 named in
the inscription as the recipient of sacrifices to be offered in the vessel. If that was
so, the "25th year" must refer to the reign of Ti Hsin (*Yin li p'u* 殷曆譜,
下, II 37). The 7 years are allotted in the list to Tsu Kêng on the evidence of an
alleged quotation in the *T'ai p'ing yü lan*, LXXXIII, though we cannot trace the
original statement in any available text of the *Shih chi*.

The years assigned in our list to the last 9 kings, when added together,
total 180. That number before c. 1050 B.C. points to a tentative estimate of
c. 1230 B.C. for the accession of Wu Ting. It is a date that tallies with Dubs's
conclusion, based on identification of certain eclipses mentioned in the Oracular
Sentences, that "King Wu-ding reigned about 1200 B.C." (*The Date of the Shang
Period* in *T'oung Pao*, XL (1951)).

CHOU DYNASTY

周代 CLAN : CHI 姬 c. 1050 – 249 B.C.

① Wu 武 (Fa 發) = I Chiang 邑姜 c. 1050 B.C.

② Ch'êng 成 (Sung 誦 or Yung 庸) c. 1047 B.C.

③ K'ang 康 (Chao 釗) c. 1017 B.C.

④ Chao 昭 (Hsia 瑕) = Fang Hou 房后 c. 992 B.C.

⑤ Mu 穆 (Man 滿) c. 973

⑥ Kung 共 or 恭 (I-hu 繄扈 or 伊扈) c. 918 B.C. ⑧ Hsiao 孝 (Pi-fang 辟方 or Fang 方) c. 900 B.C.

⑦ I 懿 (Chien 囏 or 堅) c. 903 B.C.

⑨ Yi 夷 (Hsieh 燮 or 爕) c. 893 B.C.

⑩ Li 厲 (Hu 胡) = Shên Chiang 申姜 c. 861 B.C.

Regency: Kung-ho 共和 841 – 828 B.C.

⑪ Hsüan 宣 (Ching 靜 or 靖) 827 B.C.

⑫ Yu 幽 (Kung-nieh 宮湦) = Shên Chiang 申姜 781 B.C.

⑬ P'ing 平 (I-chia 宜臼 or 宜咎) c. 772 B.C. (12A) Hsi Wang 攜王 (Yü Ch'ên 余臣) 770 – 760 B.C.

Hsieh Fu 洩父

⑭ Huan 桓 (Lin 林) = Chi Ch'i Chiang 紀季姜 719 B.C.

⑮ Chuang 莊 (To 佗 or 它 or 他) 696 B.C. = Yao 姚 (concubine)

⑯ Hsi 僖 or 釐 (Hu-ch'i 胡齊 or Hu 胡) 681 B.C. (16A) T'ui 頹 675 – 673 B.C.

⑰ Hui 惠 (Lang 閬 or Liang 涼 or Wu Liang 毋涼) 675 B.C. = Ch'ên Kuei 陳媯

⑱ Hsiang 襄 (Chêng 鄭) = Ti Wei 狄隗 c. 651 B.C. (18A) Shu Tai 叔帶. Kan Chao Kung 甘昭公 636 – 635 B.C.

⑲ Ch'ing 頃 (Jên-ch'ên 壬臣 or Wang-ch'ên 王臣 or Chü 巨 c. 618 B.C.

⑳ K'uang 匡 (Pan 班) 612 B.C. ㉑ Ting 定 (Yü 瑜) = Ch'i Chiang 齊姜 606 B.C.

CHOU DYNASTY

(continued)

(21) Ting 定 (Yü 瑜) = Ch'i Chiang 齊姜 606 B.C.

(22) Chien 簡 (I 夷) 585 B.C.

(23) Ling 靈 (Hsieh-hsin 泄心 or Ta-hsin 大心) = Ch'i Chiang 齊姜 571 B.C.

(24) Ching 景 (Kuei 貴 or I 遺) = Mu Hou 穆后 544 B.C.

(25A) Tao 悼 (Mêng 猛) Reigned 200 days 520 B.C.

(25) Ching 敬 (Kai 丐 or 匄) 519 B.C.

(26) Yüan 元 (Jên 仁 or Ch'ih 赤) c. 476 B.C.

(27) Ting 定 (Chai 介) c. 469 B.C.

(28) K'ao 考 or K'ao Chê 考哲 (Wei 嵬 or 隗) c. 440 B.C.

(29) Wei Lieh 威烈 (Wu 午) 425 B.C.

(30) An 安 or Yüan An 元安 (Chiao 驕 or Tan 耽 or Mang 駹) c. 401 B.C.

(31) Lieh 烈 or I Lieh 夷烈 (Hsi 喜) 375 B.C.

(32) Hsien 顯 or Hsien Shêng 顯聖 (Pien 扁) 368 B.C.

(33) Shên Ching 慎靚 or 慎竫 (Ting 定) 320 B.C.

(34) Nan 赧 or Wang Nan 王赧 or Yin 隱 or Jan 然 (Yen 延 or Tan 誕) 314–256 B.C.

(28A) Ai 哀 (Ch'ü-chi 去疾) Reigned 3 months c. 440 B.C.

(28B) Ssŭ 思 (Shu-hsi 叔襲) Reigned 5 months c. 440 B.C.

(28C) Hsi Chou Huan Kung 西周桓公 (Chieh 揭)

(29A) Hsi Chou Wei Kung 西周威公

(30A) Hsi Chou Hui Kung 西周惠公

(31A) Hsi Chou Wu Kung 西周武公

(32A) Hsi Chou Wên Kung 西周文公 –249 B.C.

(31B) Tung Chou Hui Kung 東周惠公 (Pan 班 or Chieh 傑) 367 B.C.

(32B) Tung Chou Wu Kung 東周武公 359 B.C.

CHOU DYNASTY

(continued)

This Table is compiled mainly from Chapters IV, XIII, XIV, and XV of the *Shih chi*. Most of the other sources used are of pre-Han date. Personal names of kings are within brackets. Ssŭ-ma Ch'ien includes in his lists the names of only 34 Chou kings belonging to 30 generations. His lead is generally followed and we follow it to the extent of numbering the same set 1 to 34. But we add certain Kings omitted from the standard series either because their reigns were too brief or because final opinion denied them kingship. Each of them, whether an ephemeral or a duplicate king, is here given the same serial number as his contemporary among the chosen 34, but to avoid confusion it is coupled with a letter of the alphabet. History of the dynasty near its close is almost as obscure as at its beginning, yet the fact is clear that after 256 B.C., when both King Nan and Prince Wu of Western Chou died, the royal house was still represented for 7 years by 2 princes who divided between them a dwindling autonomy. Accordingly our Table extends that far beyond the 34 standard kings. Ch'in 秦 aggression ended the dynasty in 249 B.C., the princes being exiled, the remnants of their possessions seized, and their subjects dispersed. In the words of Ssŭ-ma Ch'ien, "thereafter the Chou sacrifices ceased 周既不祀."

Western books of reference usually start the Chou dynasty from the defeat and death of the last Shang-Yin king, and here we conform to custom. Certainly overlapping of the two dynasties is thus avoided. Chinese opinion, however, is inclined to the view that the dynasty really began some 10 years before the conquest when the future King Wên, then Chief of the West, is reputed to have received the divine mandate. An inscription on a bronze cauldron, cast not long after that time, contains this sentence: "The illustrious King Wên received the great mandate by heaven's favour, and it fell to the lot of King Wu, having succeeded [King] Wên, to establish the state 丕顯玟王受天佑大命在珷王嗣玟作邦". Often called the "Large Yü Ting, 大盂鼎", this cauldron is said to have been unearthed early last century some 70 miles west of Ch'ang-an in Shensi together with the "Small Yü Ting" which will be mentioned later.

The notion of the divine mandate forfeited by a dynasty through misrule and transferred to its successor may have been invented by the Chou to vindicate them in their conquest and so reconcile former Shang-Yin subjects to the new régime. For years the Chou seem to have felt insecure, and the notion is echoed frequently in the classics, notably in the *To fang* 多方 of the *Shu ching*. The instance just quoted from the cauldron is not the only one among bronze inscriptions. Stress on the mandate is echoed again in a method of counting years irrespective of individual reigns. For instance, the "11th year" assigned to the conquest in the *Shu Preface* and repeated by Ssŭ-ma Ch'ien cannot mean the 11th year of King Wu's reign (*Chinese Classics*, III *Proleg.* 7; *Mém. hist.*, I 227; IV 38, 88). Nor can the "13th year" in the opening words of the Great Plan 洪範 be counted according to his reign. Two notations existed, dynastic and regnal, as certain early commentators perceived and as Wang Kuo-wei recently demonstrated. He lists examples of the dual reckoning for the 20 years just after the reputed mandate (*Kuan t'ang pieh chi*, *pu i* 觀堂別集, 補遺, 4–8).

A crucial problem of Chou chronology is the dating of the conquest. It is crucial because most of the scanty clues to absolute dating before the conquest and 2 centuries after it depend upon the date of the conquest as a basic point of reckoning. The chronological tables of Ssŭ-ma Ch'ien leave the problem unsolved; for the earliest exact date indicated in them is that of the 1st year of the Regency (Kung Ho)

CHOU DYNASTY

(continued)

corresponding to 841 B.C. In contrast to the general haziness before that date a meticulous measurement of time appears in the Bamboo Annals. It reads: "From the extinction of Yin by King Wu until King Yu there were in all 257 years." Presumably King Yu's death is meant, and, since that occurred in 771 B.C., the conquest is thus dated exactly 1027 B.C. Such precision implies an accuracy of record sustained over a long period which seems improbable. There is, too, history of the text's integrity being repeatedly imperilled during discovery, reconstruction, and survival. Fragments of the original that remain are preserved in quotations by early writers, and they sometimes disagree. We hesitate to accept for the Table this exact and solitary figure of 257 unless full support for it can be found elsewhere. A search reveals that the balance of evidence, while not actually denying it, points to a slightly larger sum of years. All considered, we prefer to adopt the round figure c.1050 B.C.

Between c.1050 for the conquest and the beginning of the Regency in 841 the years total 209. The following list and notes state how these years are apportioned among the 10 reigns, thereby explaining the approximate accession dates shown in the Table:—

KING	YEARS	AUTHORITY
Wu	3	Hung fan 洪範 and Chin t'êng 金縢 of the Shu ching
Ch'êng	30	Ch'ien Han shu
K'ang	25	Inscription on the Hsiao Yü Ting 小盂鼎
Chao	19	Bamboo Annals
Mu	55	Shih chi
Kung	15	Inscription on the Ch'io Ts'ao Ting 趞曹鼎
I	3	
Hsiao	7	Bamboo Annals
Yi	32	Inscription on the Kuo Yu Ts'ung Ting 鬲攸从鼎
Li	20	Shih chi

According to the Shu ching, King Wu died in the 13th year of the dynasty and 2 years after the one in which he had vanquished the Shang-Yin (Chinese Classics, III 320, 351–356). Though the time of his death is not clearly stated, it surely was the year he consulted the Prince of Chi 箕 and recovered from the illness as narrated in the Chin t'êng. Ssŭ-ma Ch'ien takes this view and so does the I Chou shu 逸周書 (VI 25), where it is said: "After he had smitten Chou 紂, he died in the 6th year of his reign." Thus the 1st year of King Wu was the 8th of the dynasty and 3 years before that of the conquest.

If the statement in the Ch'ien Han shu is correct, King Ch'êng and Po Ch'in 伯禽, Prince of Lu, started their reigns in the same year and Po Ch'in reigned 46 years until he died in the 16th year of King K'ang (Chapter Lü li chih 律歷志, 下, 18). That leaves 30 years for King Ch'êng's reign. For reasons to be stated presently, we give 25 years as the minimum for King K'ang's reign. Together these two come to a total of 55 years, which agrees with the Bamboo Annals statement, often repeated elsewhere, that "during the reigns of Ch'êng and K'ang the world was tranquil and punishments were not inflicted for 40 years." As quoted in the T'ai p'ing yü lan (LXXXIV), the words are "40 years and more". At both beginning and end

CHOU DYNASTY
(continued)

of the 55 years there is room for the recorded punitive campaigns without encroaching on the traditional "40 years" of peace. Early in King Ch'êng's reign 2 great rebellions were quelled and so was another in the 25th year of King K'ang as will be seen in the next paragraph.

The 25 years tentatively assigned to King K'ang in our Table is a minimum derived from an inscribed bronze cauldron often called the "Small Yü Ting" in comparison with its fellow cauldron, the so-called "Large Yü Ting" mentioned above. Jung Kêng remarks that they are thus misnamed since the capacity of the "Small" is 12 gallons while that of the "Large" is only 8 gallons. Parts of the inscription in question have perished, but enough remains to show that it commemorates 2 victorious campaigns led by Yü against rebels. Incidentally it mentions that the ti 禘 sacrifice was offered to "the King of Chou, King ...., and King Ch'êng". "The King of Chou" must be King Wên, and the obliterated name of the second king must be Wu — inferences supported by the naming of these 2 kings on the aforesaid companion cauldron. The inscription on the "Small Yü Ting" ends: "It was the King's 25th year 隹王廿又五祀", and surely that refers to King K'ang.

According to the Bamboo Annals: "King Chao in the 16th year [of his reign] invaded Ch'u-ching 楚荆, and when crossing the Han [River] encountered a large rhinoceros. In the 19th year the heavens were greatly clouded; pheasants and hares were afraid. [The King's] 6 armies perished in the Han." There is also the statement that the King came to his end while on a tour of inspection in the south 南巡, but the year is not specified. At all events, the Annals set a minimum of 19 years for King Chao's reign.

Legend assigns extreme longevity to King Mu. Ssŭ-ma Ch'ien echoes legend when he states King Mu reigned 55 years starting at the age of 50 and he identifies him with the king, mentioned in the Lü hsing 呂刑 of the Shu, who the Preface to the Shu says was King Mu (Mém. hist. I 250, 259–265). But the figures do not agree if the opening sentence of the Lü hsing is given the usual interpretation that the king had been on the throne 100 years when he charged the Prince of Lü to codify punishments (Chinese Classics, III 688). Perhaps the text known to Ssŭ-ma Ch'ien meant that the king was still on the throne a centenarian. The Bamboo Annals contain this entry: "From Chou's receiving of the mandate until King Mu there were 100 years". Should it be taken to include a reign of 55 or more years, this statement is so obviously false that some have turned to the Annals for evidence of a shorter reign. They find the following sentence and suppose the event was near the King's death: "In the 37th year he smote the Yüeh 越, and when his muster of 9 armies went westward to the Nine Rivers, turtles and alligators formed themselves into a bridge". Even taking 37 years as the maximum for Mu's reign, the tenure of his predecessors has to be lessened to an extent quite incompatible with the evidence we have cited. Moreover, the historicity of tales about King Mu is dubious because so many are romanticized. If Mu's accession is meant in the Annals statement, the previous years (according to our list) and 10 years back to the reputed mandate come to only 13 short of the 100. Ssŭ-ma Ch'ien's figure of 55 seems the best choice for a tentative estimate (Mém. hist. I 265).

For the reign of King Kung the contemporary evidence of 15 years afforded by the 2nd Ch'io Ts'ao Ting supersedes all other estimates which vary from 12

CHOU DYNASTY

(continued)

to 25 years. This cauldron's inscription presents the combination, rare on bronzes, of a king named together with the year of his reign. It records favours given Ch'io Ts'ao by King Kung on the occasion of archery practice at the New Palace in Ch'êng-Chou.

Concerning the years of King Kung's 3 immediate successors no clear indication is given by Ssŭ-ma Ch'ien. Our task being to fit them and King Li into the time yet remaining before 841 B.C., King Li may aptly be treated of first, since about him the Shih chi informs us and upon the length of his reign the other estimates depend.

Had Ssŭ-ma Ch'ien felt confident as to Li he could have fixed the date of his accession merely by counting back from the beginning of the Regency in 841 B.C. Actually he gives several conflicting figures. In Chapter IV the 30th, 34th, and 37th years of the reign are mentioned, the last being pegged to 841 B.C. when rebels caused the King's flight to Chih 彘 (Mém. hist., I 268, 272, 274). Yet elsewhere in the Shih Chi synchronization between his and certain feudal rulers' reigns presents a very different picture. Bracketed with a Ch'i 齊 prince, for instance, the length of his reign works out to some 18 years (Mém. hist., IV 41). Several princes of Wei 衛 had held the title of po 伯, often likened to "earl", until one more ambitious, named Ching 靖, on his accession bribed King Yi 夷 to raise the rank of Wei princes to that of hou 侯, often likened to "marquis". After ruling for 12 years he died and was succeeded by his son whose 13th year was the one in which King Li fled to Chih. That points to a maximum of nearly 25 years for Li's reign (Mém. hist., IV 192). The principality of Ch'ên 陳 affords yet another clue. Prince Shên 慎 was a contemporary of King Li, and it was in the 12th or 13th year of his successor, Prince Yu 幽, that the rebels drove the King from the capital. Unfortunately Ssŭ-ma Ch'ien omits to say how long Prince Shên occupied the Ch'ên throne (Mém. hist., IV 170). Though these correspondences yield no precise conclusion, they do indicate that King Li's reign lasted much nearer 20 than 37 years. Accordingly we tentatively assign to him the round number of 20 years.

Thus 42 years remain for distribution among the 3 immediate forerunners of King Li. We take the Kuo Yu Ts'ung Ting to warrant the surmise that King Yi reigned at least 32 years. A typical Second Phase piece, it has in common with a number of vessels certain names, some inscribed on one and some on another but associated in such a way that they tie the vessels together into a group. The names relevant to the present theme are those of the landowner Kuo Yu Ts'ung, his late grandfather and father, an official called K'o 克 holding the post of shan fu 善夫 (perhaps a sort of court chamberlain), and his late grandfather. Recorded on the ting is a plea for justice before the King brought by Kuo Yu Ts'ung accusing certain persons of encroaching on his land. The plaintiff dedicates the ting to his late grandfather and father by name, and mentions the "32nd year". The next link in the chain of evidence is the record of a similar plaint some 7 years before made by the same Kuo. It occurs on a food-vessel of the hsü 盨 class, and names K'o as intermediary in gaining restitution of the stolen land. Then the inscription on a cauldron, commonly called the Ta K'o Ting 大克鼎, serves to date K'o in a eulogy to his late grandfather. The words are: "in the execution of his functions he was able with devotion to protect his sovereign King Kung 肆克龔保厥辟龔王". That places K'o in the 2nd generation after King Kung and therefore lends support to

CHOU DYNASTY

(continued)

our theory that assigns not less than 32 years to the reign of King Yi.

The *Bamboo Annals* relate an event in the 7th year of King Hsiao, and we enter the length of his reign accordingly. Thus 3 years are left over for King I.

We have paid special attention to the Western Chou period because of its historical obscurity. It ended with King P'ing's flight some 200 miles eastwards to the safer capital set near the Lo River nearly 2 centuries before. Thus began the Eastern Chou period. According to Chapter XIV of the *Shih chi* this transfer of the court occurred in 770 B.C., the year after King Yu died and the same year that King P'ing was proclaimed king by the nobles who supported him. The *Bamboo Annals* state, however, that the accession of King P'ing preceded the death of King Yu, and so we enter "c. 772 B.C. in the Table. Hence there were 2 kings for a brief period and again there were 2 for about 10 years after Han, Prince of Kuo 虢公翰 put on the throne Yü Ch'ên younger brother of King P'ing, with the title Hsi Wang in the place of King Yu.

Records are still scanty until 722 B.C. when the extant annals of Lu 魯 begin. Known as the *Ch'un ch'iu* 春秋, they together with the *Tso chuan* 左傳 illumine the Eastern Chou period for nearly 2½ centuries. Ssŭ-ma Ch'ien follows these primary sources closely.

Afterwards history becomes vague again though the 2 books *Kuo yü* 國語 and *Chan Kuo ts'ê* 戰國策 provide information. Neither they nor the *Shih chi* gives a clear account of the closing years of the House of Chou that followed the deaths in 256 B.C. of King Nan and Prince Wu of Western Chou. In Chapter IV of the *Shih chi* Prince Hui of Western Chou is said to have enfeoffed his younger son with the town of Kung 鞏 and given him the title Prince Hui of Eastern Chou. It mentions no date. But the 8th-century commentary *chêng i* 正義 to Chapter XLIII of the *Shih chi* quotes the *Kua ti chih* 括地志 to say that in the 2nd year of King Hsien of Chou (367 B.C.) Prince Hui of Western Chou enfeoffed his younger son Pan 班 with Kung, to be subordinate to the royal house, with the title Prince Hui of Eastern Chou. His son, Prince Wu 武, was the one Ch'in extinguished". The *Ti wang shih chi* makes a like statement about the 1st Eastern Chou Prince. So here are 2 different names, Pan and Chieh, as we see from the following entry in the *Bamboo Annals* under the 11th year of King Hui Ch'êng 惠成 of Wei 魏 which corresponds to the 9th year of King Hsien of Chou and 360 B.C. It says: "Chieh 傑, Prince Hui of Eastern Chou, died." The *Shih pên* (II 5) calls him Pan 班.

Moreover, the lapse of time between the death in 360 B.C. of the 1st Prince and the downfall of his alleged son in 249 B.C. is 111 years. Obviously there is some muddle which precludes a neat finish to our Table.

THE RULERS OF CHINA

Explanations

At the beginning of each dynasty the top margin contains:
(a) the family name (姓 hsing) of the rulers, on the left side of the page;
(b) the capital or capitals of the dynasty, in the middle of the page;
(c) the name of the dynasty, on the right side of the page.

On the second and following pages of each dynasty the top margin has the name of the dynasty only. Here and elsewhere numbers in brackets are generally dates – of inauguration, bestowal, and such like.

1. The first column gives the posthumous Temple Title (廟號 Miao Hao); with an index letter for each Emperor, and the number of the chapter which refers to that Emperor in the History of the dynasty.
2. The second column gives the posthumous Memorial Title (謚 Shih), to which 皇帝 Huang Ti is to be added unless 侯 Hou, 公 Kung, 王 Wang, or 帝 Ti is inserted. In the later dynasties, when the Shih were very long, col. 2 has sometimes been carried forward into col. 3 to save space, the part of col. 3 so used being re-numbered 2 (e.g. on p.107). In practice the last word alone of the Shih has been commonly used, as for instance the Ch'ien-lung Emperor is known as 純皇帝 Ch'un Huang Ti.
3. The third column gives the personal name (諱 Hui or 名 Ming), sometimes followed by 小諱(名) hsiao Hui (Ming).
4. The fourth column gives the personal name (字 Tzŭ), sometimes followed or replaced by 小字 hsiao Tzŭ; and in the Yüan dynasty replaced by the name in "the native language" (國語 Kuo yü).
5. The fifth column gives the index letter or other description of the father or ancestor, and often the position in the family. (s son, gds grandson, br brother)
6. The sixth column gives the date of birth (生 shêng), day, month, year, if known. If the year only is given it is that which corresponds roughly to the lunar year.[1)]
7. The seventh column gives the date of enthronement (卽位 chi wei), followed sometimes by the date of abdication or deposition.
8. The eighth column gives the date of death (崩 p'êng).
9. The ninth column gives the Year Title (年號 nien hao); and the cycle signs (歲次 sui tzŭ) of the first year (元年 yüan nien).
10. The tenth column gives the Western day, month, and year corresponding to the first day (元, or 正, 旦 yüan, chêng, tan) of the Year Title's first year as given in the ninth column; followed by the day, month, and year when that Year Title was introduced or decreed (改元 kai yüan). When there are several Year Titles in one reign they are numbered and the later ones are brought back to columns 7 and 8, and then to 5 and 6, and so on, to save space. The explanation of 9 and 10 will of course then apply to the parts of 7 and 8, &c. which are so occupied and re-numbered 9 and 10 (e.g. on p.56).[2)]
11. Below the Tables, on the first page of each dynasty, are the authorities for that dynasty, and, on that and the following pages, footnotes.

Notes:
1) All dates (except in column 9) are Western and are calculated from P. Hoang Concord. des Chronologies &c., 1910. These dates are new style on and after 15 October 1582, when

the Gregorian kalendar was adopted in Italy. New style was adopted in France on 20 December, and in Holland on 25 December, 1582; but in England not until 14 September 1752. To change new style to old style subtract ten days from the date given from 15·10·1582 till 11·3·1700 inclusive, or subtract eleven days, from 12·3·1700 till 13·9·1752 inclusive. New style omits 29 February in 1700, 1800, and 1900. Thus 16·7·1590 N.S. = 6·7·1590 O.S.; 11·3·1700 N.S. = 29·2·1700 O.S.; 12·3·1700 N.S. = 1·3·1700 O.S.; 13·9·1752 N.S. = 2·9·1752 O.S.; and thereafter the dates given will be true for all European countries except Greece, Russia, and Turkey, which changed in this century.

The year given in the upper line in column 10 will generally be the Western year which roughly corresponds to the first lunar year (元年 yüan nien) of the Year Title in question. But in periods (as in the Ch'ien Han dynasty) when the civil year began with the 10th moon, the first day of the civil year fell in the Western year before that which on the whole corresponded to the cycle signs in column 9. Thus when a year began on 1·11·141 B.C. it was the year 140 which on the whole corresponded to the lunar year 辛丑 hsin-ch'ou and must be reckoned as approximately the first Chien-yüan year - 建元元年歲次辛丑. But when a year began on 23·1·96 B.C. it was the year 96 which so corresponded to the lunar year 乙酉 i-yu and must be reckoned as the first T'ai-shih year - 太始元年歲次乙酉.

2) When a Year Title was changed in the course of a year the new Title was usually made retrospective and reckoned (for all future documents) as in use from the first day of the first moon of that year. But it was often (especially in the Nan Sung and Ming dynasties) changed prospectively (改明年元 kai ming nien yüan), & did not come into use until the first day of the first moon of the next year. Thus a document dated in April 760 would have been dated 乾元三年 Ch'ien-yüan san nien (3rd Ch'ien-yüan year); but a later writer, referring to the same document, would date it 上元元年 Shang-yüan yüan nien (1st Shang-yüan year); while a document of December 1274 would be dated, both then and by later writers, 咸淳十年 Hsien-shun shih nien (10th Hsien-shun year), although the Title 德祐 Tê-yu had been decreed in November 1274.

The writing, done by more than one hand over the space of nine or ten years, may seem to demand apology but is, it is hoped, generally readable.

趙 Chao　　咸陽 Hsien-yang　　秦 Ch'in

1.	2.	3.	4.	5.	6.	7.	8.	9.	10.
A	始[1] Shih (221)	政 or 正 Chêng		s of 秦莊襄王 Ch'in Chuang-hsiang Wang	24, 11, 260[2]	2, 7, 247 , , 221 初并天下	18, 7, 210[3]	元年 first year 乙卯	2, 11, 247
B	二世 Êrh shih	胡亥 Hu-hai		younger s of A	-, -, 229[4]	-, 9/10, 210[5]	after 23, 9, 207[6]	壬辰	13, 11, 210
C	秦王 Ch'in Wang	子嬰 Tzŭ-ying		s of 扶蘇 Fu-su, elder s of A	—	?-, 10, 207 Ch'in Wang for 46 days	-, 1/2, 206[7]	甲午	20, 11, 208

史記 Shih chi (Sc) cc. 5, 6, 7, 15, 16; 前漢書 Ch'ien han shu (Hs) cc. 1a, 31.

1. The titles in column 2 were not posthumous in this dynasty, but used in the holder's lifetime.
2. This was the 1st day of the lunar year 壬寅 (259), and is on the authority of 宋忠 Sung Chung (Chi chieh, Sc, 6, 1a).
3. A is said to have died in his 51 year (Sc, 5, 14a), and this is wrongly changed to 49 in the K'ao chêng (5, 5a). He is said to have succeeded his father in 247 in his 13 year (Sc, 6, 1a), & so would have been in his 14 year in 246, his 1st regnal year, & in his 50 year (Chi chieh, Sc, 6, 12b) when he died in 210. The day of death is 三十七年七月丙寅 (Sc, 6, 12b). If 七月 could mean the 7th moon of the civil year, i.e. "the 4th moon, in summer", then 丙寅 would be 9, 5, 210; but if, as is most likely, it is "the 7th moon, in autumn" it included no 丙寅 day that year, & so Chavannes (Mém. hist. II, 191) has changed 寅 to 子 (丙子, 18, 7, 210). P. Hoang (Proleg. 234) agrees, making the day 18 (Julian 22), 7, 210. There can be no doubt that Sc names the moons in the normal way so that the year begins with 冬十月 "the 10th moon, in winter", though there may be apparent exceptions in cc. 5, 13b; 6, 3b. Yen Shih-ku (Hs, 1a, 8b) believed that in the Ch'in and early Han the 1st moon of the civil year (亥月) was numbered 1, the 2nd (子月) 2, & so on, though the seasons could not be moved, & that Sc & Hs had changed these to the numbering (10, 11, 12, 1, 2, &c.) in vogue after the change of kalendar in 104. Homer Dubs, Former Han Dynasty I, 154–160, does not agree with this, & quotes an inscription of 158 B.C. which is evidence that the 11th moon of the civil year was then called "8th moon" (八月) just as we find it in the books. P. Hoang (Proleg. 231–5) discusses thirteen Ch'in dates in detail.
4. The year 230-29 seems to be indicated by Sc, 6, 13a when it says that B was in his 21 year in 209. It is not likely that So yin is right in making his age then 12, so that he would have been born in 220 (Sc, 5, 14a; 6, K'ao chêng 3a).
5. Chi chieh (Sc, 6, 13a) quotes 徐廣 Hsü Kuang (352–425) that the amnesty, which often accompanied accession, was dated 17, 11, 210.
6. The last date given before the death is 23, 9, 207 – 八月己亥. The reading 己卯 (Sc, 6, 15a) would make this date 2, 11, 207, in the 9th moon. But Sc, 6, 15b; 16, 1a; Hs, 1a, 6b imply or state that B killed himself, to escape being killed by 趙高 Chao Kao, in the eighth moon, i.e. between 23, 9 and 11, 10, 207.
7. C was killed in Hsien-yang by Hsiang Yü, cf. Sc, 7, 7b; 16, 6b, K'ao chêng 6a; Hs, 1a, 8b. His age is not stated. In Sc, 6, 20b he is called a child (小子), whereupon Chavannes (Mém. hist. II, 245) says he was un homme fait because in Sc, 6, 15b, he is said to have consulted his two sons (與其子二人謀). But is it credible that A, who in 207 would have been 53, should then have had two great-grandsons old enough to be consulted on matters of state? Fu-su's younger brother (B) would have been 23 at most, and though C may just possibly have been as old as that his sons must still have been small boys.

劉 Liu 關中 Kuan-chung[1] 前 Ch'ien(西 Hsi)漢 Han[2]

1.	2.	3.	4.	5.	6.	7.	8.	9.	10.
A 高祖 Kao Tsu c.1.	高 Kao[3]	邦 Pang originally 季 Chi[4]	(國 Kuo)	not recorded[5]	-, -, 247	24, 2, 202	29, 5, 195	元年 first year ·乙未	10, 11, 207
B c.2.	孝惠 Hsiao Hui	盈 Ying[6]	(滿 Man)	s of A	-, -, 211[7]	20, 6, 195	15, 9, 188[8]	丁未	29, 10, 195
C c.3.	高后·呂氏 Kao Hou · Lü shih	雉 Chih	娥姁 O-hsü (野雞 Yeh-chi)	mother of B	?-, -, 241	-, 9, 188 regent for infant s of B	15, 8, 180	甲寅	11, 11, 188
D c.4.	孝文 Hsiao Wên	恆 Hêng	(常 Ch'ang)	2nd s of A	-, -, 202/1	1, 11, 180	3, 7, 157	(前)元年 (Ch'ien) 壬戌	12, 11, 180
								後元年 Hou	15, 11, 164 -, 9/10, 164

前漢書 <u>Ch'ien han shu</u> (<u>Hs</u>) c.1—; 史記 <u>Shih chi</u> (<u>Sc</u>) cc. 8–12.

1. Or 咸陽 Hsien-yang; 渭南 Wei (or Yü)-nan (206); 京兆尹 Ching-chao yin (105) - <u>Hs</u>, 28a, 5b.
2. The period 206-203, during which Pang was known as 漢王 Han Wang and 項籍 Hsiang Chi (羽 Yü) was independent ruler of 楚 Ch'u, is sometimes called 楚漢 'Ch'u and Han'.
3. A note by 張晏 Chang Yen (3rd cent.) says that Kao is not a possible memorial title by the rules of the <u>Li chi</u> (禮諡法), but that an exception was made for the exceptional eminence of the founder of the House (<u>Hs</u>, 1a, 1a).
4. Ssŭ-ma Chêng (<u>So yin</u> in <u>Sc</u>, 8, 1a) says that 季 Chi, meaning youngest son, must have been A's infant name (小名 or 小字) clinging to him through life; and he quotes 項岱 Hsiang Tai (2nd cent. A.D.) as saying that he changed his name to 邦 Pang when he was enthroned. (<u>Note</u>:- <u>Hs</u>, 1a, 2a, 劉季固多大言; 無如季相; 許與劉季) Notes by 荀悅 Hsün Yüeh (148–209) and 顏師古 Yen Shih-ku (581–645) indicate that 國 Kuo was used to avoid the taboo of Pang (邦之字曰國者臣下所避以相代也: cf note 6 below). Pang is not found in the text of either the <u>Shih chi</u> or the <u>Han shu</u>.
5. We are not told who A's father was, both <u>Sc</u> (8, 1a, 父曰太公) and <u>Hs</u> (1a, 1a, 父太公挂梘) using only the respectful title T'ai Kung, the <u>So yin</u> (<u>Sc</u>, 8, 1a) adding, "皇甫謐 Huang-fu Mi (215–282) says, 名執嘉 His name was Chih-chia; 王符 Wang Fu (c. A.D. 110) says, 太上皇名煓 The Emperor Father's name was T'uan", while the <u>Chêng i</u> supports Chih-chia with a quotation from 春秋握成圖 <u>Ch'un ch'iu wu ch'êng t'u</u> (4th cent.). The earliest of these authors wrote more than 300 years after the death of A; nor do they say who or what the father was.
6. A note by Yen Shih-ku (<u>Hs</u>, 2, 1a) amounts to saying that the <u>hui</u> or taboo names of the Han emperors are only deduced from the equivalents given by Hsün Yüeh (148–209): 臣下以滿字代盈者則知帝諱盈也他皆類此 "From the fact that Ministers use Man in place of Ying we know that the Emperor's name was Ying. The other [Emperors' <u>hui</u>] are all on this principle." cf note 4 above. These equivalents are given in brackets in col. 4.
7. This year is not very securely derived from <u>Sc</u>, 7, 7b, 8b; 8, 7b; and <u>Hs</u>, 2, 1a, where it is said that his father was made 漢王 Han Wang (in 207) in B's fifth year. The <u>Chi chieh</u> (<u>Sc</u>, 9, 2a) says that B was born in Shih Huang 37th year (210) and died in the 23 year of his age. <u>Li tai ming jên .. piao</u>, 507, gives his dates 207–189, age 20!
8. On the death of B, C made his son, the child of a concubine, emperor, but no name, title, or exact dates are given (<u>Hs</u>, 3, 1a). In the summer of 184 this boy was imprisoned & put to death (<u>Sc</u>, 9, 3a-b), & on 12, 6, 184 恆山王弘 i.e. 呂山 Lü Shan, later 義 I, & finally Hung Prince of Hêng-shan, became emperor, again without titles (<u>Hs</u>, 3, 2a; 4, 1a; <u>Sc</u>, 9, 3b).

1.	2.	3.	4.	5.	6.	7.	8.	9.	10.
E c.5	孝景 Hsiao Ching	啟 Ch'i	(開 K'ai)	1st s of D	-, -, 188	11, 7, 157	7, 3, 141	1. 前 Ch'ien 乙酉	29, 10, 157
								2. 中 Chung 壬辰	11, 11, 150
								3. 後 Hou 戊戌	4, 11, 144
F c.6	孝武 Hsiao Wu	徹 Ch'ê	(通 T'ung)	2nd s of E	-, -, 156	7, 3, 141	27, 3, 87	1. 建元 Chien-yüan[9] 辛丑	1, 11, 141
								2. 元光 Yüan-kuang 丁未	26, 10, 135
								3. 元朔 Yüan-shuo 癸丑	18, 11, 129
								4. 元狩 Yüan-shou 己未	12, 11, 123
								5. 元鼎 Yüan-ting 乙丑	6, 11, 117
								6. 元封 Yüan-fêng 辛未	31, 10, 111 / 15, 5, 110
								7. 太初 T'ai-ch'u 丁丑	24, 10, 105 / 25, 6, 104[10]
								8. 天漢 T'ien-han 辛巳	6, 2, 100
								9. 太始 T'ai-shih 乙酉	23, 1, 96[11]
								10. 征和 Chêng-ho 己丑	7, 2, 92
								11. 後元 Hou-yüan 癸巳	24, 1, 88
G c.7	孝昭 Hsiao Chao	弗陵 Fu(-ling)	不 Pu	younger s of E	-, -, 95	28, 3, 87	3, 6, 74[12]	1. 始元 Yüan-shih 乙未	1, 2, 86
								2. 元鳳 Yüan-fêng 辛丑	26, 1, 80 / -, 9/10, 80
								3. 元平 Yüan-p'ing 丁未	19, 2, 74

9. Year Titles are first found in the reign of F, and even then the first five Titles seem to have been made retrospectively. We read in Sc, 28, 10b (Mém. hist. I, c; III, 474), "Afterwards in the 3rd year an official said, Periods (元) ought not to be counted by numbers, as 1 & 2, but by the propitious decrees of Heaven, the first period to be called Chien, the 2nd period to be called Kuang, because of the comet (one which appeared in Sept. 135 with a tail stretching across the sky from the east - Hs, 6, 2a), the 3rd period to be called Shou, because a one-horned animal was caught at the time of the Chiao sacrifice (Ying Shao ad loc. says it was a white ch'i-lin)." This accounts for the retrospective institution of the 1st, 2nd, & 4th Titles, but nothing is said of the 3rd & 5th. P. Hoang, Conc. néom. 503, assumes that the Title Yüan-ting was decreed when an amnesty was proclaimed & a caldron found on 4(?), 6, 116; but Chavannes, Mém. hist. I, c, points out that the caldron after which the period was named was found (according to the notes in 通鑑集覽 Tung chien chi lan c.16, 1a) in the 6th moon, July, of 113 (cf. 6, 8a). Dubs, Former Han Dynasty II, 71, has a more detailed note to the same effect, based on 通鑑考異 Tung chien K'ao i, ed. S.P.T.K., 1, 9a-b, where it is shown that probably only one caldron was found, that of July 113. Thus it seems to be probable that after the suggestion had been made in 119 ("the 3rd year" above), the system was not worked out in detail, nor the Titles assigned, until the later half of 113. The omission of Yüan-shuo in Sc, 28 may be a slip, or a corruption of the text, since more than four six-year periods had elapsed between 141 & 114, & the intention was evidently to divide the reign into periods of 6 years each, as had been done in the two preceding reigns. Six-year were changed to four-year periods after 104; six-year periods resumed by G; & then four years again (or five under I), with some irregularity under Wang Mang, till A.D. 20. This change of Titles at regular intervals seems rarely to have been attempted again. There are several other examples of Chien-yüan being used as a Year Title, & not always for the first period of a reign; but the meaning "to establish a period" is also common, e.g. Chin shu, 122, 3a 建元曰太安; 123, 7a 建元曰太平; Hhs, 1a, 7a 建元為建武.

10. At the summer solstice. Mém. hist. III, 331.

11. cf. Conc. néom. 94, where the intercalary 12th moon should be in 96 (not 97) - Chavannes in TP, 1911, p. 772.

12. On the death of G, 昌邑王賀 Ho, Prince of Ch'ang-i, son of 髆 Po, the 6th son of F, was made Emperor, but after a reign of 27 days was deposed on account of his licentious conduct. No exact dates are given. - cf. Hs, 14, 19b; 63, 7a-b; 68, 2b sqq.

1.	2.	3.	4.	5.	6.	7.	8.	9.	10.
H c.8	孝宣 Hsiao Hsüan	詢 Hsün — originally 病已 Ping-chi	次卿 Tz'ŭ-ch'ing — (謀 Mou)	great-gds of F[13]	-, -, 91	8, 9, 74	8, 1, 48	1. 本始 Pên-shih 戊申	8, 2, 73
				9.	10.	9.	10.		
				6. 甘露 Kan-lu 戊辰	28, 1, 53	4. 神爵 Shên-chüeh 庚申	26, 1, 61	2. 地節 Ti-chieh 壬子	25, 1, 69
				7. 黃龍 Huang-lung 壬申	13, 2, 49	5. 五鳳 Wu-fêng 甲子	11, 2, 57	3. 元康 Yüan-k'ang 丙辰	9, 2, 65
I c.9	孝元 Hsiao Yüan	奭 Shih	(盛 Shêng)	1st s of H	-, -, 75	27, 1, 48	6, 7, 33	1. 初元 Ch'u-yüan 癸酉	1, 2, 48
				9.	10.	9.	10.		
				4. 竟寧 Ching-ning 戊子	16, 2, 33	3. 建昭 Chien-chao 癸未	11, 2, 38	2. 永光 Yung-kuang 戊寅	6, 2, 43
J c.10	孝成 Hsiao Ch'êng	驁 Ao	太孫 T'ai-sun (俊 Chün)	1st s of I	(?) -, 1, 51[14]	2, 8, 33	15, 4, 7	1. 建始 Chien-shih 己丑	4, 2, 32
				9.	10.	9.	10.		
				6. 元延 Yüan-yen 己酉	24, 1, 12	4. 鴻嘉 Hung-chia 辛丑	21, 2, 20	2. 河平 Ho-p'ing 癸巳	20, 2, 28 -, 4/5, 28
				7. 綏和 Sui-ho 癸丑	9, 2, 8	5. 永始 Yung-shih 乙巳	7, 2, 16	3. 陽朔 Yang-shuo 丁酉	6, 2, 24 11, 8, 25[15]

13. H was son of 史皇孫 the imperial grandson Shih, son of 戾太子 Li T'ai tzŭ, the second son of F (Hs, 8, 1a).

14. There is some uncertainty about this date. If J was in his third year (Hs, 10, 1a, 年三歲) when H died late in the year 49-8 (8, 1, 48), he must have been born very late in the year 52-1, i.e. after 8, 1, 51, or some time in the year 51-0. Which of these times is right will depend upon whether his third year means his third kalendar year according to the usual Chinese custom, or the third year of his life counting from his birthday, as was often done in the Han dynasty (cf. H. H. Dubs in Asia Major N.S. I. ii, 145). By this latter way of reckoning he cannot then have been in his 20th year at his accession on 2, 8, 33, as is stated by 臣瓚 Ch'ên Tsan (4th cent.) in Hs, 10, 7b, though he would have been in his 45th year when he died. If he was born at the very end of the year 52-1, he would have been by the ordinary reckoning in his 4th year in January 48, in his 20th year in 33, and in his 46th year (as calculated by Yen Shih-ku) when he died.

15. Hs, 10, 3b. But it is not certain that this date (六月庚戌) is that of the change of Title, which may have been decreed on another day between this and the end of the year.

1.	2.	3.	4.	5.	6.	7.	8.	9.	10.
K c.11	孝 哀 Hsiao Ai	欣 Hsin	(喜 Hsi)	gds of I[1]	-, -, 26	5, 5, 7	13, 8, 1	[1] 建平 Chien-p'ing 乙卯	17, 2, 6
						9.	10.		
						[3] 元壽 Yüan-shou 己未	3, 2, 2	[2] 太初元將 T'ai-ch'u-yüan-chiang[2] 丙辰	6, 2, 5 9, 7, 5
L c.12	孝 平 Hsiao P'ing	衎 K'an	(欒 Lo)	gds of I[3]	-, -, 9	15, 10, 1 B.C.	3, 2, A.D. 6[4]	元 始 Yüan-shih 辛酉	12, 2, A.D. 1
M c.99		嬰 Ying	孺子 Ju-tzŭ	gt-gt-gds of H (s of 廣戚侯 Kuang-ch'i Hou c.99a, 13a)	?-, -, A.D. 4	17, 4, 6 (皇太子) see below	-, 2/3, 25 (Hhs, 1a, 6a)	居攝 Chü-shê 丙寅	17, 2, 6 ?15, 2, 6
								始初 Shih-ch'u 戊辰	27, 1, 8 6, 1, 9[5]

1. Son of 定陶恭王 Prince Kung of Ting-t'ao.
2. This Year Title was revoked in September (八月) the same year, & Chien-p'ing was resumed.—Hs, 11, 2b-3a.
3. Son of 中山孝王興 Hsing Prince Hsiao of Chung-shan.
4. This date is 冬十二月丙午 (Hs, 12, 4b). There was no 丙午 day in the 12th moon, but the 12th moon is confirmed by c.99a, 12b, and I have guessed 丙子 (3, 2, 6). If we read, less probably, 十一月丙午, the day will be 4, 1, 6.
5. This date (Hs, 99a, 15b, 17a, 三年 . . . 十一月甲子) is consistent and possible, but a note by 劉奉世 Liu Fêng-shih (11th cent.) at the place says, "This is the winter of the second Chü-shê year. At this time he first petitioned that the third Chü-shê year should be the first Ch'u-shih year, and this seems to be a matter of the second year. I suspect that the Biography (of Wang Mang, c.99) has a mistake." This note, with the other confusing and possibly corrupt notes by Liu & by 張晏 Chang Yen (3rd cent.) on fol. 17a, b, seems to assume that it was at the end of the second Chü-shê year that Mang petitioned that the following third year should be called 初始 Ch'u-shih (or Shih-ch'u). This change of 3rd to 2nd year makes it necessary to read 十一月甲午(?), 13, 12, 7, or 十二月甲子, 12, 1, 8. But it is to be noted that all the days specified (壬子, 戊午, 甲子) actually occurred in the 11th moon of the third year (A.D. 8-9) but none of them in the 11th moon of the second year (7-8), and so I have ventured to retain the 6, 1, 9, supported too by some of the passages quoted below.

In Conc. néom. 504, the year 8-9 begins as 初始 Ch'u-shih and is changed to 始初 Shih-ch'u on 21.11.1 (6, 1, 9). Under this date Hs, 99a, 17b, has read Ch'u-shih at least since the eleventh century, and that is the only form given in modern books as far as I know. The Tzŭ chih t'ung chien, ed. 1816, 36, 24a (the text is the same in the Sung edition, ed. S.P.T.K. 36, 13b, 14b-15a), reads, 初始元年 (是年十一月莽始改元始初) "Ch'u-shih first year (Mang did not change the period to Shih-ch'u until the 11th moon of this year)." This note by 胡三省 Hu San-hsing is perhaps the source of Conc. néom.; but it seems to be clear that there was only one Title, either Shih-ch'u or Ch'u-shih, for when it comes to the 11th moon (fol. 26a-b; 14b-15a) we find 十一月甲子 . . . 以居攝三年為始初元年 "In the 11th moon chia-tzŭ (6, 1, 9) he made the third Chü-shê year into the first Shih-ch'u year", with a note quoting 通鑑考異 T'ung chien k'ao i. This K'ao i by Ssŭ-ma Kuang, ed. S.P.T.K., 2, 2b, reads 王莽始初元年 (莽傳作初始荀紀及韋莊美嘉號錄宋庠紀年通譜皆作始初今從之) "Wang Mang Shih-ch'u first year (Mang's Biography makes it Ch'u-shih. Hsün [Yüeh, Han] chi (2nd cent.), with Wei Chuang, Mei chia hao lu (c. 900), and Sung Hsiang, Chi nien t'ung p'u (11th cent.) all make it Shih-ch'u, and I now follow this.)" Ssŭ-ma Kuang does not notice that Liu Fêng-shih (see above) has read Ch'u-shih.

3

王莽 Wang Mang

1.	2.	3.	4.	5.	6.	7.	8.	9.	10.
c. 99 a, b, c	[假皇帝 Chia Huang Ti — popularly 攝皇帝 Shê Huang Ti]	莽 Mang	巨君 Chü-chün	s of 王曼 Wang Man younger br of 政君 Chêng-chün or 元后 Yüan Hou, empress of I	-, -, 45[1]	1, 7, 6 (假皇帝) — 10, 1, 9 (usurped the throne 即真)	6, 10, 23	始建國 Shih-chien-kuo 己巳	15, 1, 9 10, 1, 9
								天鳳 T'ien-fêng 甲戌	20, 1, 14
								地皇 Ti-huang 庚辰	14, 1, 20[2]
M	see above					-, 2, 25 as Emperor	-, 3/3, 25		
N	淮陽王 Huai yang Wang (known as Kêng-shih)	玄 Hsüan	聖公 Shêng-kung	cousin of A below	—	11, 3, 23 abdicated ?27, 9, 25[3]	29, 1, 26[4]	更始 Kêng-shih 癸未	10, 2, 23[5]

On -, 10, 7 劉信 Liu Hsin (s of 東平煬王 Prince Yang of Tung-p'ing) was made Emperor – Hs, 99a, 15a.
-, 1, 24 王郎 Wang Lang was made Emperor, & put to death 27, 4, 24 – Hhs, 1a, 4a, 5a.
-, 5/8, 25 公孫述 Kung-sun Shu proclaimed himself Emperor – Hhs, 1a, 6b.
-, 7/8, 25 劉盆子 Liu P'ên-tzŭ was made Emperor – Hs, 99b, 14a; Hhs, 1a, 7a.
17, 1, 26 劉永 Liu Yung proclaimed himself Emperor – Hhs, 1a, 7b.

1. A note by 劉攽 Liu Pin (11th cent.) in Hs, 99c, 14a, says, "At the age of 38 Wang Mang became 大司馬 Ta Ssŭ-ma, at 51 Regent (居攝), at 54 he usurped the throne (即真), at 68 was put to death." These ages are consistent with his birth in the year 45–4.

As from 15, 1, 9 the dynasty was called 新 Hsin (or popularly 新莽 Hsin Mang), and the year to begin with the twelfth moon (Hs, 99a, 18a); that is, the 12th moon (15, 1 – 13, 2, 9) was called the first moon (正月) of the year 9–10, so that the year 8–9 had no twelfth moon.

2. The commentary on Hhs, 1a, 1a, says "The sixth T'ien-fêng year (19) was changed to be Ti-huang." But 20 seems to be right.

3. Kêng-shih was finally defeated and fled to 高陵 Kao-ling, so ending his nominal reign, when 赤眉 Ch'ih-mei entered Ch'ang-an about 12, 10, 25 (Hs, 99c, 14a; Hhs, 1a, 7b). Ch'ih-mei is the name (hao) of the rebel 樊崇 Fan Ch'ung of 琅琊 Lang-yeh, who dyed his men's eyebrows red to distinguish them from Mang's troops (Tz'ŭ yüan & Tz'ŭ hai s.v. 赤眉; Giles, B.D. 536).

4. 十二月丙戌, Hhs, 1a, 7b. There was no ping-hsü day in the 12th moon, so it is guessed that 戌 is a mistake for 辰; ping-ch'ên was 29, 1, 26.

5. 元年正月甲子朔, Hhs, 1a, 2a. Conc. néom. 110 shows that 甲子 is a mistake for 壬子.

劉 Liu 洛陽 Lo-yang[1] 後 Hou(東 Tung)漢 Han

1.	2.	3.	4.	5.	6.	7.	8.	9.	10.
A 世祖 Shih Tsu c.1	光武 Kuang wu	秀 Hsiu	文叔[2] Wên-shu (茂 Mao)	s of 欽 Ch'in, descended in 8th generation from A (p.4)	13, 1, 5 B.C.[3]	5, 8, 25	29, 3, 57	建武 Chien-wu 乙酉	17, 2, 25 5, 8, 25
								中元[4] Chung-yüan 丙辰	5, 2, 56 14, 5, 56
B 顯宗 Hsien Tsung c.2	孝明 Hsiao Ming	莊 Chuang[5]	(嚴 Yen)	4th s of A	-, -, 28	29, 3, 57	5, 9, 75	永平 Yung-p'ing 戊午	13, 2, 58
C 肅宗 Su Tsung c.3	孝章 Hsiao Chang	炟 Ta	(著 Cho)	5th s of B	-, -, 57	5, 9, 75	9, 4, 88	[1] 建初 Chien-ch'u 丙子	24, 2, 76
						9.	10.		
						[3] 章和 Chang-ho 丁亥	21, 2, 87 12, 9, 87	[2] 元和 Yüan-ho 甲申	27, 1, 84 8, 10, 84
D 穆宗 Mu Tsung c.4	孝和 Hsiao Ho	肈 Chao[6]	(始 Shih)	4th s of C	-, -, 79	9, 4, 88	13, 2, 106	永元 Yung-yüan 己丑	30, 1, 89
								元興 Yüan-hsing 乙巳	2, 2, 105 18, 5, 105[7]

後漢書 Hou han shu (Hhs) c.1—

1. 洛(雒)陽 Lo-yang was named 河南 Ho-nan in the year 39 – Hhs, 29, 2a.
2. A note in Hhs, 1a, 1a, quotes 伏侯古今注 Fu hou ku chin chu (2nd cent.): 伯仲叔季兄弟之次長兄伯升次仲故字文叔焉 "The words po, chung, shu, chi show the order of brothers; the eldest brother was Po-shêng, the next Chung, and so Hsiu's name (tzŭ) was Wên-shu in the list." This seems to mean that Hsiu (A) was the third son of Ch'in. cf. note 4 on p. 4 above.
3. The date of birth is given in Hhs, 1b, 10b. The ages given, 28 in the year 22 (c. 1a, 1b) and 62 when he died, do not seem to be quite consistent; but by the reckoning commonly used in the Han dynasty the year 57, when he died, was actually his 62nd year (c. 1b, 10a).
4. Conc. néom. and Synchronismes both give 建武中元 Chien-wu-chung-yüan, for which Dubs, Former Han Dynasty, II, 117, says there is independent proof. But there is no indication of this in Hhs, 1b, 9b, —中元元年；四月己卯改年為中元.
5. His name at first is said to have been 陽 Yang (Li tai ming jên ... piao, 508).
6. The Harvard-Yenching Chronological Tables say that the correct form is 肇 Chao. K'anghsi tzŭ tien, s.v. says that the two words are the same, 肈同肇.
7. 四月庚午 (Hhs, 4, 8a) is impossible, and the correction to 庚子 (Conc. néom. 505), 18, 5, 105, has been adopted.

1.	2.	3.	4.	5.	6.	7.	8.	9.	10.
E c.4	孝殤 Hsiao Shang	隆 Lung	(盛 Shêng)	younger s of D	-, 11, 105[1]	13, 2, 106	21, 9, 106	延平 Yen-p'ing 丙午	21, 2, 106
F 恭宗 Kung Tsung c.5	孝安 Hsiao An	祐[2] Yu	(福 Fu)	gds of C (s of 慶 Ch'ing)	-, -, 94	23, 9, 106	30, 4, 125	1. 永初 Yung-ch'u 丁未	10, 2, 107
						9.	10.	2. 元初 Yüan-ch'u 甲寅	23, 2, 114 24, 2, 114
						4. 建光 Chien-kuang 辛酉	5, 2, 121 1, 8, 121	3. 永寧 Yung-ning 庚申	17, 2, 120 25, 5, 120
						5. 延光 Yen-kuang 壬戌	26, 1, 122 25, 4, 122		
c.5	少帝 Shao Ti (北鄉侯 Pei hsiang Hou)	懿 : 犢 I : Tu		gt-gds of C (s of 壽 Shou)		18, 5, 125 (不得上殿 Hhs, 6, 1a)	10, 12, 125		
G 敬宗 Ching Tsung c.6	孝順 Hsiao Shun	保 Pao	(守 Shou)	s of F	-, -, 115	16, 12, 125	20, 9, 144	1. 永建 Yung-chien 丙寅	10, 2, 126
						9.	10.	2. 陽嘉 Yang-chia 壬申	4, 2, 132 16, 4, 132
						4. 漢安 Han-an 壬午	13, 2, 142 26, 2, 142	3. 永和 Yung-ho 丙子	20, 2, 136 5, 3, 136
						5. 建康 Chien-Kang 甲申	22, 2, 144 3, 6, 144		
H c.6	孝沖 Hsiao Ch'ung	炳 Ping	(明 Ming)	s of G	-, -, 143	20, 9, 144	15, 2, 145	永嘉 Yung-chia 乙酉	10, 2, 145
I c.6	孝質 Hsiao Chih	纘 Tsuan	(繼 Chi)	gt-gt-gds of C (s of 鴻 Hung)	-, -, 138	6, 3, 145	26, 7, 146	本初 Pên-ch'u 丙戌	30, 1, 146

1. Hhs. 4, 8b says that E was rather more than a hundred days old (百餘日) on 13, 2, 106; i.e. born in the intercalary 9th moon, late October or early November, 105; and when it says (4, 9b) that he was in his second year when he died on 21, 9, 106, it must be reckoning by kalendar years, in the modern way.
2. The Harvard-Yenching *Chronological Tables* say that 祐 Yu should be 祜 Hu, of similar meaning.

1	2	3	4	5	6	7	8	9	10
J 威宗[1] Wei Tsung	孝桓 Hsiao Huan	志 Chih	(意 I)	gt-gds of C (s of 翼 I)	-,-,132	1, 8, 146	25, 1, 168	1. 建和 Chien-ho 丁亥	18, 2, 147
				9.	10.	9.	10.		
				6. 延熹 Yen-hsi 戊戌	16, 2, 158 17, 7, 158	4. 永興 Yung-hsing 癸巳	11, 2, 153 1, 7, 153	2. 和平 Ho-p'ing 庚寅	15, 2, 150 15, 2, 150
c.7				7. 永康 Yung-k'ang 丁未	7, 2, 167 12, 7, 167	5. 永壽 Yung-shou 乙未	20, 2, 155 5, 3, 155	3. 元嘉 Yüan-chia 辛卯	4, 2, 151 19, 2, 151
K	孝靈 Hsiao Ling	宏 Hung	(大 Ta)	gt-gt-gds of C (s of 萇)	-, -, 156[2]	17, 2, 168	13, 5, 189	1. 建寧 Chien-ning 戊申	28, 1, 168 17, 2, 168
				9.	10.	9.	10.		
c.8				4. 中平 Chung-p'ing 甲子	31, 1, 184 16, 2, 185	3. 光和 Kuang-ho 戊午	6, 2, 178 26, 4, 178	2. 熹平 Hsi-p'ing 壬子	12, 2, 172 24, 6, 172
L	弘農王 Hung nung Wang	辯 Pien		1st s of K	-, -, 173	15, 5, 189 — deposed 28, 9, 189	6, 3, 190[3]	光熹 Kuang-hsi 己巳	4, 2, 189 15, 5, 189
c.8								昭寧 Chao-ning 己巳	4, 2, 189 25, 9, 189
M	孝獻 Hsiao Hsien	協 Hsieh	伯和 Po-ho (合 Ho)	2nd s of K	-, -, 181	28, 9, 189 deposed 25, 11, 220	21, 4, 234[4]	1. 永漢 Yung-han 己巳	4, 2, 189 28, 9, 189
						9.	10.		
						4. 興平 Hsing-p'ing 甲戌	9, 2, 194 21, 2, 194	2. 中平六年 Chung-p'ing 己巳	4, 2, 189 19, 2, 190
				9.	10.				
c.9				6. 延康 Yen-k'ang 庚子	22, 2, 220 -, 4/5, 220 (?21, 4, 220)	5. 建安 Chien-an 丙子	17, 2, 196 23, 2, 196	3. 初平 Ch'u-p'ing 庚午	23, 2, 190

1. In the year 190 a petition that the Emperors D, F, G, J should not be allowed the title of 宗 Tsung was approved (Hhs, 9, 2a). The titles already given and here recorded were cancelled & not afterwards used.
2. K is said to have been in his 12th year at his accession (Hhs, 8, 1a), & so would have been born in 157, but to have died in his 34th year (Hhs, 8, 7a), that is to say, born in 156; and 156 is adopted by the modern books. I do not know on what authority.

3. The date 正月癸酉 (Hhs, 9, 1b) is impossible. In the text this date is immediately preceded by 辛亥 (4, 3, 190) and followed by 二月乙亥 (28, 3, 190), and this points to the correction 癸丑 (6, 3, 190).
4. The Annals end (Hhs, 9, 6b): "The heir (太子) died before his father; the grandson 康 K'ang reigned (立) for 51 years and died in 285 (5, 11, 285 - Chin shu 3, 10a); his son 瑾 Chin reigned for 4 years & died in 289 (11, 7, 289 - Chin shu 3, 11a); his son 秋 Ch'iu reigned for 20 years and was killed by foreign bandits in Yung-chia (309 - ? not recorded), and the dynasty was extinct."

曹 Ts'ao		洛陽 Lo-yang[1]						三國 San Kuo · 魏 Wei	
1.	2.	3.	4.	5.	6.	7.	8.	9.	10.
A 太祖 T'ai Tsu c.1	武 Wu	操 Ts'ao[2]	孟德 Mêng-tê	s of 嵩	-, -, 155	[-, 1, 190] 始起兵	15, 3, 220	used the Han Year	Titles: 190 - 220
B c.2	文 Wên	丕 P'ei	子桓 Tzŭ-huan	1st s of A	-, -, 187 (冬, 19,11,187 -14,2,188)	25,11,220	29, 6, 226	黃初 Huang-ch'u 庚子	22,2,220 10,12,220
C	明 Ming	叡 Jui.	元仲 Yüan-chung	1st s of B	-, -, 204	29, 6, 226	22, 1, 239	[1] 太和 T'ai-ho 丁未	4, 2, 227
						9.	10.		
c.3						[3] 景初 Ching-ch'u 丁巳	12, 2, 237 12, 4, 237[3]	青龍 Ch'ing-lung 癸丑	28, 1, 233 4, 3, 233

三國志·魏志(書) San kuo chih · Wei chih (shu) cc. 1–4, &c.

1. Ku chin ti ming ta tz'ŭ tien, 1931, 116, gives this (漢魏 Han Wei) dynasty five capitals, namely Ch'ang-an, 譙 Ch'iao in An-hui, 許昌 Hsü-ch'ang in Ho-nan, 鄴 Yeh in Ho-nan, & Lo-yang. The 三都賦 San tu fu takes Yeh for the Wei capital.

2. Ts'ao's other names are given as 吉利 Chi-li and 阿瞞 A-man - San kuo chih - Wei shu 1, 1a.

3. This date is taken from Conc. néom. 519. The only exact date given in the Wei chih, 3, 7a, with reference to this change is 正月壬辰, the date of the report of the appearance of a yellow dragon at 山茌 Shan-shih. In Conc. néom. 373 this day 壬辰 jên-ch'ên is the 25 day of the second moon (7, 4, 237), & on p. 519 this present date is given as the first day of second moon (14, 3, 237). But in the year 237 the Wei kalendar was changed so that the year should begin with the second astronomical moon (丑 ch'ou), which corresponds to the normal 12th moon (以建丑之月為正), and this rather complicates the question. In his Prolégomènes, 140, P. Hoang says that the change of kalendar was proposed in the second moon (where the text says 正月 "first moon", as above), but he defines the second moon as February-March, which corresponds to the normal first moon (12, 2 – 13, 3) of his own Tables (Conc. néom. 373). When he says that the change was proposed in the 2nd moon he seems to be conscious that jên-ch'ên did not occur in the normal first moon, and so by "second moon" he ought to mean the normal second moon. But when he defines the second moon as "février-mars" he describes the second moon of the changed kalendar, which again would not include jên-ch'ên, and did not in fact exist. For the change was actually made by calling the third moon fourth moon, & the new Year Title, Ching-ch'u, was apparently introduced at that time (Wei chih 3, 7a, 三月定曆改年為孟夏四月), or possibly in the 5th moon (己丑, 3 June) when the Court returned to the capital & an amnesty was proclaimed. It may be just possible that in the record of the change of kalendar & of its immediate cause, the yellow dragon, the change was made retrospective, so that by first moon (正月) the writer meant the same moon which he had, for the preceding year, called the 12th moon (十二月) in the preceding column of the same page. The day would then be 8, 2, 237. But this seems to be unlikely when it is observed that the day of the 12th moon (十二月癸巳) in the preceding column was 7, 2, 237; & it is perhaps simplest to suppose that both 壬辰 jên-ch'ên & Hoang's février-mars are slips, and that the text should read 正月壬戌, 8, 3, 237, the new Title to be decreed, as Hoang says on I do not know what authority, on 14 March.

魏 Wei

1.	2.	3.	4.	5.	6.	7.	8.	9.	10.
D c.4	少帝 Shao Ti[1] (齊王 Ch'i Wang)	芳 Fang	蘭卿 Lan-ch'ing	adopted s of C (s of 王楷 Wang Chieh)	-, -, 232[2]	21, 1, 239 — deposed 17, 10, 254	-, 10/11, 274	正始 Chêng-shih 庚申	10, 2, 240 -, 12/1, 239
								嘉平 Chia-p'ing 己巳	31, 1, 249 7, 5, 249
E c.4	高貴鄉公 Kao kuei hsiang kung	髦 Mao	彥士 Yen-shih	gds of B (s of 霖 Lin)	-, -, 241	2, 11, 254	2, 6, 260	正元 Chêng-yüan 甲戌	5, 2, 254 2, 11, 254
								甘露 Kan-lu 丙子	13, 2, 256 10, 7, 256
F c.4	元 Yüan 陳留王 (Ch'ên Liu Wang)	奐 Huan	景明 Ching-ming	gds of A (s of 宇 Yü)	-, -, 245[3]	27, 6, 260 — deposed 4, 2, 266	-, -, 302	景元 Ching-yüan 庚辰	30, 1, 260 27, 6, 260
								咸熙 Hsien-hsi 甲申	15, 2, 264 26, 6, 264

1. This title is taken from *Conc. néom.*, 374, 375, 519. *Ku chin jên ming-tz'ŭ tien*, 987, *Li tai ming jên . . piao*, 508, and Mayers *Manual*, 374, all give D as 廢帝 Fei Ti, "the deposed Emperor", and E as 少帝 Shao Ti. *San kuo chih*, *Contents*, describes D, E, F as 三少帝 "The three young Emperors"; the *Wei chih*, 4, 5*b*, calls D 皇帝芳 "The Emperor Fang" in a decree, but does not seem otherwise to record any title for D or E.

2. The *Wei chih*, 4, 6*a*, says he was in his 23 year in 254, and in 4, 6*b*, quotes the 魏世譜 *Wei shih p'u* to the effect that D died in his 43 year in the 10th T'ai-shih year (274). *Li tai ming jên . . piao*, 508, gives the year 231.

3. This date is calculated from the statement of the *Wei shih p'u* (in *Wei chih* 4, 15*b*) that F died in his fifty-eighth year in the 1st T'ai-an year (302); but the text of the *Wei chih*, 4, 15*b*, says he was deposed in his 20 year in 265-6, & would therefore have been born in 246.

劉 Liu　　　　益州 I-chou[1]　　　　三國 San Kuo 蜀漢 Shu Han

1.	2.	3.	4.	5.	6.	7.	8.	9.	10.
A c.2.	昭烈 Chao lieh (先主 Hsien Chu)	備 Pei	玄德 Hsüan-tê	s of 弘 Hung[2]	-, -, 161	15, 5, 221	10, 6, 223[3]	章武 Chang-wu 辛丑	10, 2, 221 15, 5, 221
B	思公 Ssŭ Kung (後主 Hou Chu)	禪 Shan	公嗣 Kung-ssŭ	s of A	-, -, 207	-, 6/7, 223[4] deposed -, 12/1, 263/4	-, -, 271	[1.] 建興 Chien-hsing 癸卯	18, 2, 223 ?21, 6, 223
				9.	10.	9.	10.		
c.3				[4.] 炎興[5] Yen-hsing 癸未	27, 1, 263 -, 5–10, 263	[3.] 景耀 Ching-yao 戊寅	21, 2, 258 -, -, 258	[2.] 延熙 Yen-hsi 戊午	2, 2, 238 -, 2, 238

三國志・蜀志 *San kuo chih*・*Shu chih* c.1—

1. The seat of government (治 *chih*) of I-chou was often moved, but was now at 成都 Chʻêng-tu - *Ku chin ti ming tien*, 738.
2. Hung was descended from 勝 Shêng, a son of 景帝 Ching Ti - p. 5 above.
3. The date given (*Shu chih*, 2, 8*b*, 四月癸巳) is impossible; but on the next page (9*a*) Chu-ko Liang is reported to have said, 今月二十四日奄忽升遐 "On the 24 of this moon [the Emperor] suddenly died", and that was 10 June 223 (壬午).
4. The dates are vague. The only date given for Shan's accession (*Shu chih* 3, 1*a*) is 5th moon, 16,6 - 15,7. He capitulated and was deposed in the 11th moon (18,12,263 - 16,1,264) according to the *Wei chih*, 4, 13*b*; the *Shu chih*, 3, 4*a*, merely saying that 鄧艾 Têng Ai attacked Shu in the winter (冬, 10–12 moons).
5. *Synchronismes*, 169, says that Yen-hsing was decreed in the 8 moon (21,9 - 19,10) 263, & that the dynasty ended in the 10 moon (6,11 - 5,12) 264. *Conc. néom.*, 506, agrees with the first statement. The *Shu chih*, 3, 4*a*, records the institution of Yen-hsing within the vague limits of summer & autumn (4 - 9 moons), & the installation of the 'Emperor', together with the grant of the title 公 Kung to Shan, on a day in the 3 moon (10, 5, 264) which perhaps marks the formal end of the Han dynasty.

1.	2.	3.	4.	5.	6.	7.	8.	9.	10.
A c.2	大 Ta (T'ai) (吳主 Wu Chu)	權 Ch'üan	仲謀 Chung-mu	2nd s of 堅 Chien 9. 6. 神鳳 Shên-fêng 壬申	-, -, 182 10. 29, 1, 252 -, 3, 252	23, 5, 229 9. 4. 赤烏 Ch'ih-wu 戊午 5. 太元 T'ai-yüan 辛未	-, 5, 252 10. 2, 2, 238 -, 9, 238 8, 2, 251 -, 6, 251	黃武 Huang-wu 壬寅 2. 黃龍 Huang-lung 己酉 3. 嘉禾 Chia-ho 壬子	30, 1, 222 12, 11, 222 11, 2, 229 23, 5, 229 9, 2, 232 8, 2, 232
B c.3	廢帝, Fei Ti[1] 候官侯 Hou kuan Hou (260) 會稽王 Kuei(K'uai)-chi Wang (258)	亮 Liang	子明 Tzŭ-ming	youngest s of A	-, -, 243	-, 5, 252 — deposed 9, 11, 258	-, 10/11, 260	建興 Chien-hsing 壬申 五鳳 Wu-fêng 甲戌 太平 Tai-p'ing 丙子	29, 1, 252 -, 5, 252 5, 2, 254 ?-, 12, 253 13, 2, 256 10, 11, 256
C c.3	景 Ching	休 Hsiu	子烈 Tzŭ-lieh	6th s of A	-, -, 235	30, 11, 258	3, 9, 264	永安 Yung-an 戊寅	20, 2, 258 30, [illegible], 258

三國志·吳志 *San kuo chih · Wu chih*, cc. 2, 3

1. *San kuo chih, Contents*, calls B, C, D 三嗣主 San ssŭ Chu, with their names Liang, Hsiu, and Hao. *Wu chih*, 3, followed by *Synchron.* and *Conc. néom.*, gives Ta (A), Hou (候 or 侯) kuan Hou (B), Ching (C), and Kuei ming Hou (D). Fei Ti is given by Mayers, *Manual*, 374, and *Li tai ming jên . . piao*, 509; Mo Ti by Mayers, ibid; and Wu ch'êng Ti by *Li tai ming jên . . piao*, 509. D had been made 烏程侯 Wu ch'êng Hou by B in 258 (*Wu chih*, 3, 5b). Fei Ti and Mo Ti are also given by *Chung kuo ti hao piao t'i i lan*, 77, 25.

1.	2.	3.	4.	5.	6.	7.	8.	9.	10.
D	末帝 Mo Ti 歸命侯 Kuei ming Hou 烏程帝 Wu ch'êng Ti	皓 Hao — 彭祖 P'êng-tsu	元宗 Yüan-tsung — 皓宗 Hao-tsung	gds of A (s of 和 Ho)	-, -, 242 [2]	?-, 9, 264 — deposed [3] 31, 5, 280	?-, 1, 281	1. 元興 Yüan-hsing 甲申	15, 2, 264 ?-, 9, 264
								2. 甘露 Kan-lu 乙酉	3, 2, 265 -, 5, 265
				9.	10.	9.	10.		
				7. 天璽 [6] T'ien-hsi 丙申	2, 2, 276 ?-, 8, 276	5. 鳳皇 [4] Fêng-huang 壬辰	16, 2, 272 -, -, 271/2	3. 寶鼎 Pao-ting 丙戌	22, 2, 266 -, 9/10, 266
c. 3				8. 天紀 T'ien-chi 丁酉	20, 2, 277 -, -, 276/7	6. 天册 [5] T'ien-ts'ê 乙未	13, 2, 275 -, -, 275	4. 建衡 Chien-hêng 己丑	19, 2, 269 -, 11/12, 269

2. There is some uncertainty about this date. The only indication in the text seems to be the statement (*Wu chih* 3, 5*b*) that Hao was enthroned in 264 in his 23rd year, and the year of birth is therefore given as 242. But on fol. 11*a* the text says that he died at Lo-yang in 281 (五年皓死於洛陽), a note adding a quotation from the 吳錄 *Wu lu* that he died in the 12 moon of 280 (四年十二月 *i.e.* January 281) in his 42nd year. To suppose an error of a few days in the *Wu chih* might make it agree with the *Wu lu*, that Hao died in Jan. 281; but if he was then in his 42nd year he must have been born in 239-40. *Li tai ming jên . . piao*, 509, gives the dates 243–283, age 41. *Synchron.* 169, makes him die in 283, age 42, and so born in 242. Giles *B.D.* 1807, gives 242–283. The statements in the *Wu chih*, not in themselves inconsistent, cannot be reconciled with the *Wu lu* or with the sources of the modern books. A *Wu lu* in 30 *chüan* by 張勃 Chang Po of the Chin is recorded in *Sui shu*, 33, 1*b*.

3. The date of Hao's capitulation is given both in *Wu chih*, 3, 10*b*, 11*a*, and *Chin shu*, 3, 8*b*, as 三月壬申; but the day 壬申 *jên-shên* did not occur in the 3rd moon, and as the other days given under the 3rd moon in both books were really in the 4th moon, 三月, 3rd moon, should probably be corrected to 四月, 4th moon.

4. In the third Chien-hêng year no moons or days are specified after 正月晦 "the end of the 1st moon". The year ends (3, 8*a*) with 西苑言鳳皇集改明年元 "The West Park reported a gathering of *fêng-huang*; the period for next year was changed." Thus the title Fêng-huang was decreed, like T'ien-chi below, on some day in the year before it came into use. Incidentally, the existence of a *Hsi yüan*, West Park, at this date seems to have escaped the recent geographers and lexicographers.

5. The T'ien-ts'ê year has no heading in the *Wu chih*, 3, 8*b*; but at the end of the 3rd Fêng-huang year (274) we read 天册元年吳郡言 . . . 於是大赦改年 "In the 1st T'ien-ts'ê year Wu district reported . . ; so there was a general amnesty & the year was changed". This must probably refer to the title T'ien-ts'ê, since the change to T'ien-hsi is recorded without exact date in the T'ien-hsi year. *Conc. néom.* 520, allots 275 & half of 276 to T'ien-ts'ê, but the sentence quoted above is all the notice which this year title & year receive in the Annals of the *Wu chih*.

6. *Synchron.* 172 and *Conc. néom.* 520, both say that T'ien-hsi was decreed in the 7th moon, August, 276, and I have adopted this, though I do not know what may be the authority.

司馬 Ssŭ-ma　　洛陽 Lo-yang　　西晉 Hsi Chin

1.	2.	3.	4.	5.	6.	7.	8.	9.	10.
a c.1	文宣 Wên hsüan (266) 文貞 Wên chêng (251)	懿 I	仲達 Chung-ta	2nd s of 防 Fang	-, -, 179	—	7, 9, 251	—	—
b 世宗 Shih Tsung c.2	景 Ching (266) 景王 Ching Wang 忠武公 Chung wu Kung (255)	師 Shih	子元 Tzŭ-yüan	1st s of a	-, -, 208	—	23, 3, 255	—	—
c 太祖 T'ai Tsu c.2	文 Wên (266)	昭 Chao	子上 Tzŭ-shang	s of a	-, -, 211	—	6, 9, 265	—	—
A 世祖 Shih Tsu c.3	武 Wu	炎 Yen	安世 An-shih	1st s of c	-, -, 236	8, 2, 266	16, 5, 290	泰(太)始 T'ai-shih 乙酉	3, 2, 265 8, 2, 266
								2. 咸寧 Hsien-ning 乙未	13, 2, 275 13, 2, 275
								3. 太康 T'ai-k'ang 庚子	18, 2, 280 13, 6, 280
								4. 太熙 T'ai-hsi 庚戌	28, 1, 290 28, 1, 290
B c.4	孝惠 Hsiao Hui	衷 Chung	正度 Chêng-tu	2nd s of A	-, -, 259	16, 5, 290	8, 1, 307	1. 永熙 Yung-hsi 庚戌	28, 1, 290 16, 5, 290
								2. 永平 Yung-p'ing 辛亥	16, 2, 291 16, 2, 291
								3. 元康 Yüan-k'ang 辛亥	16, 2, 291 24, 4, 291
								4. 永康 Yung-k'ang 庚申	7, 2, 300 7, 2, 300
								5. 永寧 Yung-ning 辛酉	26, 1, 301 1, 6, 301
								6. 太安 T'ai-an 壬戌	14, 2, 302 26, 1, 303
								7. 永安 Yung-an 甲子	22, 2, 304 1.29, 2, 304 2.25, 12, 304
								8. 建武 Chien-wu 甲子	22, 2, 304 10, 9, 304
								9. 永興 Yung-hsing 甲子	22, 2, 304 4, 2, 305
								10. 光熙 Kuang-hsi 丙寅	31, 1, 306 13, 7, 306
C c.5	孝懷 Hsiao Huai	熾 Chih	豐度 Fêng-tu	25th s of A	-, -, 284	11, 1, 307 deposed [2] 13, 7, 311	14, 3, 313	永嘉 Yung-chia 丁卯	19, 2, 307 [3] 19, 2, 307
D c.5	孝愍 Hsiao Min [4]	鄴 Yeh	彥旗 Yen-ch'i	gds of A (s of 晏 Yen)	-, -, 301	7, 6, 313 deposed 11, 12, 316	7, 2, 318	建興 Chien-hsing 癸酉	12, 2, 313 7, 6, 313

晉書 Chin shu cc. 1—5, &c.

1. This title is not named in Chin shu, 4, 1b; we read only 三月..壬辰大赦改元. It occurs (元康二年) in c. 6, 1a.
2. Chih was deposed by 劉聰 Liu Ts'ung (p. 35 below), & the dynasty was in abeyance for two years of confusion.
3. Conc. néom. 145 & Mélanges sur la Chronologie, 80, show that 癸丑 (c. 5, 1b) must be changed to 壬子 for the first day of this year.　4. D made 長安 Ch'ang-an his capital.

1.	2.	3.	4.	5.	6.	7.	8.	9.	10.
A 中宗 Chung Tsung c.6	元 Yüan	睿 Jui	景文 Ching-wên	gt-gds of a (s of 覲 Chin)	-, -, 276	23, 4, 318 (6, 4, 317 as 晉王 Chin Wang)	3, 1, 323	1. 建武 Chien-wu 丁丑	29, 1, 317 6, 4, 317
						9.	10.	2. 太興 T'ai-hsing 戊寅	17, 2, 318 23, 4, 318
						3. 永昌 Yung-ch'ang 壬午	3, 2, 322 3, 2, 322		
B 肅宗 Su Tsung c.6	明 Ming	紹 Shao	道畿 Tao-chi	1st s of A	-, -, 299	3, 1, 323	18, 10, 325	太寧 T'ai-ning 癸未	22, 2, 323 22, 4, 323
C 顯宗 Hsien Tsung c.7	成 Ch'êng	衍 Yen	世根 Shih-kên	1st s of B	-, -, 321	19, 10, 325	26, 7, 342	咸和 Hsien-ho 丙戌	19, 2, 326 15, 4, 326
								咸康 Hsien-k'ang 乙未	10, 2, 335 10, 2, 335
D c.7	康 K'ang	岳 Yo	世同 Shih-t'ung	s of B	-, -, 322	27, 7, 342	17, 11, 344	建元 Chien-yüan 癸卯	11, 2, 343 [11, 2,] 343
E 孝宗 Hsiao Tsung c.8	穆 Mu	聃 T'an	彭子 P'êng-tzŭ	s of D	-, -, 343	18, 11, 344	10, 7, 361	永和 Yung-ho 乙巳	18, 2, 345 18, 2, 345[1]
								升平 Shêng-p'ing 丁巳	6, 2, 357 6, 2, 357
F c.8	哀 Ai	丕 P'ei	千齡 Ch'ien-ling	1st s of C	-, -, 341	13, 7, 361	30, 3, 365	隆和 Lung-ho 壬戌	11, 2, 362 2, 3, 362
								興寧 Hsing-ning 癸亥	31, 1, 363 3, 3, 363[2]
G c.8	廢 Fei 海西公 Hai hsi Kung	奕 I	延齡 Yen-ling	s of C	-, -, 342	31, 3, 365 deposed 6, 1, 372	23, 11, 386	太和 T'ai-ho 丙寅	28, 1, 366

晉書 Chin shu cc. 6–10, &c.

1. Chin shu, 8, 1a, 正月甲戌朔. Conc. néom. 150, & Mélanges, 80, give 辛未朔 (18, 2, 345), making 甲戌 the 4th day, 21, 2, 345. The equivalent of 辛未 hsin-wei is here adopted, as there is a probability that the change was made on the 1st day (朔).
2. The date in Chin shu, 8, 6a, (二月己亥) is impossible. I presume 二月己未; but there are other possibilities.

東晉 Tung Chin

1.	2.	3.	4.	5.	6.	7.	8.	9.	10.
H 太宗 T'ai Tsung c.9.	簡文 Chien wên	昱 Yü	道萬 Tao-wan	youngest s of A	-, -, 320	6, 1, 372	19, 8, 372	咸安 Hsien-an 辛未	2, 2, 371 12, 1, 372
I	孝武 Hsiao Wu	曜 Yao	昌明 Ch'ang-ming	3rd s of H	-, -, 362	19, 8, 372	6, 11, 396	寧康 Ning-k'ang 癸酉	9, 2, 373 9, 2, 373
c.9								太元 T'ai-yüan 丙子	7, 2, 376 9, 2, 376
J	安 An	德宗 Tê-tsung	德宗 Tê-tsung	1st s of I	-, -, 383	7, 11, 396	28, 1, 419	1. 隆安 Lung-an 丁酉	13, 2, 397 13, 2, 397
						9.	10.		
c.10						3. 義熙 I-hsi 乙巳	15, 2, 405 2, 3, 405	2. 元興 Yüan-hsing 壬寅	18, 2, 402 18, 2, 402
K c.10	恭 Kung	德文 Tê-wên	德文 Tê-wên	s of I	-, -, 386	28, 1, 419 deposed 5, 7, 420	12, 11, 421	元熙 Yüan-hsi 己未	11, 2, 419 11, 2, 419

劉 Liu 建康 Chien-k'ang 南朝 Nan Ch'ao: 宋 Sung[1]

1.	2.	3.	4.	5.	6.	7.	8.	9.	10.
A 高祖 Kao Tsu cc.1–3	武 Wu	裕 Yü 寄奴(小名) Chi-nu	德輿 Tê-yü	s of 翹 Ch'iao[2]	16, 4, 363	10, 7, 420	26, 6, 422[3]	永初 Yung-ch'u 庚申	31, 1, 420 10, 7, 420
B c.4	少帝 Shao Ti 營陽王 Ying yang Wang	義符 I-fu	車兵(小字) Chü-ping	1st s of A	-, -, 406	26, 6, 422	4, 8, 424	景平 Ching-p'ing 癸亥	28, 1, 423 28, 1, 423
C 太祖 T'ai Tsu (5, 453) 中宗 (3, 453) Chung Tsung	文 Wên (5, 453) 景 Ching (3, 453) c.5	義隆 I-lung	車兒(小字) Chü-êrh	3rd s of A	-, -, 407	17, 9, 424	16, 3, 453	元嘉 Yüan-chia 甲子	16, 2, 424 17, 9, 424
D 世祖 Shih Tsu c.6	孝武 Hsiao Wu	駿 Chün	休龍 Hsiu-lung 道民(小字) Tao-min[4]	3rd s of C	19, 9, 430	20, 5, 453	12, 7, 464	孝建 Hsiao-chien 甲午	14, 2, 454 14, 2, 454
								大明 T'ai-ming 丁酉	10, 2, 457 10, 2, 457

宋書 _Sung shu_ cc.1–10, &c. 南史 _Nan shih_ cc. 1–3.

1. To distinguish it from the greater Sung, 960–1280, this dynasty is known as 前 Ch'ien Sung (_Conc. néom._), 水 Shui Sung, or commonly as 劉 Liu Sung.

2. Ch'iao was descended in the 20th generation from 交 Chiao, younger brother of Han Kao Tsu (p. 4 above).

3. _Sung shu_, 1, 1_a_, & _Nan shih_, 1, 1_a_, give the day of birth exactly. The Emperor "was born at night on the _jên-yin_ day of the third moon of the first Hsing-ning year of Ai Ti of the Chin, _kuei-hai_ in the order of years." And the _Sung shu_, 3, 4_b_, gives the day of his death, 三年…五月…癸亥上崩于西殿時六十七 秋七月… "On the _kuei-hai_ of the 5th moon of the third year the Emperor died in the West Hall, at the time 67. In the autumn, the 7th moon, …" But in 422 he was in his 60, not 67, year, and it is clear that 時六十七, with the unusual omission of 年 _nien_, "years", has been infected by the 七月 which follows & should be 時年六十 秋七月. The _Nan shih_, 1, 12_a_, in fact has 時年六十七月. Giles _B.D._ 1375, gives the dates 356–422. _Li tai ming jên.. piao_, 510, has 356–422, and the age 67. _Synchronismes_, 212, gives the age 60.

4. _Nan shih_, 2, 6_a_, reads 道人 Tao-jên. This, with 休景 Hsiu-ching for F below, is due to the taboo of 民 _min_, 丙 _ping_, &c. in the T'ang dynasty. But _Nan shih_, 3 _kao chêng_, merely records the readings 丨景, 丨炳, 景休, without comment.

宋 Sung

1.	2.	3.	4.	5.	6.	7.	8.	9.	10.
E c.7	前廢帝 Ch'ien Fei Ti	子業 Tzŭ-yeh	法師(小字) Fa-shih	1st s of D	25, 2, 449	12, 7, 464	1, 1, 466	永光 Yung-kuang 乙巳	12, 2, 465 12, 2, 465
								景和 Ching-ho 乙巳	12, 2, 465 18, 9, 465
F 太宗 T'ai Tsung c.8	明 Ming	彧 Yü	休炳 Hsiu-ping 榮期(小字) Jung-ch'i	11th s of C	9, 2, 439	9, 1, 466	10, 5, 472	泰始 T'ai-shih 乙巳	12, 2, 465 9, 1, 466
								泰豫 T'ai-yü 壬子	26, 1, 472 26, 1, 472
G c.9	[後]廢帝, Hou Fei Ti[1] 蒼梧王 Ts'ang wu Wang	昱 Yü	德融 Tê-jung 慧震(小字) Hui-chên	1st s of F	1, 3, 463	11, 5, 472	1, 8, 477	元徽 Yüan-hui 癸丑	13, 2, 473 13, 2, 473
H c.10	順 Shun	準 Chun	仲謀 Chung-mou 智觀(小字) Chih-kuan	3rd s of F	8, 8, 469	5, 8, 477 — deposed 27, 5, 479	23, 6, 479[2]	昇明 Shêng-ming 丁巳	30, 1, 477 5, 8, 477

1. *Sung shu*, 9, 1a, has Fei Ti; Hou is prefixed in *Nan shih*, 3, 3b.

2. *Sung shu*, 10, 3b, the age at the time of death is given as 13 (時年十三), presumably a misprint for 11 (十一). *Nan shih*, 3, 6b, gives no age. *Nan shih*, 3, 5b, gives the names in col. 4 as 仲謀 Chung-mo & 知觀 Chih-kuan. These forms, as well as the age 13, are given in *Chung kuo jên ming..tien* 355. Giles *B.D.* 1294, has Chung-mo. *Li tai ming jên..piao*, 510, gives the age 13, and the dates 467–479.

蕭 Hsiao 建康 Chien-k'ang Nan Ch'ao : 南齊 Nan Ch'i

1.	2.	3.	4.	5.	6.	7.	8.	9.	10.
A 太祖 T'ai Tsu c. 1, 2	高 Kao	道成 Tao-ch'êng 鬬將 (小諱) Tou-chiang	紹伯 Shao-po	s of 承之 [1] Ch'êng-chih	12, 2, 427 [2]	29, 5, 479	11, 4, 482	建元 Chien-yüan 己未	7, 2, 479 29, 5, 479
B 世祖 Shih Tsu c. 3	武 Wu	賾 Tsê 龍兒 (小諱) Lung-êrh	宣遠 Hsüan-yüan	1st s of A	17, 7, 440 [3]	11, 4, 482	27, 8, 493	永明 Yung-ming 癸亥	24, 1, 483 25, 1, 483
C c. 4	鬱林王 Yü lin Wang 廢帝 (Nan shih) Fei Ti	昭業 Chao-yeh 法身 (小諱) Fa-shên	元尚 Yüan-shang	gds of B [4]	?-, -, 473	27, 8, 493	5, 9, 494 [5]	隆昌 Lung-ch'ang 甲戌	23, 1, 494 23, 1, 494
D c. 5	海陵恭王 Hai ling Kung Wang 廢帝 (Nan shih) Fei Ti	昭文 Chao-wên	季尚 Chi-shang	gds of B [4]	-, -, 480	10, 9, 494 deposed 23, 11, 494	-, 12/1, 494	延興 Yen-hsing 甲戌	23, 1, 494 10, 9, 494

南齊書 Nan ch'i shu cc. 1—8, &c. 南史 Nan shih cc. 4, 5.

1. Ch'êng-chih was descended in the 23rd generation from Hsiao 何 Ho (+193 B.C.) who was a great supporter of Liu Pang.
2. The day & month (12, 2) are not in Nan ch'i shu or Nan shih, & I cannot now trace the source.
3. Nan ch'i shu, 3, 8b, & Nan shih, 4, 12b, record B's death in 493 in his 54 year (年五十四). If this is right he was born in 440, in his father's 14th year. But Nan shih, 4, 8b, gives an exact date of birth, "born on chi-wei of the 6th moon, the 27 Yüan-chia year" (450). The day chi-wei, however, fell in the 6th moon, as stated, in 440, but in 450 it was the first day of the 7th moon. Since B's son, who was born "before [his father] was 20" (年未弱冠), died in 493 in his 36 year (Nan ch'i shu, 21, 1a, 3a) he must have been born in 458, and we may assume that 二十七 (27, i.e. 450) in Nan shih, 4, 8b, should be 一十七 (17, i.e. 440). Synchron. 223, gives the date of death 493, age 54. Li tai ming jên ·· piao, 510, supposes a transposition of 4 & 5, making the age 45, with the dates 449 – 493.
4. C was the son of 文惠太子 Wên hui T'ai tzŭ, 458 – 493; see note 3 above. D was 2nd son of the same.
5. The day on which C was murdered is given as 二十二日壬辰 (Nan ch'i shu, 4, 3a). 壬辰 jên-ch'ên was in fact the 20, not 22, day of the 7th moon. Nan ch'i shu gives his age as 21 (i.e. born in 474), Nan shih, 5, 3a, as 22. The other indications in the Nan shih are not conclusive, though they point to 473 as the year of birth. Thus he is said to have been in his 10th year when B was enthroned (482), to have been capped (冠) on 7, 12, 487, and to have died in 494 in his 22 year. The dictionaries, following the Li chi (cf. S.B.E. xxvii, 65, 478), say that a man was capped at the age of 20 (cf. note 3 above), but here an earlier age, perhaps 15, must be meant.

南齊 Nan Ch'i

1.	2.	3.	4.	5.	6.	7.	8.	9.	10.
E 高宗 Kao Tsung c.6	明 Ming	鸞 Luan 玄度(小諱) Hsüan-tu	景栖 Ching-hsi	nephew of A (s of 道生 Tao-shêng)	-, -, 452	5, 12, 494	1, 9, 498	建武 Chien-wu 甲戌	23, 1, 494 5, 12, 494
								永泰 Yung-t'ai 戊寅	7, 2, 498 9, 5, 498
F c.7	東昏侯 Tung hun Hou 廢帝 Fei Ti (<u>Nan shih</u>)	寶卷 Pao-chüan 明賢(本名) Ming-hsien	智藏 Chih-tsang	2nd s of E	-, -, 483	1, 9, 498 — deposed 14, 4, 501	31, 12, 501	永元 Yung-yüan 己卯	28, 1, 499 28, 1, 499
G c.8	和 Ho	寶融 Pao-jung	智昭 Chih-chao	8th s of E	-, -, 488	14, 4, 501 — deposed 20, 4, 502	2, 5, 502	中興 Chung-hsing 辛巳	4, 2, 501 14, 4, 501

蕭 Hsiao　　建康 Chien-k'ang　　Nan Ch'ao : 梁 Liang

1.	2.	3.	4.	5.	6.	7.	8.	9.	10.
A 高祖 Kao Tsu c.1–3	武 Wu	衍 Yen	叔達 Shu-ta 練兒(小字) Lien-êrh	cousin of A[1] (p.22 above)	-, -, 464	30, 4, 502	12, 6, 549	1. 天監 T'ien-chien 壬午	24, 1, 502 30, 4, 502
				9.	10.	9.	10.		
				6. 中大同 Chung-ta-t'ung 丙寅	16, 2, 546 29, 5, 546	4. 中大通 Chung-ta-t'ung 己酉	25, 1, 529 17, 11, 529	2. 普通 P'u-t'ung 庚子	4, 2, 520 4, 2, 520
				7. 太清 T'ai-ch'ing 丁卯	6, 2, 547 25, 5, 547	5. 大同 Ta-t'ung 乙卯	18, 2, 535 18, 2, 535	3. 大通 Ta-t'ung 丁未	17, 2, 527 27, 4, 527
B 太宗(552) T'ai Tsung 高宗(551) Kao Tsung c.4	簡文(552) Chien wên 明(551) Ming	綱 Kang	世贊 Shih-tsan 六通(小字) Lu-t'ung	3rd s of A	2, 12, 503	7, 7, 549 deposed[2] 2, 10, 551	15, 11, 551	大寶 Ta-pao 庚午	2, 2, 550 2, 2, 550

梁書 *Liang shu* cc. 1–6, &c.　　南史 *Nan shih* cc. 6–8, &c.

1. A was son of 順之 Shun-chih, and cousin of Kao Tsu of the Nan Ch'i dynasty.

2. It is usual (cf. Mayers *Manual* 371; *Synchron.* 236; *Conc. néom.* 509; &c.) to insert between B and C the rival reign of 豫章王蕭棟 Hsiao Tung, Prince Chang of Yü, with the Year Title 天正 T'ien-chêng. It has seemed better to put it here in a note. From *Liang shu* 4, 3a, *Nan shih* 8, 2a, it seems that Tung was proclaimed by a decree purporting to come from B, but really forged by the rebel 侯景 Hou Ching, and enthroned, with the Year Title T'ien-chêng on 2, 10, 551. The long but vaguely dated biographies of Hou Ching (*Liang shu* 56, *Nan shih* 80) make these events happen "this day" or "this moon" after naming the 4 moon (*Nan shih* 80, 8b). On the next page (80, 9a) it says that Hou Ching took over the rule himself & was enthroned in the 11th moon, changing the Year Title to 太始 T'ai-shih (551-2), and finally (80, 11a) gives the exact dates of Hou Ching's brief reign, 1, 1, 552 to 28, 4, 552 when he was defeated and killed. Tung was killed four days later on 2, 5, 552 (*Liang shu* 5, 7a; *Nan shih* 8, 4b).

The Year Title 天正 T'ien-chêng had apparently been first instituted by 武陵王紀 Chi Prince of Wu-ling, 8th son of A, on 11, 6, 551 (*Nan shih* 53, 10a), when he was proclaimed Emperor in 蜀 Shu; and it was continued, or perhaps resumed on 16, 5, 552 (*Liang shu* 5, 7a), by him till he was killed on 5, 8, 553 (*Liang shu*, 5, 9a) in his 46th year. The Biographies (*Liang shu* 55, 1b–3a; *Nan shih* 53, 9b–11a) are again vague in dates. The dates are puzzling & hard to be sure of, but there seems to be nothing in the books here used to support *Synchron.* in making Ching survive to 553, or Chi to 554. The reign of Ching is stated to have lasted 120 days.

1.	2.	3.	4.	5.	6.	7.	8.	9.	10.
C 世相 Shih Tsu c.5	孝元 Hsiao Yüan ? 文 Wên (cf. Liang shu 5,1a, & also K'ao chêng)	繹 I	世誠 Shih-ch'êng 七符 (小字) Ch'i-fu	7th s of A	16, 9, 508	27, 4, 549 (secretly) —— 13, 12, 552	27, 1, 555	太清四年[1] T'ai-ch'ing (restored) 庚午	2, 2, 550
								承聖 Ch'êngshêng 壬申	11, 2, 552 13, 12, 552
D c.6	敬 Ching 江陰王 (557) Chiang yin Wang	方智 Fang-chih	慧相 Hui-hsiang 法真 (小字) Fa-chên	9th s of C	-, -, 543	29, 10, 555 —— abdicated 12, 11, 557	5, 5, 558	紹泰 Shao-t'ai 乙亥	7, 2, 555 21, 11, 555
								太平 T'ai-p'ing 丙子	28, 1, 556 19, 10, 556

1. *Nan shih* 8, 3a. C, having been secretly proclaimed Emperor (密詔授帝位) before the enthronement of of B, regarded B as a usurper & refused to recognize the Ta-pao period, calling the three Ta-pao years the 4th, 5th, and 6th T'ai-ch'ing years respectively.

1.	2.	3.	4.	5.	6.	7.	8.	9.	
A 高祖 Kao Tsu cc.1–2	武 Wu	霸先 Pa-hsien	興國 Hsing-kuo 法生(小字) Fa-shêng	s of 文讚 Wên-tsan	–, –, 503	16, 11, 557	9. 8, 559	永定 Yung-ting 丁丑	15, 2, 557 16, 11, 557
B 世祖 Shih Tsu c.3	文 Wên	蒨 Ch'ien	子華 Tzŭ-hua	1st s of 昭烈王 Chao lieh Wang, who was the elder br of A – *Ch'ên shu*, 28, 1a	–, –, 522	17, 8, 559	31, 5, 566	天嘉 T'ien-chia 庚辰	12, 2, 560 12, 2, 560
								天康 T'ien-k'ang 丙戌	5, 2, 566 4, 4, 566
C c.4	廢帝 Fei Ti 臨海王 Lin hai Wang	伯宗 Po-tsung	奉業 Fêng-yeh 藥王(小字) Yo-wang	1st s of B	20, 6, 554	31, 5, 566 abdicated 27, 12, 568	22, 4, 570[1]	光大 Kuang-ta 丁亥	26, 1, 567 26, 1, 567
D 高宗 Kao Tsung c.5	孝宣 Hsiao Hsüan	頊 Hsü	紹世 Shao-shih 師利(小字) Shih-li	2nd s of 始興昭烈王 Shih hsing Chao lieh Wang	6, 8, 528[2]	5, 2, 569	17, 2, 582	太建 T'ai-chien 己丑	2, 2, 569 5, 2, 569
E c.6	後主 Hou Chu	叔寶 Shu-pao	元秀 Yüan-hsiu 黃奴(小字) Huang-nu	1st s of D	10, 12, 553	20, 2, 582 abdicated 27, 3, 589	16, 12, 604	至德 Chih-tê 癸卯	29, 1, 583 31, 1, 583
								禎明 Chêng-ming 丁未	13, 2, 587 15, 2, 587

陳書 *Ch'ên shu* cc.1–6 南史 *Nan shih* cc. 9–10

1. The exact date is given in *Ch'ên shu* 5, 2a, & *Nan shih*, 9, 12a, 10, 1b. *Ch'ên shu* 4, 3a gives the same year & moon, but no day. Both books give the same birthday, & both say C died in his 19 (in place of 17) year. *Li tai ming jên . . piao*, 511, gives the dates 550–568, age 19. *Synchronismes*, 241, says he was killed in 570, age 19.

2. This date (*Ch'ên shu*, 5, 1a · 大通二年七月辛酉) is inconsistent with the statement that D died in his 53 year in 582. The *Nan shih*, 10, 1a, corrects this by reading 中大通二年(530). *Li tai ming jên . . piao*, 511, gives the dates 531–582, age 52; and *Synchronismes*, 247, says he died in 582, age 53. But the moon & day given in both books are correct for 528 but impossible for 530 or 531; and it is perhaps better to correct the age to 55.

拓跋 T'o-pa N.盛樂 Shêng-lo[1] S.平城 P'ing-ch'êng 北朝 Pei Ch'ao: 魏 Wei

1.	2.	3.	4.	5.	6.	7.	8.	9.	10.
a 太祖(399) c. 1. T'ai Tsu	平文 P'ing wên[2]	鬱律 Yü-lü		s of 思帝 Ssŭ Ti, br of Mu		-, -, 317	-, -, 321	元年 1st year 丁丑	29, 1, 317
b c. 1	惠 Hui	賀傉 Ho-nu		2nd s of 桓 Huan Ti		-, -, 321[3]	-, -, 325	first year 辛巳	14, 2, 321
c c. 1	煬 Yang	紇那 Ho-na		s of Huan Ti		-, -, 325 abdicated -, -, 329 restored -, -, 335 abdicated -, -, 337		元年 first year 乙酉 後元年 later 1st year 乙未	31, 1, 325 till 329 10, 2, 335
d c. 1	烈 Lieh	翳槐 I-huai		1st s of a		-, -, 329 abdicated -, -, 335 restored -, -, 337	?-, -, 338	元年 first year 己丑 後元年 later 1st year 丁酉	15, 2, 329 till 335 17, 2, 337
e 高祖 Kao Tsu c. 1	昭成 Chao ch'êng	什翼犍 Shih-i-chien		2nd s of a	-, -, 320	-, 12, 338	7, 1, 377	建國 Chien-kuo 戊戌	6, 2, 338 -, 12, 338

魏書 *Wei shu* cc. 1—12, &c. 北史 *Pei shih* cc. 1—5, &c.

1. The exact position & chronology of the capitals of Tai & Wei in the region of modern Sui-yüan and northern Shan-hsi are rather puzzling. In or about 295 穆 Mu Ti (then chieftain of one tribe) settled in the original Shêng-lo in Ting-hsiang (*Wei shu*, 1, 3a, 居定襄之盛樂故城 cf. *Ku chin ti ming tien*, 927) In 337 Lieh Ti (d) fortified New Shêng-lo, 10 *li* to the S.-E. of the old city (*Wei shu*, 1, 6a, 城新盛樂城在故城東南十里). Meanwhile Mu Ti (now prince of the whole domain) had fortified Shêng-lo in 313 as his northern capital & had repaired P'ing-ch'êng to be the southern capital. Dissatisfied with the situation, he rebuilt the latter place 100 *li* to the south, at Huang-kua tui on the north bank of the Lei river (cf. *Ku chin ti ming tien*, 519, s.v. 㶟水). The people of Chin called the new city Little P'ing-ch'êng (*Wei shu*, 1, 4b, 城盛樂以為北都修故平城以為南都帝登平城西山觀地勢乃更南百里於㶟水之陽黄瓜堆築新平城晉人謂之小平城). *Ku chin ti ming tien*, 212, seems to place the southern capital S. of Ta-t'ung, & says that Little P'ing-ch'êng is not heard of after the Ch'in, distinguishing it from New P'ing-ch'êng with which *Wei shu* identifies it. Early in 386 A settled in Shêng-lo, & in August 398, having first inspected the palaces of Yeh with a view to fixing his capital there (*Wei shu*, 2, 5b, 將有定都之意), he moved the capital to P'ing-ch'êng (*ibid.* 6a). On 10, 12, 493 G moved into the palace which he had built west of Yeh (*Wei shu*, 7b, 6a, 起宮殿於鄴西十有一月癸亥宮成徙御焉). The seat of government of Yeh seems to have been moved several times; the old walls are said to be 40 *li* W. of the modern 臨漳 Lin-chang (*Ku chin ti ming tien*, 1247). This later capital is called Lo-yang in *Li tai ming jên piao*, 511, & *Tz'ŭ hai* 南北朝.

2. Without following the descent of the Tai rulers from the Yellow Emperor or recording the first 14 or 15 chiefs, whose names & titles, without dates or exploits, are found in *Wei shu*, 1 & *Pei shih* 1, it may be noted that the succession seems to be fairly safe from 神元 Shên yüan, with title 始祖 Shih Tsu (399) or 太祖 T'ai Tsu (536 - *Pei shih* 5, 6b), who began to reign A.D. 220 & died in 277 in the 104 year of his age. He was succeeded, after 3 short reigns, by his son 昭 Chao Ti (295-307) who divided the domain into 3 tribes (分國為三部) under the rule of himself & two nephews, 桓 Huan Ti & Mu Ti, both sons of Shên yüan Ti's son 沙漠汗 Sha mo Han (文帝 Wên Ti). After the death of Chao Ti, Mu Ti (307-316) reunited the three tribes (*Wei shu* 1, 3b, 總攝三部以為一統), and was succeeded by P'ing wên Ti (a) with whom the Table begins.

3. Before Ho-nu could assume control of the government, the Empress Dowager usurped the rule, & sent envoys to Shih Lo (p. 36 below) who were nicknamed at the time "envoys from the Kingdom of Women" (*Wei shu* 1, 5a, 女國使).

1.	2.	3.	4.	5.	6.	7.	8.	9.	10.
A 太祖 T'ai Tsu	道武 (420) Tao wu	珪 Kuei		gds of e	4, 8, 371	(regency)[1] 24, 1, 399	6, 11, 409	1. 元年 first year 丁丑	26, 1, 371
						9.	10.		
烈祖 (536) Lieh Tsu	宣武 (410) Hsüan wu					4. 天興 T'ien-hsing 戊戌	3, 2, 398 24, 1, 399	2. 登國 Têng-kuo 丙戌	15, 2, 386 20, 2, 386
c.2						5. 天賜 T'ien-tz'ŭ 甲辰	28, 1, 404 15, 12, 404	3. 皇始 Huang-shih 丙申	27, 1, 396 ,8/9, 396
B 太宗 T'ai Tsung	明元 (24,1,424) Ming yüan	嗣 Ssŭ		1st s of A[2]	-, -, 392	10, 11, 409[3]	24, 12, 423	1. 永興 Yung-hsing 己酉	1, 2, 409 10, 11, 409
						9.	10.		
c.3						3. 泰常 T'ai-ch'ang 丙辰	14, 2, 416 17, 5 416	2. 神瑞 Shên-jui 甲寅	6, 2, 414 6, 2, 414
C 世祖 Shih Tsu	太武 T'ai wu	燾 Tao		1st s of B	-, -, 408	27, 12, 423[4]	11, 3, 452[5]	1. 始光 Shih-kuang 甲子	16, 2, 424
						9	10.		
						4. 太延 T'ai-yen 乙亥	14, 2, 435 11, 3, 435	2. 神䴥 Shên-chia 戊辰	·2, 2, 428 -, 3, 428
				9.	10.				
c.4a,6				6. 正平 Chêng-p'ing 辛卯	17, 2, 451 23, 7, 451	5. 太平真君[6] T'ai-p'ing-chên-chün 庚辰	19, 2, 440 4, 8, 440	3. 延和 Yen-ho 壬申	17, 2, 432 17, 2, 432

1. As Kuei was not 7 years old when his grandfather (e) died, regents took charge of the rule until his 16th year, when on 20, 2, 386 he became 代王 Prince of Tai. Tai, the old title of the domain, was changed to 魏 Wei in May or June 386, but A remained Prince (王 Wang) until 24 January 399, when he became Emperor (皇帝 Huang Ti) of Wei.
2. Pei shih 1, 10a, Wei shu 3, 1a both say that B was eldest son of A. But Pei shih 15, 7b gives a list of the 9 sons of Chao ch'êng (e), and the second of these is 明元帝, the Emperor Ming yüan, & the third 秦王翰 Han Prince of Ch'in. The major biographies which follow, agreeing with those of the sons & grandsons (子孫) of Chao ch'êng in Wei shu 15, 1-8, are those of three sons, namely 1, 3 (Wei shu 15, 1b, reads 秦明王翰, & specifies that he was the third son), and 9, and of four grandsons, the sons of the sons 5, 6, 7, & 8. The Kao chêng to Wei shu 3 says that this chapter was missing in the old copies and has been supplied from the Pei shih & other sources.
3. Wei shu 3, 1a, 壬申. Pei shih 1, 10a, reads 壬午, i.e. 20, 11, 409.
4. For the impossible 十月壬申, Pei shih 2, 1a, reads 十一月‥壬申; and this is adopted here.
5. Reading 二月 for the 三月 of both Wei shu 4b, 6a, and Pei shih 2, 8b.
6. In practice the first two words of this Year Title were sometimes omitted. cf Pei shih 2, 9a, 真君四年; Wei shu 18, 8a.

魏 Wei

<table>
<tr><th>1.</th><th>2.</th><th>3.</th><th>4.</th><th>5.</th><th>6.</th><th>7.</th><th>8.</th><th>9.</th><th>10.</th></tr>
<tr><td>恭宗
Kung Tsung
c. 4b</td><td>景穆
Ching mu</td><td>晃
Huang[1]</td><td></td><td>1st s of C</td><td>-, -, 428</td><td>—</td><td>29, 7, 451</td><td></td><td></td></tr>
<tr><td>D
c. 4b</td><td>隱
Yin
南安王 Nan an Wang</td><td>余
Yü[2]</td><td></td><td>5th s of C</td><td></td><td>11, 3, 452</td><td>?29, 10, 452</td><td>永平
Yung-p'ing[3]
壬辰</td><td>6, 2, 452
11, 3, 452</td></tr>
<tr><td rowspan="3">E 高宗
Kao Tsung
c. 5</td><td rowspan="3">文成
Wên ch'êng</td><td rowspan="3">濬
Chün</td><td rowspan="3"></td><td>gds of C
(1st s of 晃)</td><td>4, 8, 440</td><td>31, 10, 452</td><td>20, 6, 465</td><td rowspan="2">1. 興安
Hsing-an
壬辰</td><td rowspan="2">6, 2, 452
31, 10, 452</td></tr>
<tr><td>9.</td><td>10.</td><td>9.</td><td>10.</td></tr>
<tr><td>4. 和平
Ho-p'ing
庚子</td><td>8, 2, 460
8, 2, 460</td><td>3. 太安
T'ai-an
乙未</td><td>3, 2, 455
2, 7, 455</td><td>2. 興光
Hsing-kuang
甲午</td><td>14, 2, 454
15, 8, 454</td></tr>
<tr><td rowspan="2">F 顯祖
Hsien Tsu
c. 6</td><td rowspan="2">獻文
Hsien wên</td><td rowspan="2">弘
Hung</td><td rowspan="2"></td><td rowspan="2">1st s of E</td><td rowspan="2">-, 8/9, 454</td><td rowspan="2">21, 6, 465
abdicated
20, 9, 471</td><td rowspan="2">20, 7, 476</td><td>天安
T'ien-an
丙午</td><td>1, 2, 466
1, 2, 466</td></tr>
<tr><td>皇興
Huang-hsing
丁未</td><td>21, 1, 467
13, 10, 467</td></tr>
<tr><td rowspan="3">G 高祖
Kao Tsu
c. 7</td><td rowspan="3">孝文
Hsiao Wên</td><td rowspan="3">宏
Hung[4]</td><td rowspan="3"></td><td rowspan="3">1st s of F</td><td rowspan="3">23, 10, 467</td><td>20, 9, 471</td><td>26, 4, 499</td><td rowspan="2">1. 延興
Yen-hsing
辛亥</td><td rowspan="2">6, 2, 471
20, 9, 471</td></tr>
<tr><td>9.</td><td>10.</td></tr>
<tr><td>3. 太和
T'ai-ho
丁巳</td><td>30, 1, 477
30, 1, 477</td><td>2. 承明
Ch'êng-ming
丙辰</td><td>11, 2, 476
21, 7, 476</td></tr>
</table>

1. Huang, the heir of C, died before his father. Though he never reigned he is given a separate section in the histories among the Emperors, & received the posthumous titles of an Emperor from his son in 453.

2. On the murder of C, Yü was immediately set up (立 li) by the Empress and remained in some sense Emperor until he too was murdered seven months later. He is allowed no separate section as an Emperor in the histories, & received no Temple Title; but he is included here as he had a Year Title & was not apparently a mere usurper.

3. Yung-p'ing is found in Wei shu 46, 6a; 18, 8a; Pei shih 2, 8b. But Conc. néom. 521, Synchronismes 217, Mayers Manual 378, &c. give 承平 Ch'êng-p'ing.

4. Hung changed the family name from 拓跋 T'o-pa to 元 Yüan on 2, 2, 496. cf Wei shu 7b, 8b. 詔改姓為元氏.

1.	2.	3.	4.	5.	6.	7.	8.	9.	10.
H 世宗 Shih Tsung	宣武 Hsüan wu	恪 K'o		2nd s of G	?-, 6, 483.	7, 5, 499	12, 2, 515	1. 景明 Ching-ming 庚辰	15, 2, 500 19, 2, 500
				9.	10.	9.	10.		
c. 8				4. 延昌 Yen-ch'ang 壬辰	3, 2, 512 26, 5, 512	3. 永平 Yung-p'ing 戊子	17, 2, 508 26, 9, 508	2. 正始 Chêng-shih 甲申	1, 2, 504 19, 2, 504
I 肅宗 Su Tsung	孝明 Hsiao ming	詡 Hsü		2nd s of H	8, 4, 510	12, 2, 515	31, 3, 528	1. 熙平 Hsi-p'ing 丙申	18, 2, 516 18, 2, 516
						9.	10.		
						4. 孝昌 Hsiao-ch'ang 乙巳	8, 2, 525 15, 7, 525	2. 神龜 Shên-kuei 戊戌	27, 1, 518 20, 3, 518
c. 9						5. 武泰 Wu-t'ai 戊申	6, 2, 528 13, 2, 528	3. 正光 Chêng-kuang 庚子	4, 2, 520 18, 8, 520
J 敬宗 Ching Tsung	孝莊 Hsiao Chuang	子攸 Tzŭ-yu		gds of F (3rd s of 魏 Hsieh)	-, -, 507	5, 5, 528	26, 1, 531	建義 Chien-i 戊申	6, 2, 528 18, 5, 528
c. 10	武懷 Wu huai							永安 Yung-an 戊申	6, 2, 528 19, 10, 528

1. On the death of I a great-grandson of G, 幼主 Yu Chu "the young Lord", was enthroned without delay on 2 April 528. He was the heir of 寶暉 Pao-hui who was a son of 京兆王愉 Yü Prince of Ching-chao, second son of G. Less than seven weeks later he & the Empress Dowager were put to death. cf. Wei shu 9, 12a-b; Pei shih 4, 9b.

It was a time of great disorder, and Synchronismes, 229, 232, gives a list, which could be extended, of no less than thirteen rebels, of whom some maintained independence for several years.

Name	Date	Year Title	Authority
破落汗拔陵 P'o-lo han Pa-ling	524·3 moon	真王 Chên-wang	Wei shu 9, 7a, 9a.–
莫折念生 Mo-chê Nien-shêng	524·6	天建 T'ien-chien	Wei sh. 9, 12a Pei shih 4, 7-8.
元法僧 Yüan Fa-sêng	525·1	天啟 T'ien-ch'i	Wei shu 9, 8a
杜洛周 Tu Lo-chou	525·8 — 528·2	真王 Chên-wang	Wei shu 9, 9b–12b
劉蠡升 Liu Li-shêng	525·12 — 527·1	神嘉 Shên-chia	Wei sh. 9, 10a .. Pei shih 4, 8b
鮮于修禮 Hsien-yü Hsiu-li	526·1–8	魯興 Lu-hsing	Wei sh. 9, 10a .. Pei shih 4, 8b
葛榮 Ko Jung	526·6 — 528·9	廣安 Kuang-an	Wei shu 9, 11a — 10, 3a
劉獲 Liu Huo	527·7	天授 T'ien-shou	Wei shu 9, 11b
蕭寶夤 Hsiao Pao-yin (486–530)	527·10 — 530·4	隆緒 Lung-hsü dynasty: 齊 Ch'i	Wei shu 9, 12a, 59, 3b–8b
北海王顥 Ao Prince of Pei-hai	529·4	孝基 Hsiao-chi 建武 Chien-wu	Wei shu 21a, 14b
邢杲 Hsing Kao	528·6	天統 T'ien-t'ung	Wei shu 10, 2b
万俟醜奴 Mo-ch'i Ch'ou-nu	528·7	神獸 Shên-shou	Wei sh. 10, 3a .. Pei shih 5, 1b
汝南王悅 Yüeh Prince of Ju-nan	529	更興 Kêng-hsing	Wei shu 22, 3b

The references given to authorities are far from being complete.

魏 Wei

1.	2.	3.	4.	5.	6.	7.	8.	9.	10.
K c. 19c, 8a	東海王 Tung hai Wang	曄 Yeh	華興 Hua-hsing 盆子(小字) P'ên-tzŭ	gt-gds of D (2nd s of 怡 I)		5, 12, 530 ——— deposed[1] 1, 4, 531	26, 12, 532	建明 Chien-ming 庚戌	13, 2, 530 5, 12, 530
L c. 11	前廢帝 or 節文 Ch'ien Fei Ti : Chieh wên	恭 Kung	修業 Hsiu-yeh	gds of F (s of 羽 Yü)	-, -, 498	1, 4, 531 abdicated 1, 6, 532	21, 6, 532	普泰 P'u-t'ai 辛亥	3, 2, 531 1, 4, 531
M c. 11, 3b	後廢帝 Hou Fei Ti	朗 Lang	仲哲 Chung-chê	gt-gds of F (3rd s of 融 Jung)	-, -, 513	31, 10, 531 (at 信都 Hsin-tu) abdicated 6, 6, 532	26, 12, 532	中興 Chung-hsing 辛亥	3, 2, 531 31, 10, 531
N c. 11, 4b	孝武 Hsiao Wu 出帝 Ch'u Ti	修 Hsiu	孝則 Hsiao-tsê	gds of G (3rd s of 懷 Huai)	-, -, 510	13, 6, 532	3, 2, 535	1. 太昌 T'ai-ch'ang 壬子	23, 1, 532 13, 6, 532
						9.	10.		
						3. 永熙 Yung-hsi[2] 壬子	23, 1, 532 ? 8, 2, 533	2. 永興 Yung-hsing 壬子	23, 1, 532 7, 2, 533

1. Pei shih 5, 3b, 二月己巳, correctly, for Wei shu 11, 1a, 三月己巳. Synchron. 232, has 敬 Ching for K.
2. It was remembered just too late that Yung-hsing had been B's first Year Title, & so it was changed at once. – Wei shu 11, 6b.

O: 東魏 Tung Wei, cap. 鄴 Yeh — P–R: 西魏 Hsi Wei, cap. 長安 Ch'ang-an

1.	2.	3.	4.	5.	6.	7.	8.	9.	10.
O[1] c. 12	孝靜 Hsiao Ching 中山王 (550) Chung shan Wang	善見 Shan-chien		1st s of 亶 T'an	-, -, 524	8, 11, 534 ——— abdicated 7, 6, 550	21, 1, 552	1. 天平 T'ien-p'ing 甲寅	30, 1, 534 8, 11, 534
								2. 元象 Yüan-hsiang 戊午	15, 2, 538 21, 2, 538
						9.	10.		
						4. 武定 Wu-ting 癸亥	21, 1, 543 21, 1, 543	3. 興和 Hsing-ho 己未	4, 2, 539 9, 12, 539
P Pei shih 5, 6a	文 Wên	寶炬 Pao-chü		gds of G (s of 愉 Yü)	-, -, 507	18, 2, 535	28, 3, 551	大統 Ta-t'ung 乙卯	18, 2, 535 18, 2, 535
Q Pei shih 5, 8b	廢帝 Fei Ti	欽 Ch'in		1st s of P		?28, 3, 551 deposed -, 2/3, 554	? -, 2/3, 554	元年 first year 壬申	11, 2, 552
R Pei shih 5, 8b	恭 Kung	廓 Kuo		4th s of P		-, 2/3, 554 deposed 14, 2, 557	? -, 2/3, 557	元年 first year 甲戌	18, 2, 554

1. In the Wei shu this reign ends the Annals (帝紀); but in the Pei shih 5, 9a, as well as in Western chronological tables, it is reckoned as an usurpation forming the Eastern Wei dynasty, while the three following reigns which form the Western Wei are regarded as the legitimate successors of the original Northern, T'o-pa, Wei.

1.	2.	3.	4.	5.	6.	7.	8.	9.	10.
a 高祖(565) Kao Tsu 太祖(550) T'ai Tsu c.1–2	神武(565) Shên wu 獻武(547) Hsien wu	歡 Huan	賀六渾 Ho-lu-hun	s of 樹 Shu	-, -, 496	—	13, 2, 547		
b 世宗 Shih Tsung c.3	文襄 Wên hsiang	澄 Ch'ên	子惠 Tzŭ-hui	1st s of a	-, -, 521	—	15, 9, 549		
A 顯祖(570) Hsien Tsu 威宗(560) Wei Tsung c.4	文宣 Wên hsüan	洋 Yang	子進 Tzŭ-chin	2nd s of a	-, -, 529	9, 6, 550	25, 11, 559[1]	天保 T'ien-pao 庚午	2, 2, 550 9, 6, 550
B c.5	廢帝 Fei Ti	殷 Yin	正道 Chêng-tao	1st s of A	-, -, 545	4, 12, 559 deposed 8, 9, 560	-, 9/10, 561	乾明 Ch'ien-ming 庚辰	12, 2, 560 12, 2, 560
C c.6	孝昭 Hsiao Chao	演 Yen	延安 Yen-an	6th s of a	-, -, 535	8, 9, 560	-, -, 561 (between 24, 11 – 3, 12)	皇建 Huang-chien 庚辰	12, 2, 560 8, 9, 560
D 世祖 Shih Tsu c.7	武成 Wu ch'eng	湛 Chan		9th s of a	-, -, 537	3, 12, 561 abdicated 8, 6, 565	23, 1, 569	大寧[2] T'ai-ning 辛巳 河清 Ho-ch'ing 壬午	1, 2, 561 3, 12, 561 19, 2, 562 24, 5, 562
E c.8	後主 Hou Chu 温公 Wên Kung	緯 Wei	仁綱 Jên-kang	1st s of D	29, 5, 556	8, 6, 565 abdicated 3, 2, 577	-, 4, 577	天統 T'ien-t'ung 乙酉 武平 Wu-p'ing 庚寅 隆化 Lung-hua 丙申	16, 2, 565 8, 6, 565 22, 1, 570 22, 1, 570 15, 2, 576 17, 1, 577
F c.8	幼主 Yu Chu 温國公 Wên kuo Kung	恒 Hêng		1st s of E	-, 7/8, 570	4, 2, 577 deposed 5, 4, 577	-, 4, 577	承光 Ch'êng-kuang 丁酉	4, 2, 577 4, 2, 577

北齊書 Pei ch'i shu cc. 1–8   北史 Pei shih cc. 6–8.

1. In Pei ch'i shu 5, 1b for 十一月 read 十月, as in c. 4, 10a.

2. Synchronismes 242, & Conc. néom. 424, 523, read 太寧, but Pei ch'i shu & Pei shih consistently print 大.

宇文 Yü-wên　　　長安 Ch'ang-an　　　Pei Ch'ao: 周 Chou

1.	2.	3.	4.	5.	6.	7.	8.	9.	10.
a 太祖 T'ai Tsu	c.1–2 文 Wên	泰 T'ai	黑獺 Hei-t'a	s of 肱 Kung	-, -, 505		21, 11, 556		
b c.3	孝閔 Hsiao Min	覺 Chüeh	陁羅尼 T'o-lo-ni	3rd s of a	-, -, 542	15, 2, 557 deposed -, 11, 557	-, 11/12, 557		
A 世宗 Shih Tsung	明 Ming	毓 Yü 統萬突(小名) Tung-wan-t'u		1st s of a	-, -, 534	5, 11, 557	30, 5, 560	元年 first year 丁丑	15, 2, 557
c.4						as Emperor 1, 10, 559		武成 Wu-ch'êng 己卯	24, 1, 559 1, 10, 559
B 高祖 Kao Tsu	武 Wu	邕 Yung	禰羅突 Mi-lo-t'u	4th s of a	-, -, 543[1]	31, 5, 560	1, 7, 578	[1] 保定 Pao-ting 辛巳	1, 2, 561 1, 2, 561
c.5–6				9. [4] 宣政 Hsüan-chêng 戊戌	10. 24, 1, 578 17, 4, 578	9. [3] 建德 Chien-tê 壬辰	10. 31, 1, 572 12, 4, 572	[2] 天和 T'ien-ho 丙戌	6, 2, 566 10, 2, 566
C c.7	宣 Hsüan	贇 Yün	乾伯 Ch'ien-po	1st s of B	-, -, 559	2, 7, 578 abdicated 1, 4, 579	22, 6, 580	大成 Ta-ch'êng 己亥	12, 2, 579 12, 2, 579
D	靜 Ching	衍 Yen		1st s of C	-, 7/8, 573	1, 4, 579	10, 7, 581	大象 Ta-hsiang 己亥	12, 2, 579 1, 4, 579
c.8		闡 Shan						大定 Ta-ting 辛丑	21, 1, 581 21, 1, 581

周書 Chou shu cc.1–8　　北史 Pei shih cc. 9, 10

1. This date is given as 大統元年 (535), but the age in 578 as 36 (Chou shu 5, 1a; 6, 7a). As the older brother (b) was born in 542, the Pei shih 10, 1a is certainly right in reading 九年, 9th year (543).

楊 Yang　　長安 Ch'ang-an　　隋 Sui

1.	2.	3.	4.	5.	6.	7.	8.	9.	10.
A 高祖 Kao Tsu c. 1, 2	文 Wên	堅 Chien		s of 忠 Chung	21, 7, 541	4, 3, 581[1]	13, 8, 604	開皇 Kai-huang 辛丑	21, 1, 581 4, 3, 581
								仁壽 Jên-shou 辛酉	8, 2, 601 8, 2, 601
B c. 3, 4	煬 Yang	廣 Kuang 英 Ying	阿𡡉 A-ma	2nd s of A	-, -, 569	13, 8, 604 deposed 17, 12, 617	11, 4, 618	大業 Ta-yeh 乙丑	25, 1, 605 25, 1, 605
C c. 5	恭 Kung	侑 Yu		gds of B (s of 昭 Chao)	-, -, 605	18, 12, 617 deposed 30, 5, 618	-, 64, 619	義寧 I-ning 丁丑	11, 2, 617 18, 12, 617

隋書 *Sui shu* cc. 1–5, &c.　*Pei shih* cc. 11, 12 (the Sui is not, however, counted among the *Northern dynasties*.)

1. The Ch'ên dynasty was not finally subdued until 2, 2, 589 (*Sui shu* 2, 2a), or 27, 3, 589 (*Ch'ên shu* 6, 6a).

十六國 Shih liu Kuo

劉 Liu　　長安 Ch'ang-an (318)　　XVI. 1. 前趙 Chien Chao

1.	2.	3.	4.	5.	6.	7.	8.	9.	10.
A 高祖 Kao Tsu	光文 Kuang wên	淵 Yüan	元海 Yüan-hai	s of 豹 Pao		20,12,304 (as 漢王 Han Wang) —, 11,308	-, 7/8,310	1. 元熙 Yüan-hsi 甲子	22, 2,304 ? -, 11/12,304
						9.	10.		
						3. 河瑞 Ho-jui 己巳	28, 1,309	2. 永鳳 Yung-fêng 戊辰	8, 2,308 -, 11,308
B 烈宗 Lieh Tsung		聰 Ts'ung	玄明 Hsüan-ming	4th s of A		-, 7/8,310	-, 8/9,318	1. 光興 Kuang-hsing 庚午	16, 2,310 -, 9/10,310
				9.	10.	9.	10.		
		(一名) 載 Tsai		4. 麟嘉 Lin-chia 丙子	10, 2,316	3. 建元 Chien-yüan 乙亥	20, 2,315	2. 嘉平 Chia-p'ing 辛未	5, 2,311
C	隱 Yin	粲 Ts'an	士光 Shih-kuang	s of B		-, 8/9,318	-, 9/10,318	漢昌 Han-ch'ang 戊寅	17, 2,318 -, 8/9,318
D		曜 Yao	永明 Yung-ming	?cousin of A		19,11,318 deposed 6, 2,329	-, -,329	光初 Kuang-ch'u 戊寅	17, 2,318 -, 11/12,318
								太和 T'ai-ho[1] 戊子	28, 1,328

晉書 Chin shu cc. 4–7, 101–103　　魏書 Wei shu c. 95

1. Synchronismes 183, assigns this Year Title to Shih Lo, founder of the Hou Chao (see below); but Wei shu 95, 3b, explicitly says that both Kuang-ch'u and T'ai-ho were proclaimed by Liu Yao. Chung kuo ti hao.. (nien piao) 11, has the Title under Hou Chao.

1.	2.	3.	4.	5.	6.	7.	8.	9.	10
A 高祖 Kao Tsu		勒 Lo	世龍 Shih-lung		-, -, 274	9, 12, 319[3] (as 趙王 Chao Wang)	17, 8, 333	元年 first year 己卯	6, 2, 319
			匐勒 (小字) Fu-lo			-, 9, 330		建平[4] Chien-p'ing 庚寅	5, 2, 330 -, 9, 330
B	海陽王 Hai yang Wang	弘 Hung	大雅 Ta-ya	2nd s of A	-, -, 313	17, 8, 333 deposed -, -, 334	-, 12/1, 334	延熙 Yen-hsi 癸巳	1, 2, 333 -, 9, 333
C 太祖 T'ai Tsu		虎 Hu	季龍 Chi-lung	gt. nephew of A	-, -, 295[5]	-, 12/1, 334[6] see note 6	-, 5, 349	1. 建武 Chien-wu 乙未	10, 2, 335
						9.	10.		
						3. 太寧 T'ai-ning 己酉	4, 2, 349	2. 龍興 Lung-hsing 丙申	30, 1, 336

晉書 Chin shu cc. 6–8, 104–107 魏書 Wei shu cc. 1, 95 僞趙將相大臣年表 Wei chao chiang hsiang ta ch'ên nien piao (in 二十五史補編 Êrh shih wu shih pu pien III), quoted as Wei chao with page & column of ... pu pien.

1. Shih Lo, a member of the 羯 Hsieh clan of Hsiung-nu, sinicized his name after his rise to power by taking 石 Shih as his family name (姓) and 勒 Lo as his personal name (名). - Wei shu 95, 3b.

2. Lo made Hsiang-kuo in modern Ho-pei his capital, but also fortified the palace at Yeh in Ho-nan, employing several hundred thousand men day & night on the work. - Wei shu 95, 4b. C definitely moved the capital to Yeh in Oct. 335 (Wei chao 4038 d), but Hsiang-kuo was retained as an important point, & G was enthroned there in 350.

3. Reading 戊申 for the impossible 十一月戊寅 of Chin shu 6, 4b. Lo's enthronement as Emperor is put in 9, 330 by Chin shu 7, 3a & Wei shu 95, 4b, but in 328 by Chin shu 107, 6a, & the length of the dynasty is there reckoned as 23 years from 328 to 350. Wei chao 4038 a has 建平元年二月 (March 330) 石勒僭稱帝號. The exact day of Lo's death is found in Chin shu 7, 3b.

4. Before Chien-p'ing several modern books insert T'ai-ho without quoting the source (see note 1, p. above). Thus the 十六國年表 Shih liu kuo nien piao (Êrh shih wu shih pu pien III, 4008 a) has: 石勒伐曜當之改元太和.

5. This date is obtained from C's age as given in Wei shu 95, 5a.

6. C's accession as 居攝趙天王 Chü shê Chao T'ien Wang is put in the 11 moon (12, 12, 334 – 10, 1, 335) of the 9 Hsien-ho year in Chin shu 7, 4a, & with this Shih liu kuo nien piao (4008 b) agrees. Wei shu 1, 5b gives 334/5 with no moon, & c. 95 has no exact date. But Chin shu 106, 1b, 107, 3b both give 335/6, the latter place stating C's reign as 始以咸康元年 (335) 僭位至此太 (read 永) 和六年 (350) 凡在位十五歲, & so putting the year of death also later. Chin shu 105, 9b also gives 335/6 as the year of B's death. But Wei chao 4038 c puts C's accession in Yen-hsi 1 (333/4), perhaps agreeing with Shih liu kuo nien piao (4008 b) in making Yen-hsi 1 = 334/5; while Chin shu 105, 8b puts B's accession & the Title Yen-hsi both in 332!

Chin shu 8, 2a says that C was enthroned as Emperor at Yeh on 16, 2, 349.

1.	2.	3.	4.	5.	6.	7.	8.	9.	10.
D		世 Shih		youngest s of C		-, 5, 349	-, 6, 349[1]		
E		遵 Tsun		elder br of D		-, 6, 349	9, 12, 349		
F		鑒 Chien		elder br of E		-, 12, 349	-, 3, 350	青龍 Ch'ing-lung 己酉	4, 2, 349 -, 12, 349
G		祗 Chih[2]		younger br of F		-, 3, 350	-, 5/6, 351	永寧 Yung-ning 庚戌	25, 1, 350
H	武悼天王 Wu tao T'ien Wang	冉] 閔 [Jan] Min (一名) 良 Liang	永曾 Yung-tsêng 棘奴 Chi-nu	adopted gds of C (s of 瞻 Chan)		-, 3, 350[3]	-, 5, 352	永興 Yung-hsing 庚戌	25, 1, 350 ? -, 3, 350

1. D is said to have reigned 33 days (*Chin shu* 107, 4*b*); E 183 days (*Id.* 107, 5*a*); and F 103 days (*Id.* 107, 6*a*), so having been enthroned perhaps on 17 or 18 December 349.

2. Chih, whose name is also written 秖 or 秪, does not seem to be mentioned in *Wei shu* 1, 6*b*, or 95. His dates are here taken from *Chin shu* 8, 2*b*. Not only the whole family of 石 Shih but as many as possible of the members of their tribe, with many Chinese who were mistaken for foreigners, were destroyed in an indescribable massacre ordered by Jan Min within the closed gates of Hsiang-kuo (*Chin shu* 107, 5*b*–6*a*).

3. Min (who is often called by his adopted surname, 石 Shih Min) was enthroned in March (*Chin shu* 8, 2*b*) or Feb.y (*Wei chao* 4040*a* · 正月) 350, and changed the Dynastic Title from Chao to 魏 Wei in 350 (*Chin shu* 8, 2*b*). The date of his death (May 352) is confirmed by *Chin shu* 8, 3*a*, 107, 6*a*; *Wei shu* 1, 6*b*. His son 智 Chih surrendered Yeh in September 352.

慕容 Mu-jung 中山 Chung-shan[1] 鄴 Yeh XVI·3. 前燕 Ch'ien Yen

1.	2.	3.	4.	5.	6.	7.	8.	9.	10.
A 烈祖 Lieh Tsu	景昭 Ching chao	儁 Chün	宣英 Hsüan-ying	3rd s of 皝 Huang	-, -, 319	25, 10, 348[2] as Emperor -, 5, 352	15, 2, 360	元年 first year 己酉	4, 2, 349
								元璽 Yüan-hsi 壬子	2, 2, 352 -, 12/1, 352
								光壽 Kuang-shou 丁巳	6, 2, 357
B	幽 Yu	暐 Wei	景茂 Ching-mao	3rd s of A	?-, -, 337	-, 2, 360 deposed -, 12, 370	?-, -, 371	建熙 Chien-hsi	3, 2, 360 -, 2, 360

晉書 Chin shu cc. 8, 110, 111 魏書 Wei shu cc. 1, 95 北史 Pei shih c. 93

1. A was enthroned at 中山 Chung-shan (the modern 定州 Ting Chou in Ho-pei), - Chin shu 8, 3a; but Tz'ŭ hai s.v. 五胡十六國, gives 大棘 Ta-chi in Manchuria as the first capital; transferred to Yeh in 353 (Pei shih 93, 3b).

2. This date is given in Chin shu 8, 2a; & Wei shu 1, 6b, also gives 348. But Chin shu 110, 1a, gives 349, and says (5b) that A died in 360 in his 42nd year, having reigned 11 years. Synchron. 186, gives 349 & the age 53. The Year Title 天璽 T'ien-hsi in Pei shih 93, 3b may be a mere misprint. Chün is written 雋, 儁, or 㑺; Giles B.D. 1550, reads Tsun.

苻 Fu 長安 Ch'ang-an XVI·4. 前秦 Ch'ien Ch'in

1.	2.	3.	4.	5.	6.	7.	8.	9.	10.
A	三秦王 San Ch'in Wang	洪 Hung	廣世 Kuang-shih	s of 懷 Huai	-, -, 285		-, 12/1, 350		
B 高祖 Kao Tsu 世宗 (355) Shih Tsung	明 Ming	健 Chien	建業 Chien-yeh	3rd s of A	-, -, 317	17, 2, 351 (as 天王) -, 2, 352	-, 7, 355	皇始 Huang-shih 辛亥	13, 2, 351
C	厲王 Li Wang	生 Shêng	長生 Ch'ang-shêng	3rd s of B	-, -, 335	-, 7, 355[1]	-, 7, 357	壽光 Shou-kuang 乙卯	30, 1, 355 -, 7, 355
D 世祖 Shih Tsu	宣昭 Hsüan chao	堅 Chien 文玉 (小名) Wên-yü	永固 Yung-ku	gds of A (s of 雄 Hsiung, A's youngest s)	-, -, 338	-, 7, 357	-, 8/9, 385	[1] 永興 Yung-hsing 丁巳	6, 2, 357 -, 7, 357
						9.	10.		
						[3] 建元 Chien-yüan 乙丑	7, 2, 365	[2] 甘露 Kan-lu 己未	14, 2, 359

晉書 Chin shu cc. 8, 9, 112–115 魏書 Wei shu cc. 1, 2, 95

1. Chin shu 112, 3a, gives the date of accession & of Shou-kuang as 永和十三年 (357). There was no thirteenth Yung-ho year, & 三 (3) is probably a slip or misprint for 一 (1), as in c. 8, 4a & Wei shu 1, 7a.

前秦 Ch'ien Ch'in

1.	2.	3.	4.	5.	6.	7.	8.	9.	10.
E	哀平 Ai p'ing	丕 P'ei	永叔 Yung-shu	s of D		-,9/10,385	?-,1/12,386	太安 T'ai-an 乙酉	27,1,385
F 太宗 T'ai Tsung	高 Kao	登 Têng	文高 Wên-kao	gt-nephew of D	-,-,343	-,12/1,386	-,8/9,394	太初 T'ai-ch'u 丙戌	15,2,386 -,12/1,386
G		崇 Ch'ung		s of F		-,8/9,394	-,11,395[1]	延初 Yen-ch'u 甲午	17,2,394 -,8/9,394

1. *Chin shu* 115,6b says that the dynasty, excluding Ch'ung, lasted 44 years, 351-394. On the assassination of his father Ch'ung fled to 湟中 Huang-chung in Kuku-nor, where he was enthroned.

姚 Yao 長安 Ch'ang-an XVI. 5. 後秦 Hou Ch'in

1.	2.	3.	4.	5.	6.	7.	8.	9.	10.
A 太祖 T'ai Tsu	武昭 Wu chao	萇 Ch'ang	景茂 Ching-mao	24th s of 弋仲 I-chung	-,-,330	-,5,384	-,1/2,394[1]	白雀 Po-ch'iao 甲申	8,2,384
						as Emperor -,6/7,386		建初 Chien-ch'u 丙戌	15,2,386 -,6/7,386
B 高祖 Kao Tsu	文桓 Wên huan	興 Hsing	子略 Tzŭ-lüeh	1st s of A	-,-,366	?-,3/4,394	-,-,416[2]	皇初 Huang-ch'u 甲午	17,2,394
								弘始 Hung-shih 己亥	22,2,399 -,8/9,399
C	後主 Hou Chu	泓 Hung	元子 Yüan-tzŭ	1st s of B	-,-,388	-,-,416[3]	-,8,417	永和 Yung-ho 丙辰	14,2,416

晉書 *Chin shu* cc. 9,10,116-119 魏書 *Wei shu* cc. 2,3,95 北史 *Pei shih* c. 93

1. *Chin shu* 9,8a, has 十月 (Nov.-Dec. 393), but *Wei hou ch'in* .. 4051a, followed by *Synchron.* 194, gives 12th moon (Jan.-Feb. 394); while *Chin shu* 116,6b & *Wei shu* 2,3a-b, give the year 393/4 but no moon. On his accession in 386 A had changed Ch'ang-an to be written 常安 Ch'ang-an.

2. *Chin shu* 10,6a, has 義熙十一年二月丁未 (18,3,415), and this precise date is possible for 415 but not for 416. In c. 118,6a however it has 義熙十二年興死時年五十一在位二十二年, so making the reign 394-416. *Wei shu* 3,4a, & *Pei shih* 93,7b, support the year 416, but give no moon; *Synchron.* 199, has 2nd moon of 416. *Wei shu* 2,3b supports *Synchron.* again in putting A's death in 393/4 and B's accession in 394/5, while *Wei hou ch'in* .. 4051a puts both events in the 12 moon (1/2,394). On the whole the evidence seems to favour the Spring of 394/5 for B's accession & the Spring of 416 for his death.

3. See note 2 above. For the date of C's defeat, capture, & execution (in the market-place of Chien-k'ang) *Chin shu* 10,6b, gives the 7th moon (August, 417), *Wei shu* 3,4b, the 8th (September), and *Synchron.* 206, the 9th (October). The duration of the dynasty is reckoned as 32 years (386-417), but the founder of the family seems to have been I-chung who died in 352 in his 73rd year, the father of 42 sons.- *Chin shu* 116,1a-2a.

李 Li 郫城 P'i ch'êng[1] XVI. 6. 蜀 Shu[2]

1.	2.	3.	4.	5.	6.	7.	8.	9.	10.
A 始祖(305) Shih Tsu	景 Ching	特 T'ê	玄休 Hsüan-hsiu			-, 11/12, 301	-, 4, 303	建初 Chien-ch'u 壬戌	14, 2, 302
	秦文王 Ch'in wên Wang	流 Liu[3]	玄通 Hsüan-t'ung	4th br of A	-, -, 248	-, -, 303	-, -, 303		
B 太宗 T'ai Tsung	武 Wu	雄 Hsiung	仲儁 Chung-chün	3rd s of A	-, -, 274	-, 5, 303[4] as 成都王 Ch'êng-tu Wang 20, 12, 304 as Emperor 11, 7, 305	-, 7/8, 334	1. 建興 Chien-hsing 甲子	22, 2, 304
								2. 太武 T'ai-wu[5] 乙丑	11, 2, 305 11, 7, 305
						9.	10.		
						4. 玉衡 Yü-hêng 辛未	5, 2, 311	3. 晏平 Yen-p'ing 丙寅	31, 1, 306

晉書 Chin shu cc. 4–8, 120, 121 魏書 Wei shu c. 96

1. The site of P'i ch'êng is said to be 50 li N. of the modern P'i N.-E. of 成都 Ch'êng-tu. Ch'êng-tu itself is sometimes spoken as if it was the capital.

2. Hsiung chose the dynastic Title Shu in 305 (Chin shu 4, 6b). He assumed the title 大成帝 Ta ch'êng Ti, and the dynasty is also called Ch'êng, or 漢 Han (338).

3. On the death of A Liu seems to have assumed power for a short time before the accession of B. Chin shu 120, 4b–5a; cf. c. 4, 4b, where B re-occupies I chou after A's execution (四月特子雄復據益州), & Liu is not mentioned.

4. There is some uncertainty in the dates of B's accession & death. Chin shu 4, 6a: [永興元年(304)十一月]辛丑李雄僭號成都王; 121, 1a: 永興元年稱成都王. The first of these extracts dates the assumption of the title Prince of Ch'êng-tu on 21, 12, 304. Wei shu 96, 9b puts the accession of A in the 7th year of Chao Ti (301), of B in the 10th year (304), & finally (as Emperor) in the 12th year (306). Chin shu 120, 1b, 3b, seems very vaguely to put A's accession in the 1st Yung-k'ang year (300). Chin shu 4, 4b, puts B's succession of A in May 303 (see note 3 above), & in 4, 6b B's enthronement as Emperor is exactly dated 11, 7, 305. When it comes to B's death, Chin shu 121, 3a says: 咸和八年(333)雄生瘍於頭六日死時年六十一在位三十年. This would put his birth in 273 and his accession in 304. But Chin shu 7, 4a, has 咸和九年(334)六月; & Wei shu 96, 9b, 烈帝六年(334). The more exact dates of the Chin shu annals (-, 5, 303; 20, 12, 304; 11, 7, 305; & -, 7/8, 334) are here adopted, supposing that the 30 years reign is calculated from the enthronement, 305–334, & the 61 years of age from 274. Synchronismes 176, 179, gives T'ê 302–303; Liu 303; Hsiung 304, 306, 334.

5. Chin shu 121, 1, gives the Year Titles Chien-hsing, T'ai-wu (on B's accession as Emperor), & Yü-hêng, without dates. Chung kuo ti hao .. i lan, 16, has T'ai-wu with cross-reference to Yen-p'ing, & on p. 58 Yen-p'ing (晏平(成) 306-310) with cross-reference to T'ai-wu. Synchron. 179, & Chung kuo jên ming .. tien 430 omit T'ai-wu. The note to Chin shu 121, 1b, says that 華陽國志 Hua yang kuo chih (4th cent.) & 後蜀錄 Hou shu lu read 大成 Ta-ch'êng for T'ai-wu, but does not mention Yen-p'ing. Wei shu 96, 9b, has 十二年僭稱皇帝號大成改年為晏平; & this suggests a possible explanation of the Ta-ch'êng in Hua yang kuo chih, of which T'ai-wu may be a corruption.

蜀 Shu

1.	2.	3.	4.	5.	6.	7.	8.	9.	10.
C		班 Pan	世文 Shih-wên	nephew of B[1]	-, -, 288	-, 7/8, 334	-, 11/12, 334		
D	幽公 Yu Kung	期 Ch'i	世運 Shih-yün	4th s of B	-, -, 313	-, 11/12, 334	-, 5, 338[2]	玉恆 Yü-hêng 乙未	10, 2, 335
E 中宗 Chung Tsung	昭文 Chao wên	壽 Shou	武考 Wu-k'ao	nephew of A[3]	-, -, 300	-, 5/6, 338	-, 9, 343[4]	漢興 Han-hsing 戊戌	6, 2, 338
F		勢 Shih	子仁 Tzŭ-jên	1st s of E		-, 9, 343[5] deposed 13, 4, 347	-, -, 361	太和 T'ai-ho 甲辰	31, 1, 344
								嘉寧 Chia-ning 丙午	8, 2, 346

1. C was 4th son of B's elder brother 蕩 T'ang.
2. *Chin shu* 7, 4b, says D was murdered by E in May 338. *Wei shu* 96, 9b, says he was deposed by E & killed himself.
3. E was son of A's brother 驤 Hsiang.
4. *Chin shu* 7, 6a; but c. 121, 5b: 咸康八年(342) 時年四十四在位五年. If 342 is right the year of birth may be 299.
5. *Chin shu* 121, 6b, seems to put the accession in 343 (在位五年); & in the same place the dates of the dynasty are given as 302 to 347. For the dates given throughout one must rely chiefly on the *annals* (cc. 4–8) of the *Chin shu*, or else on other books which are not at my disposal. The later chapters (120, 121) give very few dates, & do not seem to mention day or moon at all except in the date of the deposition of Shih (F) - 三月十七日(乙亥), 13, 4, 347; and this differs from c. 8, 1b, where day 丁亥, 25, 4, 347, is specified. *Wei shu* 96, 9a–10b, mentions years corresponding to 301, 304, 306, 334, 338, 347.

1.	2.	3.	4.	5.	6.	7.	8.	9.	10.
A 太祖 T'ai Tsu	懿武 I wu	光 Kuang	世明 Shih-ming	s of 婆樓 P'o-lou	-, -, 337	-, 9/5, 386 涼州牧 -, 3/4, 389 三河王 -, 7/8, 396 天王 abdicated -, 1/2, 400	-, 1/2, 400[1] (on the day of his abdication)	太安 T'ai-an 丙戌 麟嘉 Lin-chia 己丑 龍飛 Lung-fei 丙申	15, 2, 386 -, 4/5, 386 12, 2, 389 -, 3/4, 389 27, 1, 396 -, 7/8, 396
B	隱王 Yin Wang	紹 Shao		s of A		-, 1/2, 400 reigned 5 days	-, 1/2, 400		
C		纂 Tsuan	永緒 Yung-hsü	1st s of A		-, 1/2, 400	1?, 3, 401[2]	咸寧 Hsien-ning 己亥	22, 2, 399 -, 1/2, 400
D		隆 Lung	永基 Yung-chi	nephew of A (s of 寶 Pao)		-, 3, 401	-, -, 404[3]	神鼎 Shên-ting 辛丑	30, 1, 401 -, 3, 401

晉書 Chin shu cc. 9, 10, 122. 魏書 Wei shu cc. 2, 95

1. For the years of accession (396) & death (399 400) see Chin shu 9, 8a; 10, 2a, with which Wei shu 95, 20a, agrees. Synchronismes 201, following the reconstructed Shih liu kuo ch'un ch'iu, gives these years as 395 & 398, noting however that 晉記 Chin chi (18th cent.) & 十六國春秋輯補 Shih liu kuo ch'un ch'iu chi pu (?) agree with Chin shu and Wei shu.

2. Chin shu 10, 2b; Wei shu 2, 8b. But Chin shu 122, 8a, has 402; & Synchron. 201, 400.

3. Chin shu 122, 9a, where also the duration of the dynasty, counting from 387 to Lung (至隆), is given as 13 years. Chin shu 10, & Wei shu, 2 & 95, give no date for D's death. Synchron. 201 says August 403.

慕容 Mu-jung　　中山 Chung-shan　　XVI·9. 後燕 Hou Yen

1.	2.	3.	4.	5.	6.	7.	8.	9.	10.
A 世祖 Shih Tsu	成武 Chêng wu	垂 Ch'ui	道明 Tao-ming	5th s of 皝 Huang	-, -, 326	15, 3, 386	-, 5, 396	燕元 Yen-yüan 癸未	19, 2, 383
						-, -, 383[1] 燕王		建興 Chien-hsing 丙戌	15, 2, 386
B 烈宗 Lieh Tsung	惠愍 Hui min	寶 Pao	道祐 Tao-yu	4th s of A	-, -, 355	-, 5, 396	-, 6, 398[3]	永康 Yung-k'ang 丙申	27, 1, 396 -, 5, 396
C 中宗 Chung Tsung	昭武 Chao wu	盛 Shêng	道運 Tao-yün	1st s of B	-, -, 373	-, -, 399	-, 8, 401[3]	建平 Ch'ien-p'ing 戊戌	3, 2, 398 -, 11, 398
						-, 11, 398 長樂王		長樂 Ch'ang-lo 己亥	22, 2, 399
D	昭文 Chao wên	熙 Hsi	道文 Tao-wên	youngest[4] s of A	-, -, 385	-, 8, 401	-, 8/9, 407[5]	光始 Kuang-shih 辛丑	30, 1, 401 -, 8, 401
			長生 (小字) Ch'ang-shêng					建始 Chien-shih 丁未	25, 1, 407
E	惠懿 Hui i	雲 Yün	子雨 Tzŭ-yü	adopted s of B (s of 高拔 Kao Pa)		-, 8/9, 407	7, 10, 409	正始 Chêng-shih 丁未	25, 1, 407 -, 8/9, 407

晉書 Chin shu cc. 9, 10, 123, 124　魏書 Wei shu cc. 1, 2, 95　北史 Pei shih c. 93

1. Chin shu 123, 3a. But Wei shu 2, 1b, Synchron. 193, make the year 384. The day of death may be 27, 5, 396, reading 丁丑 for the impossible 丁卯 of Chin shu 9, 8a. Pei shih 93, 4b says that 垂 was originally 缺.
2. Chin shu 10, 1b; but c. 124, 3a: "3rd Lung-an year" 399).
3. Chin shu 10, 2b gives 七月, 7th moon, both for accession (30, 7 – 28, 8, 398) and death (27, 7 – 24, 8, 401). Wei shu 2, 8b gives no moon. Synchron. 199, has 8th moon (September) 401.
4. Pei shih 93, 5b, says eldest son (長子).
5. Pei shih 1, 9b. Chin shu & Wei shu agree in the year, but give no moon. Chin shu 124, 7a gives D's age as 23.
6. Chin shu 10, 5a, 九月戊辰. As mou-ch'ên did not fall in the 9 moon in 409, we may read 戊戌 (7, 10, 409) or, since the 8 moon has not been mentioned, 八月戊辰 (7, 9, 409); or again, to conform with Synchron. 206, 十月戊辰 (6, 11, 409), even though the next entry is the formal 冬十月. Pei shih has no exact dates here.

乞伏 Ch'i-fu 勇士城 Yung-shih ch'êng, 金城 Chin ch'êng, 苑川 Wan-ch'uan (in Kansu), 枹罕 Pao-han **XVI.** 10. 西秦 Hsi Ch'in

1.	2.	3.	4.	5.	6.	7.	8.	9.	10.
A 烈祖 Lieh Tsu	宣烈王 Hsüan lieh Wang	國仁 Kuo-jên	–	s of 司繁 Ssŭ-fan	–	–, –, 385	–, 7/8, 388	建義 Chien-i 乙酉	27, 1, 385
B 高祖 Kao Tsu	武元王 Wu yüan Wang	乾歸 Ch'ien-kuei	–	younger br of A	–	–, 7/8, 388 deposed –, 8, 400 restored –, 8, 409	–, 6, 412[2]	太初 T'ai-ch'u[3] 戊子	25, 1, 388 –, 7/8, 388
								更始 Kêng-shih 己酉	1, 2, 409 –, 8, 409
C 太祖 T'ai Tsu	文昭王 Wên chao Wang	熾磐 Chih-p'an	–	1st s of B	–	–, 6, 412	–, 6, 428[4]	永康 Yung-k'ang 壬子	30, 1, 412 –, 6, 412
								建弘 Chien-hung 庚申	31, 1, 420
D –	–	慕末 Mu-mo (暮 or 末)	安石跋[5] An-shih-p'o	s of C	–	–, 6, 428	–, 2, 431[6]	永弘[7] Yung-hung 戊辰	2, 2, 428 –, 7, 428

晉書 Chin shu cc. 9, 10, 123, 124. 魏書 Wei shu cc. 1, 2, 95. 北史 Pei shih c. 93.

1. Chin shu c. 10, 5a nearly agreeing with Synchron. p. 207 where the 3rd moon is given. Pei shih c. 1, 10 gives 409. But Chin shu c. 125, 4b gives the year as 義熙三年 (407), where 三 is perhaps a misprint for 五; but see the next Note.
2. Chin shu c. 10, 5b, 八年五月 (27, 5 – 24, 6); Synchron. p. 195 says 6th moon (25, 6 – 24, 7). Chin shu c. 125, 5a again puts the date two years earlier, twice specifying 義熙六年 (410).
3. From 8, 400 to 8, 409 the title Hung-shih (see p. 39) was used; and from 407 to 8, 409 the Title I-hsi (see p. 19) was also used.
4. Pei shih c. 2, 2a. Wei shu c. 4a, 3a gives 428, without moon; Chin shu c. 125, 6b says 元嘉四年 (427). Chih-p'an's death is not mentioned in the Sung shu, c. 5, 3.
5. Chung kuo jên ming ta tzŭ tien p. 14 has 安石 An-shih, as also Ku chin jên wu. p. 321. Wei shu c. 99, 3b: 字安石跋卽立 改年為永洪; and so also Pei shih c. 93, 9a.
6. Pei shih c. 2, 2b; c. 93, 9a.
7. Wei shu c. 99, 3b: 建洪 and 永洪.

馮 Fêng　　　　昌黎 Ch'ang-li　　　　XVI. 11. 北燕 Pei Yen

1	2	3	4	5	6	7	8	9	10
A 太祖 T'ai Tsu	—	跋 Po	文起 Wên-ch'i 乞直 Ch'i-chih (小字)	s of 安 An	—	—, 11, 409[1] [?—, 9, 409]	—, 10, 430	太平 T'ai-p'ing 己酉	1, 2, 409
B —	昭成 Chao ch'êng	弘 Hung	文通 Wên-t'ung	youngest br of A	—	—, —, 430 deposed —, 10, 436	—, 4/5, 436	太興 T'ai-hsing 庚午	9, 2, 430[2]

晉書 Chin shu cc. 10, 11, 125. 魏書 Wei shu cc. 2, 3, 97. 北史 Pei shih c. 93.

1. Chin shu c. 10, 5a says this took place after the day 戊辰 in the 9th moon. As there was no 戊辰 in the 9th moon 409, and the next entry is "winter 10th moon", it would be natural to read here "8th moon" or September; but as Synchron. has 10th moon, November is also possible. See p. 45 above, Note 6. Pei shih c. 1, 10a records the day 十月戊辰 but does not mention this incident.
2. Synchron. p. 212 gives 辛未 431; but I see no confirmation of this in Chin shu, Wei shu, or Pei shih.

禿髮 T'u-fa　　　　樂都 Lo-tu (397, 402) 西平 Hsi-p'ing (399)　　　　XVI. 12. 南涼 Nan Liang

1	2	3	4	5	6	7	8	9	10
A 烈祖 Lieh Tsu	武王 Wu Wang	烏孤 Wu-ku	—	s of 壽闐 Shou-t'ien	—	—, 3/4, 397	—, 9/10, 399	太初 T'ai-ch'u 丁酉	13, 2, 397
B —	康王 K'ang Wang	利鹿孤[1] Li-lu-ku	—	younger br of A	—	—, 9/10, 399	—, 4/5, 402	建和 Chien-ho 己亥	22, 2, 399
C —	景王 Ching Wang	傉檀 Nu-t'an	—	younger br. of A & B	—, —, 365	—, 4/5, 402 deposed —, —, 404 restored —, 12, 408 deposed —, 7, 414	—, 7/8, 415	弘昌 Hung-ch'ang 壬寅 嘉平 Chia-p'ing 戊申	18, 2, 402 —, 4/5, 402 13, 2, 408 —, 12, 408

晉書 Chin shu cc. 10, 126. 魏書 Wei shu cc. 2, 99.

1. In Chin shu c. 129, 1b called 鹿孤 Lu-ku; cf. Wei shu c. 2, 7b.

慕容 Mu-jung　　滑臺 Hua-t'ai　廣固 Kuang-ku　XVI·13 南燕 Nan Yen

1	2	3	4	5	6	7	8	9	10
A 世宗 Shih Tsung	獻武 Hsien Wu	德 Tê	玄明 Hsüan-ming	youngest s. of 皝 Huang (cf. p. 38 above)	-, -, 336	-, 2, 398 -, -, 400 (as 皇帝)	-, 5/6, 405[1]	燕元年 Yen yüan 戊戌	3, 2, 398
								建平 Chien-p'ing 庚子	11, 2, 400
B	昭文 Chao wên	超 Ch'ao	祖明 Tsu-ming	s. of 納 Na, elder br. of A	-, -, 385	-, 12/1, 405	-, 3/4, 410	太上 T'ai-shang 乙巳	15, 2, 405 -, 12/1, 405

晉書 Chin shu cc. 10, 127, 128. 魏書 Wei shu cc. 2, 95.

1. *The months (4th and 11th moon) of the death of Tê and accession of Chao are taken from Synchron. p. 202; the other dates from the Chin shu and Wei shu. Synchron. p. 202 puts the assumption of the title Huang ti and the fixing of the capital at Kuang-ku in 398 and, following 紀元編 Chi yüan pien (19th century), makes the first Year Title 燕平 Yen-p'ing in place of Yen yüan, which simply means "the first year of the Yen".*

李 Li　　燉煌 Tun-huang 酒泉 Chiu-ch'üan (405)　XVI·14 西涼 Hsi Liang

1	2	3	4	5	6	7	8	9	10
A 太祖 T'ai Tsu	武昭王 Wu chao Wang	暠 Kao	玄盛 Hsüan-shêng 長生(小字) Ch'ang-shêng	s. of 昶 Ch'ang	-, -, 351	-, -, 400	-, 3, 417	元年 First year 庚子	11, 2, 400
								建初 Ch'ien-ch'u 乙巳	15, 2, 405
B	後主 Hou Chu	歆 Hsin	士業 Shih-yeh 桐椎(小字) Tung-ch'ui	s of A		-, 3, 417	-, 8, 420	嘉興 Chia-hsing 丁巳	3, 2, 417 -, 3, 417
C		恂 Hsün		younger s of A		-, 8, 420	-, -, 421	永建 Yung-chien 庚申	31, 1, 420 -, 8, 420
D		重耳 Ch'ung-êrh		s. of B		-, -, 421	-, -, 423		

晉書 Chin shu cc. 10, 87. 魏書 Wei shu cc. 2, 3, 99.

1. Chin shu c. 87, 7a

沮渠 Chü-ch'ü　　張掖 Chang-i (401) 姑臧 Ku-tsang (412)　　XVI·15. 北涼 Pei Liang

1	2	3	4	5	6	7	8	9	10
A	「建康公 Chien k'ang Kung」	段業 Tuan Yeh				–,–,397	–, 6, 401	神璽 Shên-hsi 丁酉	13, 2, 397
								天璽 T'ien-hsi[1] 己亥	22, 2, 399
B	武宣王 Wu hsüan Wang	蒙遜 Mêng-hsün			–, –, 368	–, 6, 401 –, 12/1, 412 (河西王)	–, 5, 433	永安 Yung-an 辛丑	30, 1, 401 –, 6, 401
								玄始 Hsüan-shih 壬子	30, 1, 412 –, 12/1, 412
								承玄 Ch'êng-hsüan 戊辰	2, 2, 428
								義和 I-ho 辛未	29, 1, 431
C	哀王 Ai Wang	茂虔 Mao-ch'ien (or 牧犍 Mu-chien)		s. of B		–, 5, 433 deposed 18, 10, 439	–, –, 440[2]	永和 Yung-ho 癸酉	6, 2, 433

晋書 *Chin shu* cc. 10, 129　魏書 *Wei shu* cc. 2–4, 99　北史 *Pei shih* c. 93

1. *Synchron.* p. 200; but I do not see this title in the *Chin shu*, *Wei shu*, or *Pei shih*.

2. *Synchron.* p. 213; The dynasty ended on 18.10.439 with the submission of C and his nephew 萬年 Wan-nien; but C's younger brother seems to have maintained some independence at 晋陽 Chin-yang and 酒泉 Chiu-ch'üan until 20.12.441. See *Wei shu* cc. 4a, 9a; 4b, 1b.

赫連 Ho-lien (鐵弗 T'ieh-fu). 朔方 Shuo-fang, 統萬 T'ung-wan, 長安 Ch'ang-an (418) XVI·16. 夏 Hsia

1.	2.	3.	4.	5.	6.	7.	8.	9.	10.
A 世祖 Shih Tsu	武烈 Wu lieh	勃勃 Po-po (or 敦敦)	屈孑 Ch'ü-chieh[1]	3rd s of 衛辰 Wei-chên	–, –, 381	–, 7/8, 407 (夏天王)	–, 9, 425	龍昇 Lung-shêng 丁未	25, 1, 407
								鳳翔 Fêng-hsiang 癸丑	17, 2, 413
						–, –, 418 (皇帝)		昌武 Ch'ang-wu 戊午	21, 2, 418
								真興 Chên-hsing 己未	11, 2, 419
B		昌 Ch'ang (or 折 Chê)	還國 Huan-kuo	2nd s. of A[2]		–, 9, 425	–, 3, 428	承光 Ch'êng-kuang 乙丑	4, 2, 425 –, 9, 425
C		定 Ting	直獖 Chih-fên	5th s of A		–, 3, 428	–, 7, 431	勝光 Shêng-kuang 戊辰	2, 2, 428

晉書 Chin shu cc. 10, 130. 魏書 Wei shu cc. 2-4a, 95. 北史 Pei shih c. 93.

1. The Wei shu reads 屈丐 Ch'ü-kai, and calls the name 名 ming. The Pei shih c. 93, 2a also uses the form Ch'ü-kai, and says that the family name was changed from T'ieh-fu to Ho-lien in or soon after 407.

2. Pei shih c. 93, 2a. Wei shu c. 95, – 3rd son.

A TABLE OF THE SIXTEEN KINGDOMS

The Table beneath is divided into five Sections (I–V), each containing 28 years; & each Section is divided into eleven vertical columns. Of these the first column gives the Emperors of the West & East Chin (Ch.) or, at the end, Sung (S.) dynasty; the second those of the Wei (W.); and the third the years (A.D. 301–440). The remaining 8 columns are marked a, b, c, d, e, f, g, h, & contain the Sixteen Kingdoms. Each Kingdom begins with its proper number opposite its first year, and a thick vertical line, ending with ▾ opposite its last year, shows how long it lasted. Thus Hou Chao (2.) begins in Section I b with 2. opposite the year 319, and its line ends with ▾ opposite the year 352 in Section II b.

1.	前趙 Ch'ien Chao (304–329)	p.35:	Section	I a — II a
2.	後趙 Hou Chao (319–352)	p.37:	"	I b — II b
3.	前燕 Ch'ien Yen (348–370)	p.38:	"	II a — III a
4.	前秦 Ch'ien Ch'in (352–410)	p.38:	"	II c — IV c
5.	後秦 Hou Ch'in (384–417)	p.39:	"	III a — V a
6.	蜀 Shu (301–347)	p.40:	"	I d — II d
7.	前涼 Ch'ien Liang (302–376)	p.42:	"	I e — III e
8.	後涼 Hou Liang (386–404)	p.44:	"	IV b
9.	後燕 Hou Yen (386–409)	p.45:	"	IV g
10.	西秦 Hsi Ch'in (389–431)	p.46:	"	IV d — V d
11.	北燕 Pei Yen (409–436)	p.47:	"	IV g — V g
12.	南涼 Nan Liang (397–414)	p.47:	"	IV e — V e
13.	南燕 Nan Yen (398–410)	p.48:	"	IV c
14.	西涼 Hsi Liang (400–423)	p.48:	"	IV f — V f
15.	北涼 Pei Liang 397–439)	p.49:	"	IV h — V h
16.	夏 Hsia (407–431)	p.50:	"	IV b — V b

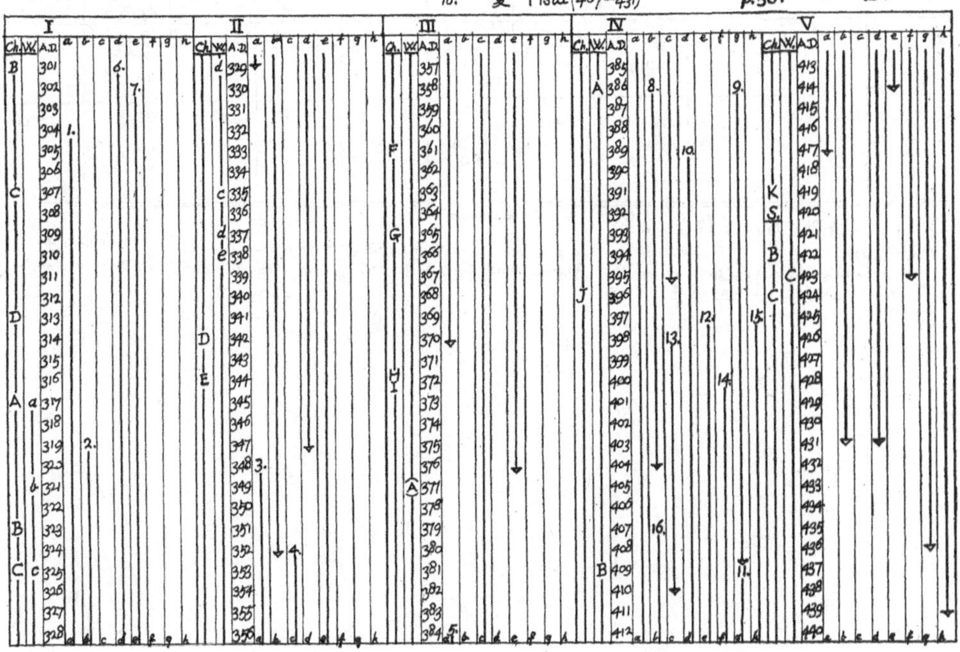

慕容 Mu-jung 長子 Ch'ang-tzŭ 阿房 A-fang[1] (385) 17. 西燕 Hsi Yen

	1.	2.	3.	4.	5.	6.	7.	8.	9.	10.
A			泓 Hung				–,4/5,384	–,6/7,384	燕興 Yen-hsing 甲申	8,2,384
B			沖 Ch'ung		younger br. of 暐 Wei		–,1,385 (甲申)	29,3,386	更始 Kêng-shih 乙酉	27,1,385
C			段] 隨 Tuan] Sui				–,–,386	–,–,386	昌平 Ch'ang-p'ing 丙戌	15,2,386
D			覬 Chi		s of 宜都王 I tu Wang		–,–,386	–,–,386	建明 Chien-ming 丙戌	15,2,386
E			望 Wang		s of B		–,–,386	–,–,386	建平 Chien-p'ing 丙戌	15,2,386
F			忠 Chung		s of A		–,–,386	–,–,386	建武 Chien-wu 丙戌	15,2,386
G			永 Yung	叔明 Shu-ming	gds of 運 Yün, br of 廆 Wei, father of 皝 Huang (p.38)		–,–,386	–,9/10,396[2]	中興 Chung-hsing 丙戌	15,2,386

晉書 <u>Chin shu</u> c.9. 魏書 <u>Wei shu</u> cc. 2, 95

1. <u>Chin shu</u> c.9, 6a.

2. The death of Yung does not seem to be recorded in <u>Chin shu</u> c.9 or <u>Wei shu</u> c.2. The names given above are taken from <u>Wei shu</u> c.95, 10b, 11a. <u>Synchron</u>. reads 顗 I for D, and 瑤 Yao for E. 顗 and 瑤 are given as names (人名) in <u>K'ang hsi tzŭ tien</u>, but not 覬.

蕭 Hsiao

18. 後梁 Hou Liang

1.	2.	3.	4.	5.	6.	7.	8.	9.	10.
A 中宗 Chung Tsung	宣 Hsüan	詧 Ch'a	理孫 Li-sun	3rd s. of 統 T'ung, s. of A (p. above)	–, –, 519	–, 2/3, 555	2, 4, 562[1]	大定 Ta-ting 乙亥	7, 2, 555
B 世宗 Shih Tsung	孝明 Hsiao ming	巋 K'uei	仁遠 Jên-yüan	3rd s. of A	–, –, 542	–, 4, 562	–, 6, 585	天保 T'ien-pao 壬午	21, 1, 562 –, 4, 562
C		琮 Ts'ung	温文 Wên-wên	s. of B		–, –, 585 deposed –, –, 587		廣運 Kuang-yün 丙午 乙巳	25, 1, 586 5, 2, 585

陳書 Ch'ên shu cc. 2, 3. 北史 Pei shih c. 93.

1. It is not certain that the exact day (癸丑) is meant to apply to the death of Ch'a, which in any case occurred in the intercalary 2nd moon as given in Concord. néom. p. 177. The Chou shu c. 5, 2a and Synchron. both say "second moon", but the former puts the intercalary moon before the 2nd moon so that its 2nd moon is the same as the intercalary 2nd moon of Concord. néom. p. 177.

李 Li

Ancestors of 唐 T'ang

1.	2.	3.	4.	5.	6.	7.	8.	9.	10.
a 西涼太祖 T'ai Tsu of Hsi Liang (p. 46 above)	武昭王 Wu chao Wang	暠 Kao			–, –, 351		–, –, 417		
b	涼王 Liang Wang	歆 Hsin		s. of a			–, –, 420		
c		重耳 Ch'ung-êrh		s. of b			–, –, 423		
d 獻祖 Hsien Tsu	宣簡公 Hsüan chien Kung (618): 宣 Hsüan (674)	熙 Hsi		s. of c			buried 建初陵 Chien ch'u Ling		
e 懿祖 I Tsu	光 Kuang (674)	天賜 T'ien-tz'ŭ		1st s. of d			buried 啓運陵 Ch'i yün Ling		
f 太祖 T'ai Tsu	襄(相) Hsiang: 景 Ching (618)	虎 Hu		2nd s. of e			buried 永康陵 Yung k'ang Ling		
g 世祖 Shih Tsu	仁 Jên: 元 Yüan (618)	昞 Ping		3rd s. of f			buried 興寧陵 Hsing ning Ling		

舊唐書, 新唐書 Chiu & Hsin t'ang shu c. 1, 1a 唐會要 T'ang hui yao c. 1

1	2	3	4	5	6	7	8	9	10
E 睿宗 Jui Tsung c.6,7; c.5	玄真大聖大興孝 (754) Hsüan chên ta shêng ta hsing hsiao 大聖貞 (716) Ta shêng chêng	旦 (678)[2] Tan originally (旭)輪 (Hsü-) lun	—	8th s. of C and F	22,6,662	27,2,684 — deposed 16,10,690[3]	13,7,716 [14, thy]	文明 Wên-ming 甲申	23,1,684 27,2,684 [17,3,685 thy]
F c.6; c.4	則天順聖皇后 (749) Tsê t'ien shun shêng Huang hou 大聖則天皇后 (705) Ta shêng tsê t'ien Huang hou 天后 (710) T'ien Hou 大聖天后 (710) Ta shêng t'ien Hou 天后聖帝 (712) T'ien hou shêng Ti 聖后 (712) Shêng Hou 則天皇后 (716) Tsê t'ien Huang hou 「commonly known as 武后 Wu Hou. one of her titles in her lifetime was: 金輪皇帝 Chin lun Huang ti」	曌 Chao	則天 Tsê-t'ien	daughter of 武士彠 Wu Shih-huo	–, –, 623[4]	16,10,690[5] — abdicated 21,2,705	16,12,705 [15, 1, 706 thy]	1. 光宅 Kuang-chê 甲申	23,1,684 19,10,684 [18, 10 thy]

9	10	9	10	9	10	9	10
15. 久視 Chiu-shih 庚子	27,11,699 27,5,700	11. 萬歲登封 Wan-sui-têng-fêng 丙申	12,12,695 20,1,696	7. 長壽 Ch'ang-shou 壬辰	26,11,691 23,10,692	2. 垂拱 Ch'ui-kung 乙酉	9,2,685 9,2,685
16. 大足 Ta-tsu 辛丑	13,2,701 15,2,701	12. 萬歲通天 Wan-sui-t'ung-t'ien 丙申	12,12,695 22,4,696	8. 延載 Yen-tsai 甲午	3,12,693 9,6,694	3. 永昌 Yung-ch'ang 己丑	27,1,689 27,1,689
17. 長安 Ch'ang-an 辛丑	13,2,701 26,11,701	13. 神功 Shên-kung 丁酉	30,11,696 29,9,697	9. 證聖 Chêng-shêng 乙未	23,11,694 22,1,695	4. 載初 Tsai-ch'u 庚寅	18,12,689[6] 18,12,689
		14. 聖曆 Shêng-li 戊戌	20,12,697 20,12,697	10. 天冊萬歲 T'ien-ts'ê-wan-sui 乙未	23,11,694 22,10,695	5. 天授 T'ien-shou 庚寅	18,12,689 16,10,690
						6. 如意 Ju-i 壬辰	26,11,691 22,4,692

1. From 16,10,690 until 2,3,705 inclusive the Title of the dynasty (國號) was changed from T'ang to 周 Chou.
2. 681 in T'ang hui yao c.1,5b.
3. Hsin t'ang shu c.4,4a, T'ang hui yao c.1,5b.
4. Chiu t'ang shu c.6,6b; 625 according to T'ang hui yao c.3,3a.
5. Hsin t'ang shu c.4,4a, T'ang hui yao c.3,2b,3a. Her reign had in effect begun in 684 with the deposition of Chung Tsung.
6. From 689/90 until 700/1 inclusive the civil year began with the 11th moon.

1.	2.	3.	4.	5.	6.	7.	8.	9.	10.
D 中宗 Chung Tsung (continued) c.7; c.4	See p. 55 above					restored,[1] 23, 2, 705		神龍 Shên-lung 乙巳	30, 1, 705 21, 2,[2] 705
								景龍 Ching-lung 丁未	7, 2, 707 5, 10, 707
G — c.7; c.5	「温王 Wên Wang」	重茂 Ch'ung-mao	—	s. of D & 韋皇后 Wei Huang hou	–, –, 695	8, 7, 710 — deposed 22, 7, 710	—	唐隆 T'ang-lung 庚戌	4, 2, 710 5, 7, 710
E 睿宗 Jui Tsung (continued) cc.6,7; c.5	See p. 56 above					25, 7, 710 abdicated as Regent 8, 9, 712[3] — retired from being Regent 30, 7, 713		景雲 Ching-yün 庚戌	4, 2, 710 19, 8, 710
								太極 T'ai-chi 壬子	12, 2, 712 1, 3, 712
								延和 Yen-ho 壬子	12, 2, 712 21, 6, 712

1. <u>Chiu t'ang shu</u> c.7, 1a, <u>Hsin t'ang shu</u> c.4, 9a; 22, 2, 705 according to <u>T'ang hui yao</u> c.1, 4b.
2. <u>Hsin t'ang shu</u> c.4, 9a.
3. 30, 9, 712 in <u>T'ang hui yao</u> c.1, 6b.

1.	2.	3.	4.	5.	6.	7.	8.	9.	10.
H 玄宗 Hsüan Tsung c.8,9; c.5	至道大聖大明孝 (762) Chih tao ta shêng ta ming hsiao [commonly known as 唐明皇 T'ang Ming Huang, and in his life as 武皇 Wu Huang]	隆基 Lung-chi	—	3rd s. of E	8, 9, 685	8, 9, 712 abdicated 16, 9, 756 [12, 8, 756] thy 1, 7a [13, 9, 756] thy 1, 7b	3, 5, 762[1]	先天 Hsien-t'ien 壬子	12, 2, 712 12, 9, 712
								開元 K'ai-yüan 癸丑	31, 1, 713 22, 12, 713
								天寶 T'ien-pao[2] 壬午	10, 2, 742 10, 2, 742
I 肅宗 Su Tsung	文明武德大聖大宣孝 (762) Wên ming wu tê ta shêng ta hsüan hsiao	亨 (744) Hêng 嗣昇 Ssü-shêng 浚 (727) Chün 璵 (735) Yü 紹 (738) Shao	—	3rd s. of H	–, –, 711[3] [7, 10, 712 read 19, 10, 711? thy]	12, 8, 756[4]	16, 5, 762	1. 至德 Chih-tê 丙申	5, 2, 756 12, 8, 756
								2. 乾元 Ch'ien-yüan 戊戌	13, 2, 758 18, 3, 758 [17, 4, thy]
								3. 上元 Shang-yüan[5] 庚子	23, 1, 760 7, 6, 760 [28, 5, 760 thy]
						9 5. 寶應 Pao-ying 壬寅	10 ?29, 4, 762 14, 5,[6] 762	4. 元年 Yüan-nien 壬寅	2, 12, 761 23, 10, 761 [4, 10, thy]

1. Hsin t'ang shu c.5, 12b gives this date as 元年建巳月, the 4th moon in 762 (see note 5 below); likewise also T'ang hui yao c.1, 7a. Chiu t'ang shu c.9, 11a has 上元二年四月甲寅; but in 761 (二年) 甲寅 was the last day of the 3rd moon, so that 二年 (761) may be a misprint for 三年 (762). Both Hsin and Chiu t'ang shu give the Emperor's age as 78.
2. Years were called 載 tsai instead of 年 nien in dates from 20, 1, 744 till 18, 3, 758.
3. Chiu t'ang shu c.10, 1a gives the date of birth as 景雲二年乙亥, omitting the moon. T'ang hui yao, c.1, 8a, where 三年 seems to be a misprint for 二年, supplies the moon and day 九月三日. In 711 乙亥 fell on 21, 2; 22, 4; 21, 6; 20, 8; 19, 10; and 18, 12.
4. News of the enthronement, which took place at 靈武 Ling-wu, did not reach Hsüan Tsung at 蜀 Shu till 10, 9, 756. See Chiu t'ang shu c.9, 11a.
5. On 23, 10, 761 (4, 10, 761 in T'ang hui yao c.1, 8b) it seems to have been decreed that the next year should begin with the 11th moon (2, 12, 761) and should be called 元年 "First year" without a Year Title, and the moons named 子 tzŭ, 丑 ch'ou, &c. (see note 1 above). This decision was reversed on 14, 5, 762, so that the year 761 had only 10 moons, and 762 fourteen. — Chiu t'ang shu c.10, 10b, 11a. See P. Hoang, Prolégomènes à la Concordance Néoménique pp. 141-2, where, however, the date of death of H (3, 5, 762) is mistaken for that of I (16, 5, 762).
6. The Year Title Pao-ying was decreed only two days before I's death.

1	2	3	4	5	6	7	8	9	10
J 代宗 Tai Tsung c.11; c.6	睿文孝武 (779) Jui wên hsiao wu	豫 (758) Yü 俶 (732) Shu	—	1st s. of I	9,1,727	18,5,762 [19, thy]	10,6,779 [9, thy]	廣德 Kuang-tê 癸卯	19,1,763 24,8,763 [2,9, thy]
								永泰 Yung-t'ai 乙巳	26,1,765 26,1,765
								大曆 Ta-li 丙午	14,2,766 18,12,766 [18,11, thy]
K 德宗 Tê Tsung cc.12,13; c.7	神武孝文 (805) Shên wu hsiao wên¹	适 K'uo	—	1st s. of J	27,5,742	12,6,779	25,2,805	建中 Chien-chung 庚申	11,2,780 11,2,780
								興元 Hsing-yüan 甲子	27,1,784 27,1,784
								貞元 Chêng-yüan 乙丑	14,2,785 14,2,785
L 順宗 Shun Tsung c.14; c.7	至德弘道大聖大安孝 (849) Chih tê hung tao ta shêng ta an hsiao 至德大聖大安孝 (806) Chih tê ta shêng ta an hsiao	誦 Sung	—	1st s. of K	–,2/3,761 [21,2,761 thy]	28,2,805 abdicated 4,9,805	11,2,806	永貞 Yung-chêng 乙酉	3,2,805 1,9,805
M 憲宗 Hsien Tsung cc.14,15; c.7	昭文章武大聖至神孝 (849) Chao wên chang wu ta shêng chih shên hsiao 聖神章武孝 (820) Shêng shên chang wu hsiao	純 (805) Ch'un 淳 (788) Ch'un	—	1st s. of L	–,3,778 [17,3, thy]	5,9,805	14,2,820	元和 Yüan-ho 丙戌	24,1,806 25,1,806
N 穆宗 Mu Tsung c.16; c.8	睿聖文惠孝 (824) Jui shêng wên hui hsiao	恒 (806) Hêng 宥 (805) Yu	—	3rd s. of M	–,7/8,795 [26,7, thy]	20,2,820	25,2,824	長慶 Ch'ang-ch'ing 辛丑	6,2,821 9,2,821

1. Chiu t'ang shu c.12,1a, c.13;15b; also T'ang hui yao. Hsin t'ang shu c.7,1a has 神武聖文 Shên wu shêng wên.

1.	2.	3.	4.	5.	6.	7.	8.	9.	10.
O 敬宗 Ching Tsung c.17a; c.8	睿武昭愍孝(827) Jui wu chao min hsiao	湛 Chan	—	1st s. of N	22,7,809 [24,7 thy]	26,2,824	9,1,827	寶曆 Pao-li 乙巳	23,1,825 29,1,825
P 文宗 Wên Tsung c.17a, b; c.8	元聖昭獻孝(840) Yüan shêng chao hsien hsiao	昂(827) Ang 涵(821) Han	—	2nd s. of N	20,11,809	13,1,827	10,2,840[1]	太和[2] T'ai-ho 丁未	31,1,827 14,3,827
								開成 K'ai-chêng 丙辰	22,1,836 22,1,836
Q 武宗 Wu Tsung c.18a; c.8	至道昭肅孝(846) Chih tao chao su hsiao	炎(846) Yen 澧(821) Li [thy]	—	5th s. of N	2,7,814 [1,7 thy]	20,2,840	22,4,846	會昌 Hui-ch'ang 辛酉	27,1,841 4,2,841[3]

1. Chiu T'ang shu c.17b, 20a, Hsin T'ang shu c.8, 6a give the age as 33 instead of 32.
3. Hsin T'ang shu c.8, 6b. Chiu T'ang shu c.18a, 2a by some mistake replaces 癸酉, the 1st day of the 1st moon, by 壬寅, which was the 1st day of the 2nd moon, and dates the institution of Hui-ch'ang on 庚戌, which was the 9th day, not of the 1st, but of the 2nd moon.
2. Sir Percival David kindly points out the misprint 永和 Yung-ho in Mathews's Chinese-English Dictionary, 1931, 1947, p.1172. All sources give T'ai- or 大 Ta-ho.

1.	2.	3.	4.	5.	6.	7.	8.	9.	10.
R 宣宗 Hsüan Tsung c.18b : c.8	元聖至明成武獻文睿智章仁神聰懿道大孝(872) Yüan shêng chih ming ch'êng wu hsien wên jui chih chang jên shên ts'ung i tao ta hsiao 聖武獻文孝 Shêng wu hsien wên hsiao (859)	忱(846) Shên 怡(821) I		13th s of M	27, 7, 810 [28, 7 *thy* 2, 2]	23, 4, 846	7, 9, 859[1]	大中 Ta-chung 丁卯 ——— 丙寅 [*thy* 2, 3] but 13 year is 己卯 859	21, 1, 847 6, 2, 847 ——— 31, 1, 846
S 懿宗 I Tsung c.19a : c.9	睿文昭聖恭惠孝(873) Jui wên chao shêng kung hui hsiao[2]	漼(859) Ts'ui 温(847) Wên		1st s of R	28, 12, 833	13, 9, 859 [7, 9, *thy*]	15, 8, 873	咸通 Hsien-t'ung 庚辰	27, 1, 860 17, 12, 860[3]
T 僖宗 Hsi Tsung c.19b ; c.9	惠聖恭定孝(888) Hui shêng kung ting hsiao	儇(873) Huan originally 儼 Yen		5th s of S	8, 6, 862	16, 8, 873[4]	20, 4, 888	1. 乾符 Ch'ien-fu 甲午	22, 1, 874 17, 12, 874
						9.	10.		
						4. 光啓 Kuang-ch'i 乙巳	20, 1, 885 2, 4, 885	2. 廣明 Kuang-ming 庚子	14, 2, 880 14, 2, 880
						5. 文德 Wên-tê 戊申	16, 2, 888 5, 4, 888[5]	3. 中和 Chung-ho 辛丑	3, 2, 881 9, 8, 881

1. The dates are taken from the *Chiu t'ang shu* c. 18b, 1^{a}, 14^{b}. The *Hsin t'ang shu* cc. 8, 8^{a}, 9^{b}; 9, 1^{a} gives 三月甲子 (22, 4) for the enthronement, and 八月癸巳 (10, 9) both for the death of R and for the enthronement of S.
2. *Chiu t'ang shu* c. 19a, 16^{a}. At the beginning of the chapters both books (c. 19a, 1^{a}; c. 9, 1^{a}) omit the first two words of this title.
3. *Hsin t'ang shu* c. 9, 1^{b}. Here again *Chiu t'ang shu* c. 19a, 1^{b} has the cycle signs wrong, putting 丙午, 丁未 for 1, 2 of the 11th moon in place of 丙子, 丁丑.
4. *Chiu t'ang shu* c. 19^{b}, 1^{a}, 二十日. *Hsin t'ang shu* c. 9, 3^{a} says 辛巳 (15, 8).
5. *Chiu t'ang shu* c. 19^{b}, 17^{b}, 戊子. *Hsin t'ang shu* c. 9, 8^{b}, 庚寅 (7, 4).

1.	2.	3.	4.	5.	6.	7.	8.	9.	10.
usurper c.19b; c.9	「襄王 Hsiang Wang」	熅 Yün	—	great gds. of I	—	31,10,886[1]	–,1,887	建貞 Chien-chêng 丙午	8,2,886 7,6,886
U 昭宗 Chao Tsung	聖穆景文孝 (904) Shêng mu ching wên hsiao	曄 (888) Yeh 傑 (872) Chieh 敏 (888) Min	—	7th s. of S	31,3,867 [30,4, thy]	22,4,888	22,9,904	1. 龍紀 Lung-chi 己酉	4,2,889 4,2,889
				9	10	9	10	2. 大順 Ta-shun 庚戌	25,1,890 25,1,890
				7. 天祐 T'ien-yu 甲子	21,1,904 28,5,904	5. 光化 Kuang-hua 戊午	26,1,898 16,9,898	3. 景福 Ching-fu 壬子	2,2,892 2,2,892
						6. 天復 T'ien-fou 辛酉	23,1,901 13,5,901[2]	4. 乾寧 Ch'ien-ning[3] 甲寅	10,2,894 10,2,894
c.20a; c.10									
V 景宗 (c.930) Ching Tsung (cancelled) c.20b; c.10	哀 Ai 昭宣光烈孝 (c.930) Chao hsüan kuang lieh hsiao (not used)	柷 (904) Chu 祚 (897) Tso	—	9th s. of U	27,9,892	26,9,904 [23,9, thy] deposed 1,6,907 [–,4/5, thy]	25,3,908		

1. *Chiu t'ang shu* c.19b, 15b, 五月庚辰 (7,6). But *Hsin t'ang shu* c.9, 8a, with which the *T'ung chien kang mu* is said to agree (cf. *Chiu t'ang shu* c.19b, 考證 1a), gives the date of enthronement, without mentioning the Year Title, as 31,10,886. *Chiu t'ang shu* l.c. shows that Yün lost his life in the 12th moon on, or soon after, 辛酉 (14,1,887); and in c.175, 7a, 熅四月監國至十二月死凡在僞位九月矣 "Yün established his rule in the 4th moon and died when it came to the 12th moon, having occupied the usurped throne for 9 moons." — having said above (fol. 6b) that he was not enthroned as Emperor until the 10th moon, when he changed the Year Title to 永貞 Yung-chêng (*sic*). The *Hsin t'ang shu* c.82, 7a confirms the form Chien-chêng, but gives no exact dates. *Synchronismes* p.305 makes Yün reign from the 5th to the 10th moon.
2. *Chiu t'ang shu* c.20a, 17a, 四月甲戌. *Hsin t'ang shu* c.10, 5b 四月丙子 (15,5).

3. In the 3rd moon of the 2nd year of Ch'ien-ning (4,895) the rebel 董昌 Tung Ch'ang called his country Lo-p'ing and proclaimed the Year Title Ta-shêng 僭號稱羅平國年稱大聖, — *Chiu t'ang shu* c.20a, 8a.

十國 Shih kuo

楊 Yang 揚州 Yang chou 1. 淮南 Huai-nan or 吳 Wu

1.	2.	3.	4.	5.	6.	7.	8.	9.	10.
A 太祖 (919) T'ai Tsu	孝武 Hsiao Wu	行密 Hsing-mi	化源 Hua-yüan	—	–,–,852	–,–,902	24,12,905	壬戌	11,2,902
B 烈宗 (919) Lieh Tsung	景 Ching	渥 Wu	奉天 Fêng-t'ien	1st s. of A	–,–,886	–,–,905	–,7,908[1]		
C 高祖 Kao Tsu	惠 Hui[2] 宣 Hsüan[3]	渭 Wei or (1) 瀛 Ying (2) 隆演 Lung-yen	鴻源 Hung-yüan	2nd s. of A	–,–,897	–,–,908 –,5,919 (as 吳王)	–,5/6,920	武義 Wu-i 己卯	4,2,919 –,5,919
D —	睿 Jui	溥 P'u	—	4th s. of A	–,–,901	–,8/9,920 29,11,927 (as 皇帝) deposed –,11,937	–,12/1,938[4]	1. 順義 Shun-i 辛巳	11,2,921 –,3/4,921
						9	10	2. 乾貞 Ch'ien-chêng 丁亥	5,2,927 29,11,927
						4. 天祚 T'ien-tso 乙未	6,2,935 –,10,935	3. 大和 Ta-ho[5] 己丑	13,2,929 –,12,929

舊五代史 Chiu wu tai shih c.134. 五代史 Wu tai shih c.61.

1. Wu tai shih c.61, 3, 5a reads Lieh Tsung and Lieh 祖 Tsu; 承天 Ch'êng-t'ien for Fêng-t'ien; and 五月 (6,908) for the date of death.
2. Chiu wu tai shih c.134, 2b.
3. Wu tai shih c.61, 5b.
4. Wu tai shih c.61, 6a, 三年 (937)…十月…禪位…十二月溥卒; but in c.62, 2a it speaks of P'u as alive in May 938 and implies that he died in or after the 11th moon (25,11 – 24,12) 938. Chiu wu tai shih c.134, 3a, 天福二年 (937)…遜位…年餘以幽死.
5. Chiu wu tai shih c.134, 4a reads 太和 T'ai-ho.

十國 Shih kuo

徐 Hsü (李 Li) 金陵(西都) Chin-ling 廣陵(東都) Kuang-ling 2. 南唐 Nan T'ang (-,5,938)

1.	2.	3.	4.	5.	6.	7.	8.	9.	10.
A 義祖 (938) I Tsu 太祖 (935) T'ai Tsu	忠武孝 Chung wu hsiao	温 Wên	敦美 Tun-mei	—	-,-,862		20,11,927[1]		
B 烈祖 Lieh Tsu	光文肅武孝高 (943) Kuang wên su wu hsiao kao	昪 Pien[2] originally 知誥 Chih-kao	正倫 Chêng-lun	s. of 徐榮 Hsü Jung (adopted by A)	-,-,888	-,11,937 (succeeded D-p.63 above) -,5,938 (as 皇帝)	-,-,943	昪元 Shêng-yüan 丁酉	13,2,937 -,11,937
C 元宗 Yüan Tsung	明道崇德文宣孝 (961) Ming tao ch'ung tê wên hsüan hsiao [宣 hsüan omitted in Sung Shih c. 478, 2a]	景 Ching[3] originally 景通 Ching-t'ung or 璟 Ying	伯玉 Po-yü	1st s. of B	-,-,916	-,-,943	-,7/8,961	保大 Pao-ta 癸卯 中興 Chung-hsing[4] 戊午 交泰 Chiao-t'ai 戊午	8,2,943 — 23,1,958 -,½,958 23,1,958 -,½,958
D —	後主 Hou Chu 「吳王 (978) Wu Wang」	煜 Yü originally 從嘉 Ts'ung-chia	重光 Ch'ung-kuang	6th s. of C	-,-,937	-,7/8,961 deposed 1,1,976	15,8,978[5]	From 958 to 973 inclusive the Titles of the Chou and Sung were used. The last two years of the dynasty, 974 & 975 were simply 甲戌, 乙亥	

舊五代史 Chiu wu tai shih c. 134. 五代史 Wu tai shih c. 62. 宋史 Sung shih c. 478.

1. Wu tai shih c. 61, 7a, 順義十年(930)温又請溥卽皇帝位溥未許而温病卒. As P'u (p.   above) was enthroned on 29,11,927, it is probable that 十年 (930) is a misprint for 七年 (927); and 七年 is indeed given on fol. 5b. The exact day is given incidentally in Chiu wu tai shih c. 134, 4a.
2. Lieh Tsu changed his surname (姓) from 徐 Hsü to 李 Li, his name (名) from 知誥 Chih-kao to 昪 Pien, and his kingdom (國號) from 齊 Ch'i (937) to 唐 T'ang on his accession in May 938. — Chiu wu tai shih c. 134, 4a. Sung shih c. 478, 1a has 昇 Shêng in place of Pien.
3. Chiu wu tai shih c. 134, 4a says that Ying was the original name, changed to Ching for reasons of taboo; and Sung shih c. 478, 1a has (1) Ching-t'ung, (2) Ying, (3) Ching.
4. Sung shih c. 478, 1b, where it is said that it was immediately changed again to Chiao-t'ai; but it does not seem to be mentioned in Chiu wu tai shih cc. 81, 134, 4b (where the change to Chiao-t'ai in the 1st moon is recorded on the authority of 南唐書 Nan t'ang shu), or in Wu tai shih cc. 62, 71; nor is it mentioned in the intricate note on the chronology of Ching's reign at the end of c. 62.
5. The dates of birth, deposition, and death, and the posthumous Title Wu Wang (追封吳王) are taken from Sung shih cc. 3, 4a; 4, 3b; 478, 4b.

十國 Shih kuo

王 Wang 成都 Ch'êng-tu 3.前蜀 Ch'ien Shu (漢 Han, in 917 only)

1.	2.	3.	4.	5.	6.	7.	8.	9.	10.
A 高祖 Kao Tsu	神武聖文孝德明惠 Shên wu shêng wên hsiao tê ming hui [verified by his seal found in the 永陵 Yung Ling tomb]	建 Chien	光圖 Kuang-t'u	—	–,–,847	10,10,907	–,7/8,918	「天復 T'ien-fou	901–907
								1.武成 Wu-ch'êng 戊辰	5,2,908 ?5,2,908
						9	10		
						4.天漢 T'ien-han 丁丑	26,1,917 –,1,917	2.永平 Yung-p'ing 辛未	2,2,911 –,1,911
						5.光天 Kuang-t'ien 戊寅	14,2,918 –,½,918	3.通正 T'ung-chêng 丙子	6,2,916 –,11,916
B _	「順正公 (927) Shun chêng Kung」	衍 (918) Yen originally 宗衍 Tsung-yen	化源 Hua-yüan	11th s. of A	–,–,899	–,7/8,918 deposed 9,12,925	?–,5,926	乾德 Ch'ien-tê 己卯	4,2,919 ?4,2,919
								咸康 Hsien-k'ang 乙酉	27,1,925 –,–,925

舊五代史 Chiu wu tai shih c.136. 五代史 Wu tai shih c.63.

十國 Shih kuo

孟 Mêng 成都 Ch'êng-tu 4.後蜀 Hou Shu

1.	2.	3.	4.	5.	6.	7.	8.	9.	10.
A 高祖 Kao Tsu	文武聖德英烈明孝 Wên wu shêng tê ying lieh ming hsiao	知祥 Chih-hsiang	保裔 Pao-i	—	–,–,874	?–,–,926 (入蜀) –,2/3,934 (as 皇帝)	–,8/9,934	明德 Ming-tê 甲午	18,1,934 –,5/6,934
B _	楚王 Ch'u Wang	昶 Ch'ang originally 仁贊 Jên-tsan	保元 Pao-yüan	3rd s. of A	–,–,919	–,8/9,934 deposed 17,2,965	12,7,965	廣政 Kuang-chêng 戊戌	2,2,938 –,1,938

舊五代史 Chiu wu tai shih c.136. 五代史 Wu tai shih c.64.

劉 Liu 廣州 Kuang chou 十國 Shih kuo

5. 南漢 Nan Han (918) 越 Yüeh (917)

A _	襄 (917) Hsiang 南平王 (909) Nan p'ing Wang 南海王 (911) Nan hai Wang	隱 Yin	—	1st s. of 謙 Ch'ien	?-,-,873	-,-,905 (廣州節度使)	-,4/5,910		
B 高祖 Kao Tsu	天皇大帝 T'ien huang ta Ti	龑 (925) Yen originally 陟 Chih 巖 Yen[2]	—	3rd s. of Ch'ien	-,-,889	-,8/9,917	-,5/6,942[3]	乾亨 Ch'ien-hêng 丁丑	26,1,917 -,8/9,917
								白龍 Po-lung 乙酉	27,1,925 ?-,10/12,925
								大有 Ta-yu 戊子	26,1,928 -,2/4,928
C _	殤 Shang	玢 (942) Pin originally 洪度 Hung-tu	—	1st s. of B	-,-,920	-,5/6,942	-,4/5,943	光天 Kuang-t'ien 壬寅	20,1,942 ?-,5/6,942
D 中宗 Chung Tsung	文武光聖明孝 (958) Wên wu kuang shêng ming hsiao	晟 Shêng originally 洪熙 Hung-hsi	壽儁 Shou-chün	2nd s. of B	-,-,920	-,4/5,943	-,9/10,958	應乾 Ying-ch'ien 癸卯	8,2,943 ?-,4/5,943
								乾和 Ch'ien-ho 癸卯	8,2,943 ?-,12,943
E _	南越王 Nan Yüeh Wang	鋹 Ch'ang originally 繼興 Chi-hsing	—	1st s. of D	-,-,942	-,9/10,958 deposed 4,3,971[4]	3,4,980	大寶 Ta-pao 戊午	23,1,958 -,9/10,958

舊五代史 Chiu wu tai shih c.135. 五代史 Wu tai shih c.65.

1. Chiu wu tai shih c. 135, 4b. But Wu tai shih c.65, 1b, 911.
2. Wu tai shih c.65, 2a, 初名巖又更曰陟九年(925)…. 又更名龑.
3. Chiu wu tai shih c.135, 5a; Wu tai shih c.65, 2b. But Synchronismes p.314 gives 944.
4. Sung shih c.2, 5a gives 22,3,971 as the date of the capture of Kuang chou.

馬 Ma 長沙 Ch'ang-sha 十國 Shih kuo 6. 楚 Ch'u

1.	2.	3.	4.	5.	6.	7.	8.	9.	10.
A –	武穆 Wu mu (931)	殷 Yin	霸圖 Pa-t'u	–	–,–,854	–,–,927[1]	21,12,931[2]	Year of 後唐 (p. 64)	Titles Hou T'ang below)
B –	衡陽王 (932) Hêng yang Wang	希聲 Hsi-shêng	若訥 Jo-no	2nd s of A	–,–,899	?–,12,931	–,8,932		
C –	文昭王 Wên chao Wang	希範 Hsi-fan	寶規 Pao-kuei	4th s of A	–,–,899	–,8,932	–,5/6,947		
D –	—	希廣 Hsi-kuang	德丕 Tê-p'ei	s of A (younger br of C)	–	–,–,947	?–,–,950		
E –	—	希萼 Hsi-o	–	s of A	–	–,–,950	–	Year 南唐 (p. 64)	Titles of Nan T'ang above)
F –	—	希崇 Hsi-ch'ung	–	s of A	–	–,–,951 deposed[3] –,–,956	–		

舊五代史 Chiu wu tai shih c.133. 五代史 Wu tai shih c.66.

1. Wu tai shih c.66,2b; Synchronismes p.321. Chiu wu tai shih c.133,3b gives 923.
2. Chiu wu tai shih c.133,3b gives this year, and Yin's age as 78. Wu tai shih c.66,2b gives 930, and the age 79. This year and age, given also in Synchronismes p.321 and noted in the notes (考證) to Chiu wu tai shih c.133, would put back the year of birth to 852.
3. Wu tai shih c.66,4a. The domains and succession of D,E,F appear to be vague; nor do they seem to have been really independent rulers.

錢 Ch'ien　　杭州 Hang chou　　十國 Shih kuo　　7. 吳越 Wu Yüeh

1	2	3	4	5	6	7	8	9	10
A 太祖 Tai Tsu[1]	武肅 (932) Wu su	鏐 Ch'iu[2]	具美 Chü-mei	s of 寬 K'uan[3] (835 – 16,5,895)	20,3,[4]852	3,7,902 as 越王 7,6,904 as 吳王,[5] 16,6,907 as 吳越王	6,5,932	天寶 T'ien-pao[6] 戊辰	5,2,908
								Year Titles of Hou Liang (p. 74 below)	6,2,916
								寶大 Pao-ta 甲申	8,2,924
								寶正 Pao-chêng 丙戌	15,2,926

1. 舊五代史 Chiu wu tai shih c.133. 2. 五代史 Wu tai shih c.67. 3. 宋史 Sung shih cc.4,5, 480. 4. 吳越備史 Wu yüeh pei shih 5. 錢氏家乘 Ch'ien shih chia ch'êng.

1. This and the other Temple Titles are given in Synchronismes, but have not been found by Professor G. Haloun or myself in any Chinese source.
2. 鏐 is read both Ch'iu and Liu. At Hang-chou it is to this day pronounced Ch'iu; and that this is traditionally correct has been stated by the living representatives of the family. On the other hand a decree was made in 992 that all persons of the name of 劉 Liu in Chê-chiang should cease to change it to 金 Chin, as they had been obliged to do to avoid the taboo of 鏐 Liu (Sung shih c. 480, 6a); and the name is given under the sound Liu in K'ang hsi tzŭ tien. cf. T'oung Pao, 1937, pp. 110, 111 n.
3. The name and dates of the father of A are supplied from sources 4 and 5 by Professor G. Haloun, to whose very great kindness all details which cannot be found in sources 1, 2, & 3 are owed.
4. Sources 4 & 5 agree in the moon, but 5 misprints 十六日 (10,3) for 二十六日 (20,3).
5. The exact dates, which do not seem to be given in detail in sources 1–5 nor in either of the T'ang shu, are supplied by Professor Haloun from the Tzŭ chih t'ung chien cc. 263, 8b; 264, 29b; 266, 14a respectively.
6. This and the two following Year Titles are taken 容齋隨筆 (四筆, preface 1197, c.5, 9a–10b; ed. 四部叢刊續編) Jung chai sui pi by 洪邁 Hung Mai, 1123–1202, who in turn seems to have found them in the collection of inscriptions by his contemporary 王厚之, 順伯, Wang Hou-chih, Shun-po, 1131–1204. Inscriptions are quoted which prove the dates T'ien-pao 908–912; Pao-ta 924, 925; Pao-chêng 926–931; but the statement by Wang Hou-chih (fol. 10a) that the Liang Calendar was used from 913 to 923 inclusive does not seem to be so well established. The examples quoted range only from early 916 (丙子正月) to 923 (龍德三年). Professor Haloun kindly tells me that in the list of Year Titles in the 玉海 Yü hai c.13 the same three Titles (T'ien-pao, fol. 12b; Pao-ta or Pao-t'ai, and Pao-chêng, fol. 33a) with the addition of 廣初 Kuang-ch'u (fol. 22b) are attributed to Ch'ien Ch'iu without exact dates. It thus seems that the author, 王應麟 Wang Ying-lin, 1223–1296, may have found a source for these Titles independent of Wang Hou-chih; and it is possible that Kuang-ch'u is to be fitted in between 912 and 916. An inscription still extant near Hang-chou speaks of the Liang years 907–912 (梁單閼至涒灘 — covering the T'ien-pao period, which is not mentioned) and is dated simply 甲申六月十五日 (19,7,924), perhaps showing that Pao-ta was not decreed until after 19 July 924 (cf.

7. 吴越 Wu Yüeh

1	2	3	4	5	6	7	8	9	10
B 世宗 Shih Tsung	文穆 (21,12,943[1]) Wên mu 莊穆 (941) Chuang mu	元瓘 Yüan-kuan	明寶 Ming-pao	7th[2] s of A	30,11,887	15,5,932 as 吴越國王	17,9,941	Year Titles of Hou T'ang (p. 79 below)	9,2,932
C 成宗 Chêng Tsung	忠獻 Chung hsien	弘佐 Hung-tso[3]	玄祐 Hsüan-yu[4]	6th[5] s of B	14,8,928	26,9,941	22,6,947		
D _	忠遜 Chung hsün or 忠讓 Chung jang[6]	弘倧 Hung-tsung[3]	隆道 Lung-tao[7]	7th s of B	15,8,929	30,7,947 deposed 12,2,948	?-,-,972[8]		

G.E. Moule, Hangchow past and present, 1907, frontispiece). These Year Titles are not mentioned in either of the Wu tai shih, and the Chiu wu tai shih c.133,5b says that the rulers were independent sovereigns in every other respect except the change of Year Titles (但不改年號而已). But in his preface to the chronological tables of the period (Wu tai shih c.71, 1a) Ou-yang Hsiu says that he had heard from old people that the title Ti, "Emperor", and Year Titles had been used in Wu Yüeh, though he had found it hard to obtain exact evidence beyond the existence of one document dated 寶正六年辛卯 "6th Pao-chêng year hsin mao", i.e. 931.

1. Chiu wu tai shih c.82,2a.
2. Wu yüeh pei shih, followed by Ch'ien shih chia ch'êng. Chiu wu tai shih says fifth son; Wu tai shih gives no number. The day and month of birth and the day of accession are also taken from Wu yüeh pei shih.
3. In the Sung dynasty the character 弘 Hung was dropped from the names of Tso and his brothers out of respect to the taboo of 弘殷 Hung-yin, the name of 宣祖 Hsüan Tsu, father of the founder of the Sung dynasty. Synchron. p.327 gives 仁佐 Jên-tso as an alias for Hung-tso.
4. Wu tai shih c.67, 3b says 宇祐, omitting 玄.
5. The position in the family, and the day and month of birth, accession, and death are all taken from Wu yüeh pei shih. Chiu wu tai shih c.133, 7b gives no date of birth, or age; Wu tai shih c.67,3b,4a gives the age as 13 in 941, and 20 in 947.
6. The variant Chung jang is found in Wu yüeh pei shih c.3,1a.
7. This name, and the date of birth, are taken from Ch'ien shih chia ch'êng; the position in the family and the exact day of accession and deposition from Wu yüeh pei shih, followed by the chia ch'êng.
8. The Ch'ien shih chia ch'êng says he died in 875 (開寶八年) aged 44 years. As the date of his birth in 929 must be approximately correct, he must have died either in 872 or at the age of 47 years. The Sung shih c.480,6a says that he died after living more than 20 years at Yüeh-chou (居越州二十餘年卒); and from the Wu yüeh pei shih, followed by the chia ch'êng, we learn that he was sent to live in Yüeh-chou in the 4th moon of the 1st Kuang-shun year (i.e. May or June 851). It seems safe to conclude that he died in 872 at the age of 44 years; and this is confirmed by the 十國春秋 Shih kuo ch'un ch'iu c.80,11a (年四十四). (G.H.)

吳越 Wu Yüeh

1	2	3	4	5	6	7	8	9	10
E _	忠懿 Chung i	弘俶 Hung-shu[1]	文德 Wên-tê	9th s of B	30,9,929	17,2,948 abdicated 12,6,978[2]	7,10,988[3]		

1. See note 3 on the previous page.
2. Professor G. Haloun has collected the following data from Wu yüeh pei shih. Hung-shu left Hang-chou 14,3,978 and reached the capital on 3,5,978. His first petition to be allowed to abdicate, dated 5,6,978, was refused. He petitioned again on 12,6. This was accepted on 14,6; and he was made 淮海國王 Huai hai kuo Wang and given the insignia on 21,6,978. He was subsequently made 漢南國王 Han nan kuo Wang 4,1,985; 南陽國王 Nan yang kuo Wang c.3,986; 許王 Hsü Wang c.3,987; 鄧王 Têng Wang c.3,988. The Sung shih c.4,3a makes him reach the capital to do homage on 3,5,978; petition to resign the title of Wu yüeh kuo Wang on 7,6; petition the second time to be allowed to abdicate on 9,6; and says that this was accepted with his appointment as Huai hai kuo Wang on 11,6,978.
3. This was the 24th day of the 8th moon; and it was noticed with surprise that Hung-shu was born on the 24th day of the 8th moon in 929, and that his father, Yüan-kuan, had died on that day in 941 (Sung shih c.480,5a). From the Wu yüeh pei shih, however, the following dates of birth are obtained: cc. 1,62b; 2,5b, 八月己酉 i.e. 18,9,929; c.4,1a, 八月二十五日 i.e. 30,9,929; c.4,39b, 八月二十四日 i.e. 29,9,929. Professor Haloun thinks that 己酉 is a misprint for 辛酉, and that the correct date is 25th day of the 8th moon (30,9,929); and he adds: "These dates come from the original work of 范坰 Fan Chiung and 林禹 Lin Yü as the entries run 今大元帥 .... 生 (The present Ta yüan shuai .... was born). The third date originates in the supplement and has certainly been adjusted from the day of death so as to give a complete cycle. The entry runs: 天成四年八月二十四日四鼓而生端拱元年八月二十四日四鼓而薨以生訖薨實治周一甲子." The posthumous titles Chung i and 秦國王 Ch'in kuo Wang were granted on 5,1,989.

十國 Shih kuo

王 Wang 長樂 Ch'ang-lo, 福州 Fu chou 8. 閩 Min (932 or 933)

1	2	3	4	5	6	7	8	9	10
A 太祖(933) T'ai Tsu	昭武孝 (933) Chao wu hsiao 忠懿 (925) Chung i	審知 Shên-chih	信通 Hsin-t'ung	younger s of 恁 Jên, and younger br of 潮 Ch'ao	–,–,862	–,–,898 (governor of 福建 on death of 潮 2,1,898) –,–,907 (閩王)	–,12/1,925[1]	Year Titles of 後梁 Hou Liang (p. 74 below)	
B –	–	延翰 Yen-han	子逸 Tzŭ-i	1st s of A	–	–,11,926[2] (建國)	–,1,927	Year Titles of 後唐 Hou T'ang (p. 75 below)	
C 太宗 T'ai Tsung	惠 Hui	鏻 (927) Lin originally 延鈞 Yen-chün	–	2nd s of A	–	–,1,927[3] (閩王) –,–,932 (as 皇帝)	–,1/12,934[4]	龍啓 Lung-ch'i 壬辰	9,2,932 –,–,932
								永和 Yung-ho 甲午	18,1,934 —
D 康宗 K'ang Tsung	—	昶 Ch'ang originally 繼鵬 Chi-pêng	–	1st s of C	–	–,11,935 –,–,937[5] (as 閩王)	–,5/7,938[6]	通文 T'ung-wên 乙未	6,2,935 —

舊五代史 Chiu wu tai shih c. 134. 五代史 Wu tai shih c. 68.

1. Wu tai shih c. 68, 1b, 同光三年卒年六十四. Chiu wu tai shih c. 134, 6a, 同光元年卒 with no age. Neither book gives the moon. Synchron. p. 315 gives 925, 12th moon. Wu tai shih c. 68, 5a makes the dynasty begin in 886 and last exactly one cycle, reckoning from the appointment of 王潮 Wang Ch'ao as governor of Ch'üan chou; but prefers to reckon from Ch'ao's appointment as 觀察史 Kuan ch'a shih in 892.
2. Wu tai shih c. 68, 1b. –,–, 925 according to Wu tai shih c. 71, 2b.
3. Wu tai shih c. 71, 2b, 丙戌 (926 = 1,927) 是歲鏻立.
4. Wu tai shih c. 68, 3a, adding "reigned 10 years" (立十年) inconsistently. Chiu wu tai shih c. 134, 6a, 清泰元年 (934).
5. Wu tai shih c. 68, 3a says that on his accession Chi-pêng changed his name to Ch'ang and changed the Year Title to 通文 T'ung-wên, and adds that in 937 he presented tribute and received the title 閩王 Min Wang. Chiu wu tai shih c. 134, 6a says very vaguely that in 938 he presented tribute and received the title Min Wang, and changed the Year Title to 通大 T'ung-ta (sic).
6. Wu tai shih c. 68, 3b seems to put the assassination of Chi-pêng in "the summer of the 3rd year" (三年夏 i.e. 5-7, 938). Chiu wu tai shih c. 134, 6a, after recounting the tribute, etc. of 938, simply says, "afterwards he was killed" (後遇弒). Synchron. p. 322 gives 939, 6th moon.

閩 Min

1	2	3	4	5	6	7	8	9	10
E 景宗 Ching Tsung	—	曦 Hsi originally 延羲 Yen-hsi	—	youngest s of A	—	–,6,938[1]	–,4,943[2]	永隆 Yung-lung 戊戌	2,2,938 –,6,938
F _	—	延政 Yen-chêng	—	s of A	—	–,–,942[3] (殷國) –,–,944 deposed –,–,946	—	天德 Tien-tê 癸卯	20,1,942 —

1. Wu tai shih c.68,3b. –,6,939 according to c.71,3b.
2. Wu tai shih c.68,4a. –,4,944 according to c.71,4a.
3. Wu tai shih c.68,4a puts the establishment of Yen-chêng at 建州 Chien chou as Emperor of 殷 Yin, the year before the assassination of Hsi, and dates this event in "the 6th [Yung-lung] year" (?943). Thus the accession of Yen-chêng at Chien chou and the Year Title Tien-tê would both be dated 942. The vaguer notice in Chiu wu tai shih c.134,6a is not inconsistent with this. Synchronismes p.329 also gives 942 for both events, although it dates Yung-lung as 939 and the death of Hsi in 944. Synchron. also ends the dynasty in 944, against the text of Chiu wu tai shih c.134,6a, and the note on Wu tai shih c.68,4b and 5a, 諸家記其國滅丙午是也, and also Wu tai shih c.71,4b, 是歲(丙午)延政為南唐所虜王氏滅. Wu tai shih c.71,4a, however, dates the accession of Yen-chêng at Chien chou 癸卯 (943).

十國 Shih kuo

高 Kao 荊州 Ching chou 9. 南平 Nan p'ing

1	2	3	4	5	6	7	8	9	10
A _	武信王 Wu hsin Wang	季興 Chi-hsing originally 季昌 Chi-ch'ang	貽孫 I-sun	—	–,–,858	–,–,907 (governor of 荊南) –,–,925 (as 南平王)	–,½,929	Year Titles of 後吳 Hou Wu (p.63 above)	
B _	文獻王 Wên hsien Wang	從誨 Ts'ung-hui	遵聖 Tsun-shêng	1st s of A	–,–,891	–,½,929[1]	–,12,948[2]	Year Titles of 後唐 Hou T'ang (p.75 below)	
C _	貞懿王 Chêng i Wang	保融 Pao-jung	德長 Tê-ch'ang	3rd s of B	–,–,920	–,12,948	–,8/9,960		
D _	–	保勖 Pao-hsü	省躬 Hsing-kung	10th s of B	–,–,924	–,8/9,960	–,12,962		
E _	–	繼沖 Chi-ch'ung	成和 Chêng-ho	s of C	–,–,943	?–,12,962 deposed –,9/10,963	–,–,973		

舊五代史 Chiu wu tai shih c.133. 五代史 Wu tai shih c.69.

1. Wu tai shih c.71,3a, 戊子.
2. Chiu wu tai shih c.133,2a. Wu tai shih c.69,2b says 10th moon, November.

十國 Shih kuo

10. 東漢 Tung Han

劉 Liu

1	2	3	4	5	6	7	8	9	10
A 世祖 Shih Tsu	—	旻 (951) Min originally 崇 Ch'ung	—	br of 高祖 Kao Tsu of Hou Han (p.. below)	–,–, 896	–, 2/3, 951	–, 12/1, 955	Year Titles of 後漢 Hou Han (p. 76 below)	
B 睿宗 Jui Tsung	孝和 Hsiao ho	承鈞 Chêng-chün	—	2nd s of A	—	?–, 12/1, 955[1]	–, 8, 968[1]	天會 T'ien-hui 丁巳	3, 2, 957 —
C —	—	繼恩 Chi-ên	—	s of 薛釗 Hsieh Chao (adopted by A)	—	–, 8, 968	–, 10[2], 968		
D —	英武 Ying wu	繼元 Chi-yüan	—	br of C	—	?–, 10, 968 deposed –, 6, 979	–,–, 991	廣運 Kuang-yün 甲戌	26, 1, 974[3]

舊五代史 Chiu wu tai shih c.135. 五代史 Wu tai shih c.70.
宋史 Sung shih c.482.

1. Wu tai shih c.70, 3b, 承鈞立十三年 might put his death in 967; but that his accession may not have followed at once upon his father's death is suggested on fol. 2b, 承鈞既立始赦境内改乾祐十年(957)曰天會元年.

2. Wu tai shih c.70, 3b implies the 9th moon (October); Synchron. p.341 says 10th moon (November).

3. Wu tai shih c.70, 4a says 立改元曰廣運, not suggesting an interval of 5 years or more, 968–974.

朱 Chu　　洛陽 Lo-yang (909-13) 開封 K'ai-fêng (907-23)　　五代 Wu tai
1. 梁 Liang

1.	2.	3.	4.	5.	6.	7.	8.	9.	10.
A 太祖 T'ai Tsu cc. 1–7; cc. 1, 2	神武元聖孝 Shên wu yüan shêng hsiao	晃 (907) Huang originally 溫 Wên 賜名全忠 Ch'üan-chung [Wthy]	—	3rd s of 誠 Ch'êng (烈祖文穆 907, Lieh Tsu-wen mu)	5,12,852	1,6,907[1]	18,7,912 [21,7 Wthy]	開平 K'ai-p'ing 丁卯	15,2,907 5,6,907
								乾化 Ch'ien-hua 辛未	2,2,911 31,5,911
B —	—	友珪 Yu-kuei	—	5 of A	—	21,7,912	27,3,913	鳳歷 Fêng-li 癸酉	9,2,913
C — cc. 8–10; c. 3	末帝 Mo Ti	瑱 (915; 913– Wthy) T'ien 鍠 (913) Huang originally 友貞 Yu-chêng	—	4th s of A[2]	20,10,888	–,¾,913[3]	18,11,923	乾化三年 Ch'ien-hua 3 癸酉	9,2,913 –,¾,913
								貞明 Chêng-ming 乙亥	18,1,915 17,12,915[4]
								龍德 Lung-tê 辛巳	11,2,921 9,6,921

舊五代史 Chiu wu tai shih c. 1–. 五代史 Wu tai shih c. 1–. 五代會要 Wu tai hui yao (Wthy).

1. Tzŭ hai s.v. 戊 says that in 907 the cycle sign 戊 mou was changed to 武 wu to avoid the taboo of A's great grandfather 茂琳 Mao-lin, and ever after 戊 has generally been read wu; K'ang-hsi to same effect, but explicitly says that wu is wrong.
2. Wu tai shih c. 3, 1a says 3rd son.
3. Between 27 March and 9 April. Both texts say 是月 "this month", and a note in Wu tai shih c. 3, 1a points out that the loss of the exact day is proof of the extreme confusion of the times. Wu tai hui yao, however, gives 27 March, and, for the Year Title Chêng-ming, reads 正 for 貞.
4. Tzŭ chih t'ung chien k'ao i c. 29, 2a quotes Wu yüeh pei shih 二月壬辰朔改元 (misprint for 三月 etc.; 19,3,915), but prefers the date here given from Chiu wu tai shih.

李 Li 東京魏州 Wei chou; 西京太原 T'ai-yüan; 北都鎮州 Chên chou.[1] 五代 Wu tai

2. 唐 T'ang (13,5,923)

1.	2.	3.	4.	5.	6.	7.	8.	9.	10.
A 太祖 (923) T'ai Tsu cc. 25, 26; —	武 (923) Wu	克用 K'o-yung	—	3rd[2] s of 朱邪(耶)國昌 Chu-hsieh (yeh) Kuo-ch'ang originally (名) 赤心 Ch'ih-hsin (獻祖文 923, Hsien Tsu-wên)	24,10,856	–, 4/5, 888 (隴西郡王) 1, 1, 896 (晉王)	23, 2, 908		
B 莊宗 Chuang Tsung cc. 27-34; cc. 4, 5	光聖神閔孝 (926) Kuang shêng shên min hsiao	存勗 Ts'un-hsü (小名) 亞子 Ya-tzŭ	—	1st s of A	2,12,885[3] [30, 1, 886 Wthy]	–, 2, 908 (晉王) 13, 5, 923 (皇帝)	15, 5, 926[3]	同光 T'ung-kuang 癸未	20, 1, 923 13, 5, 923
C 明宗 Ming Tsung cc. 35-44; c. 6	聖德和武欽孝 (934) Shêng tê ho wu ch'in hsiao	亶 (926) Tan originally 嗣源 Ssŭ-yüan 邈佶烈 Mo-chi-lieh	—	adopted s of A 1st s of 孝成皇帝	10,10,867	3. 6, 926	15,12,933	天成 T'ien-ch'êng 丙戌 長興 Ch'ang-hsing 庚寅	15, 2, 926 11, 6, 926 2, 2, 930 23, 3, 930
D — c. 45; c. 7	閔 (936) Min[4]	從厚 Ts'ung-hou 菩薩奴 (小字) P'u-sa-nu	—	3rd s of C	17,12,914	20,12,933 deposed 22, 5, 934	24, 5, 934	應順 Ying-shun 甲午	18, 1, 934 24, 1, 934
E — cc. 46-48; c. 7	末 (or 廢) Mo (or Fei)	從珂 Ts'ung-k'o	阿三 A-san[5]	adopted s of C 姓王氏 s of Wang	11, 2, 885	20, 5, 934[6] [21, 5. Wthy]	11, 1, 937[7] [26, 1 Wthy]	清泰 Ch'ing-t'ai 甲午	18, 1, 934 31, 5, 934

舊五代史 *Chiu wu tai shih* c. 25–. 五代史 *Wu tai shih* c. 4–. 五代會要 *Wu tai hui yao* (*Wthy*).

1. *Wu tai hui yao* c. 19: 同光元年 (923).... 復為西京京兆府 (fol. 3a); 同光三年 (925).... 今後依舊以洛京為東都魏州改為鄴都興唐府興(與?)北都太原府並為次府 (fol. 2b); 長興三年 (932).... 本朝都長安以京兆府為上[今]都洛陽以河南府為上 (fol. 2b).
2. *Chiu wu tai shih* c. 25, 1b. 1st son according to *Wu tai hui yao* c. 1, 14a.
3. *Wu tai shih* c. 5, 4a note, 年四十三. This would put the year of birth back to 884. *Wu tai hui yao* c. 1, 3b says 年四十二.
4. *Wu tai shih* c. 7, 1a has 愍 Min, and says he was 5th son of C.
5. *Wu tai shih* c. 7, 1b. *Chiu wu tai shih* c. 46, 1a reads 二十三 Êrh-shih-san.
6. *Wu tai shih* c. 7, 2a gives 21, 5, 934 in agreement with *Wu tai hui yao* c. 1, 6a; and 19, 5, 934 for the deposition of D.
7. *Wu tai shih* c. 7, 3a note, 年五十一. This would put the year of birth forward to 886. *Wu tai hui yao* c. 1, 6a has 年五十二.

石 Shih

五代 Wu tai
3. 晉 Chin

1.	2.	3.	4.	5.	6.	7.	8.	9.	10.
A 高祖 KaoTsu cc.75-80; c.8	聖文章武明德孝 Shêng wên chang wu ming tê hsiao	敬瑭 Ching-t'ang	–	2nd s of 臬捩鷄 Nieh-li-chi (憲祖孝元 Hsien Tsu-hsiao yüan)	30,3,892	28,11,936[1] [28,12 Wthy]	28,7,942	天福 T'ien-fu 丙申	27,1,936 30,11,936
B _ cc.81-85; c.9	少 or 出 Shao or Ch'u	重貴 Chung-kuei	–	s of 敬儒 Ching-ju, elder br of A	22,7,914	–,7,942[2] [28, Wthy] deposed[3] 11,1,947	(alive in 954)	開運 K'ai-yün[4] 甲辰	28,1,944 23,7,944

舊五代史 Chiu wu tai shih c.75–. 五代史 Wu tai shih c.8–. 五代會要 Wu tai hui yao (Wthy).

1. Chiu wu tai shih c.48,5a says 閏十一月丁卯 (28,12,936) in agreement with Wu tai hui yao c.1,6b; but c.75,4b, Wu tai shih cc.7,3a, 8,1b, Liao shih c.3,4b all have 十一月丁酉 (28,11,936). The accession of A in 936 (天顯九年) is confirmed in Wu tai shih c.72,4b, but no month is named.
2. The day does not seem to be exactly stated in either book, but Wu tai hui yao c.1,7b gives 28,7.
3. Wu tai hui yao c.1,7b says 三年正月 (–,2,946) but adds "aged 34" (年三十四), i.e. 947 (fol.8a).
4. 開通 K'ai-t'ung in Chiu wu tai shih c.82,2b seems to be a mere misprint.

劉 Liu

汴州 Pien chou

五代 Wu tai
4. 漢 Han

1.	2.	3.	4.	5.	6.	7	8.	9.	10.
A 高祖 KaoTsu cc.99,100; c.10	睿文聖武昭肅孝[1] (948) Jui wên shêng wu chao su hsiao	暠 (948; 947-Wthy) Kao originally 知遠 Chih-yüan	–	1st s of 琠 T'ien (顯祖章聖 Hsien Tsu-chang shêng)	4,3,895	10,3,947	10,3,948	天福十二年 T'ien-fu 12 丁未 乾祐 Ch'ien-yu 戊申	25,1,947 13,2,948 17,2,948
B _ cc.101-103; c.10	隱 (951) Yin	承祐 Ch'êng-yu	–	2nd s of A	28,3,931 [30,3 Wthy]	14,3,948	2,1,951 [1,1 Wthy]		

舊五代史 Chiu wu tai shih c.99–. 五代史 Wu tai shih c.10–. 五代會要 Wu tai hui yao (Wthy).

1. Wu tai hui yao c.1,8b transposes 文聖, but 8a agrees with this.
2. Wu tai shih c.10,3a note explains that B would naturally have changed the Year Title at the beginning of 949, but his subjects (臣民) were pleased with the likeness of Ch'ien-yu to his name Ch'êng-yu, and so it was left unchanged.

郭 Kuo 汴州 Pien chou 五代 Wu tai

5. 周 Chou

1.	2.	3.	4.	5.	6.	7.	8.	9.	10.
A 太祖 T'ai Tsu cc.110-113; c.11	聖神恭肅文武孝 (954) Shêng shên kung su wên wu hsiao	威 Wei	文仲 Wên-chung	1st s of 郭簡 Kuo Chien (慶祖章肅 Ch'ing Tsu-chang su)	10,9,904	13,2,951	22[1],2,954	廣順 Kuang-shun 辛亥	9,2,951 13,2,951
								顯德 Hsien-tê 甲寅	6,2,954 6,2,954
B 世宗 Shih Tsung cc.114-119; c.12	睿武孝文 (959) Jui wu hsiao wên	榮 Jung	—	s of 柴守禮 Ch'ai Shou-li adopted by A	27,10,921	26,2,954 [25,2 Wthy]	27,7,959		
C c.120; c.12	恭 (973) Kung	宗訓 Tsung-hsün	—	4th s of B	14,9,953	28,7,959 [17,7 Wthy] deposed 3,2,960	6,4,973		

舊五代史 Chiu wu tai shih cc.110-120. 五代史 Wu tai shih cc.11,12.
五代會要 Wu tai hui yao (Wthy).

1. The day is given in both books as 是日 ("this day"). Here and elsewhere I have taken this to refer to the last day recorded (here 壬辰); and this is confirmed by the explicit mention of 壬辰 in Wu tai shih c.12,1a. But c.11,3a has the note, 書是日連上文嫌無崩日.-"no day of death"

Table of the Wu tai & Shih kuo

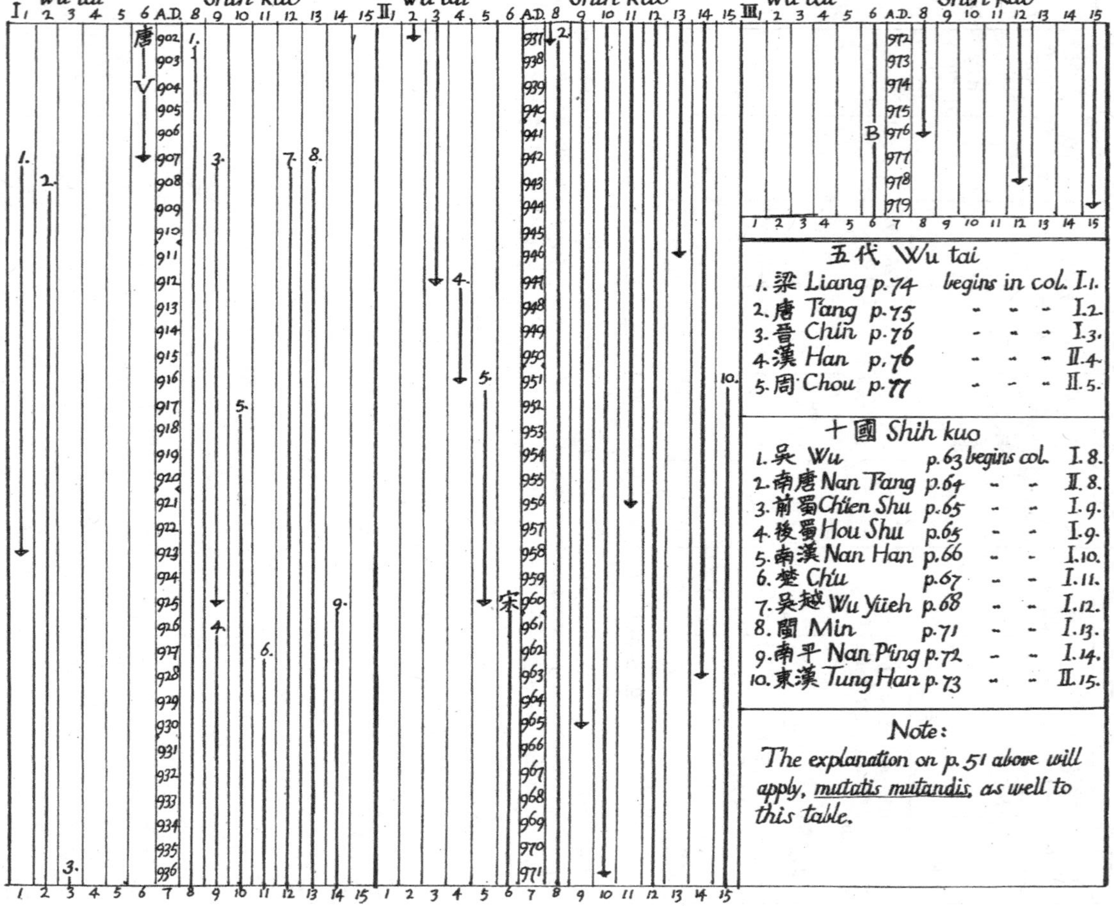

五代 Wu tai

1. 梁 Liang	p. 74	begins in col.	I. 1.
2. 唐 Tang	p. 75	- - -	I. 2.
3. 晉 Chin	p. 76	- - -	I. 3.
4. 漢 Han	p. 76	- - -	II. 4.
5. 周 Chou	p. 77	- - -	II. 5.

十國 Shih kuo

1. 吳 Wu	p. 63	begins col.	I. 8.
2. 南唐 Nan Tang	p. 64	- -	II. 8.
3. 前蜀 Ch'ien Shu	p. 65	- -	I. 9.
4. 後蜀 Hou Shu	p. 65	- -	I. 9.
5. 南漢 Nan Han	p. 66	- -	I. 10.
6. 楚 Ch'u	p. 67	- -	I. 11.
7. 吳越 Wu Yüeh	p. 68	- -	I. 12.
8. 閩 Min	p. 71	- -	I. 13.
9. 南平 Nan P'ing	p. 72	- -	I. 14.
10. 東漢 Tung Han	p. 73	- -	II. 15.

Note:

The explanation on p. 51 above will apply, *mutatis mutandis*, as well to this table.

拓跋 To-pa 李 Li (882 and 986) 趙 Chao (982) 夏州 Hsia chou 長安 Ch'ang-an (1218) 西夏 Hsi Hsia

1.	2.	3.	4.	5.	6.	7.	8.	9.	10.
a –	–	思恭[1] Ssŭ-kung	–	–	–	–, –, 882[2] as 夏國公	–, –, 895[3]		
b –	–	思諫 Ssŭ-chien	–	younger br of a	–	–, –, 895[4]	–, –, 908		
c –	–	彝昌 I-ch'ang	–	gds of a[5]	–	–, –, 908	–, –, 909		
d –	虢王 (933) Kuo Wang	仁福 Jên-fu	–	cousin of c[6]	–	–, –, 909	–, 4, 933		
e –	–	彝超 I-ch'ao	–	2nd s of d	–	–, –, 933	–, –, 935		
f –	夏王 (967) Hsia Wang	彝興 (960)[7] I-hsing originally 彝殷 I-yin	–	younger br of e	–	–, –, 935 – –, –, 954 as 西平王 Hsi p'ing Wang	–, –, 967		
g –	–	克睿[8] K'o-jui originally 光睿 Kuang-jui	–	s of f	–	–, –, 967	–, –, 978		
h –	–	繼筠 Chi-yün	–	s of g	–	–, –, 978	–, –, 980		
i –	–	繼捧(奉) Chi-fêng[9] 趙保忠 Chao Pao-chung	–	younger s of g	–	–	–, –, 1004		

舊唐書 Chiu t'ang shu c. 20a. 唐書 T'ang shu cc. 10, 221a.
舊五代史 Chiu wu tai shih c. 132. 五代史 Wu tai shih cc. 40, 72, 73.
宋史 Sung shih cc. 1–44, 485, 486. 遼史 Liao shih cc. 1–30, 70, 115. 金史 Chin shih c. 134.

1. Wu tai shih c. 40, 3b gives 思敬 Ssŭ-ching by confusion with the younger brother of 思孝 Ssŭ-hsiao.
2. T'ang shu c. 221a, 3a.
3. Wu tai shih c. 40, 3b 乾寧二年. But T'ang shu c. 221a, 3a seems to indicate 886, i.e. 光啓二年.
4. 886 according to T'ang shu c. 221a, 3a. Chiu t'ang shu c. 20a, 9b mentions him on 5, 9, 895; T'ang shu c. 10, 3b same date mentions him along with 李思孝 Li Ssŭ-hsiao.
5. According to Chiu wu tai shih c. 132, 4b and Wu tai shih c. 40, 4a: son of b.
6. Wu tai shih c. 40, 4a says relation to c is not known.
7. His name was changed to avoid the taboo of 宣祖 Hsüan Tsu (p. 84).
8. Changed to avoid the taboo of 太宗 T'ai Tsung (p. 85).
9. He was loyal to Sung from 982 onwards and was constantly at war with A.

西夏 Hsi Hsia

<table>
<tr><th>1</th><th>2</th><th>3</th><th>4</th><th>5</th><th>6</th><th>7</th><th>8</th><th>9</th><th>10</th></tr>
<tr><td>A
太祖
(1032)
T'ai Tsu
武宗[1] (1012)
Wu Tsung</td><td>神武 Shên wu (1032)
應運法天神智仁聖至道廣德光孝 (1012)
Ying yün fa t'ien shên chih jên shêng chih tao kuang tê kuang hsiao[2]</td><td>繼遷
Chi-ch'ien
保吉 (990)
Pao-chi[3]</td><td>—</td><td>s[4] of 光儼 Kuang-yen and cousin (族弟) of 繼捧 Chi-fêng</td><td>-,-,963[5]</td><td>, ,986[6]
as 夏國王</td><td>26,1,1004[7]</td><td></td><td></td></tr>
<tr><td>B
太宗
T'ai Tsung</td><td>光聖
Kuang shêng</td><td>德明
Tê-ming
德昭
Tê-chao[8]</td><td>(小字)
阿移
A-i</td><td>s of A</td><td>-,-,982[9]</td><td>21,7,1004[10]
as 西平王
—
10,9,1013[11]
as 大夏國王</td><td>-,10/11,1031[12]</td><td></td><td></td></tr>
<tr><td rowspan="5">C
景宗
Ching Tsung</td><td rowspan="5">武烈
Wu lieh</td><td rowspan="5">曩霄
Nang-hsiao
originally
元昊
Yüan-hao[13]</td><td rowspan="5">嵬理
(小字)
Wei-li</td><td rowspan="5">s of B</td><td rowspan="5">7,6,1003[14]</td><td rowspan="2">28,12,1032[15]
—
-,-,1038[16]
as 皇帝
Huang Ti</td><td rowspan="2">-,½,1048[17]</td><td>1. 顯道[18]
Hsien-tao
壬申</td><td>14,2,1032
—</td></tr>
<tr><td rowspan="2">2. 開運[19]
K'ai-yün
甲戌</td><td rowspan="2">23,1,1034
—</td></tr>
<tr><td>9</td><td>10</td></tr>
<tr><td rowspan="2">5. 天授禮法延祚
T'ien-shou-li-fa-yen-tsu
戊寅</td><td rowspan="2">7,2,1038
—</td><td>3. 廣民[20]
Kuang-min
甲戌</td><td>23,1,1034
—</td></tr>
<tr><td>4. 大慶
Ta-ch'ing
乙亥</td><td>11,2,1035
—</td></tr>
</table>

1. *Sung shih* c.485,5a, where 太祖 is prefixed to 應運 etc.
2. *Sung shih* c.485,5a. On fol. 4a, ... 孝光 hsiao kuang.
3. *Sung shih* c.485,3a.
4. A was descended from 思忠 Ssŭ-chung, younger brother of 思恭 Ssŭ-kung (a). See *Sung shih* c.485,2b.
5. *Sung shih* c.485,2b
6. *Sung shih* c.485,3a, but *Liao shih* c.115,3b gives -,12/1,990 but says 潛附于宋 -,1,992.
7. *Sung shih* c.485,4a; but c.7,1b gives -,3,1004; and *Liao shih* c.14,2b says he died 30,6,1003 as 西平王.
8. *Liao shih* c.14,2b, c.115,3b.
9. *Sung shih* c.485,4a
10. *Liao shih* c.14,2b, c.115,3b.
11. *Liao shih* c.15,3b; but c.115,3b says 1010; and *Sung shih* c.485,4b gives 1008.
12. *Sung shih* c.485,5b; but c.10,1b gives 29,12,1032; and *Liao shih* c.18,2a and c.115,4a gives 28,12,1032.
13. so usually in *Liao shih*.
14. *Sung shih* c.485,8b
15. *Liao shih* c.18,2a and c.115,4a.
16. *Sung shih* c.485,6b
17. *Sung shih* c.485,9a; but -,4,1048 according to *Liao shih* c.20,1b, c.115,4a.
18. changed from the Sung Year Title 明道 Ming-tao for taboo of B (德明 Tê-ming).
19. changed after a month because K'ai-yün was the Year Title under which the Hou Chin dynasty (p. 76 above) had ceased to exist.
20. *Sung shih* c.485,6a; but on fol. 9a 廣運 Kuang-yün, as also *Synchronismes*.

1.	2.	3.	4.	5.	6.	7.	8.	9.	10.
D 毅宗 I Tsung	昭英 Chao ying	諒祚 Liang-tsu	寧令哥 Ning-ling-ko	1st s of C	5,3,1047[1]	-,½,1048[2]	-,1,1068[3]	1. 延嗣寧國 Yen-ssu-ning-kuo 戊子 [己丑]	18,1,1048 [5,2,1049 Synchronism.] —
						9	10	2. 天祐垂聖 T'ien-yu-ch'ui-shêng 己丑 [庚寅]	5,2,1049 [26,1,1050 Synchr.] —
						4. 奲都 Ch'ê-tu 丙申 [丁酉]	20,1,1056 [7,2,1057 Synchr.] —		
						5. 拱化 Kung-hua 壬寅 [癸卯]	12,2,1062 [1,2,1063 Synchr.] —	3. 福聖承道 Fu-shêng-ch'êng-tao 壬辰 [癸巳]	4,2,1052 [23,1,1053 Synchr.] —
E 惠宗 Hui Tsung	康靖 K'ang ching	秉常 Ping ch'ang	—	1st s of D	-,-,1061	-,1,1068[4] [-,3,1069 Synchr.] — 26,11,1068[5] 夏國王	21,8,1086[6]	1. 乾道 Ch'ien-tao 丁未 [己酉]	18,1,1067 [26,1,1069 Synchr.] —
								2. 天賜禮盛國慶 T'ien-tz'ŭ-li-shêng-kuo-ch'ing 己酉 [辛亥]	26,1,1069 [3,2,1071 Synchr.] —
						9	10		
						4. 天安禮定 T'ien-an-li-ting 乙丑 [丙寅]	29,1,1085 [18,1,1086 Synchr.] —	3. 大安 Ta-an 甲寅 [丙辰]	30,1,1074 [8,2,1076 Synchr.] —

1. Sung shih c.485,9a
2. Sung shih c.485,9a
3. Liao shih c.22,2b and c.115,4b. Sung shih c.485,10a makes this -,12,1066 or -,12/1,1067, but says aged 21, reigned 20 years, thus making it -,1,1068 in agreement with Liao shih.
4. Sung shih c.486,1a.
5. Liao shih c.22,3a and c.115,4b. Sung shih c.486,1a gives -,3,1069 as 夏國主.
6. Sung shih c.486,4b. Liao shih c.115,4b gives -,11,1086. Sung shih c.17,3a,b says news of the death was reported 16,11,1086.

1	2	3	4	5	6	7	8	9	10
F 崇宗 Ch'ung Tsung	聖文 Shêng wên	乾順 Ch'ien-shun	—	1st s' of E	–,–,1084[1]	11,11,1086 –,2,1087 as 夏國主[2] –,7/8,1088 as 八王[3] –,7,1122 as 夏國皇帝[4]	1,7,1139[5]	1. 天儀治平 T'ien-i-chih-p'ing 丙寅	18,1,1086 [6,2,1087 Synchr.] —
								2. 天祐民安 T'ien-yu-min-an 庚午	3,2,1090 —
								3. 永安 Yung-an 戊寅	4,2,1098 [24,1,1099 Synchr.] —
				9	10	9	10		
				8. 大德 Ta-tê 乙卯	16,1,1135 —	6. 元德 Yüan-tê 己亥	12,2,1119 [1,2,1120 Synchr.] —	4. 貞觀 Chêng-kuan 辛巳	31,1,1101 [21,1,1102 Synchr.] —
						7. 正德 Chêng-tê 丁未	13,2,1127 —	5. 雍寧 Yung-ning 甲午	8,2,1114 [28,1,1115 Synchr.] —
G 仁宗 Jên Tsung	聖德 Shêng tê	仁孝 Jên-hsiao	—	1st s of F	–,–,1124	–,7,1139[6]	16,10,1193[7]	大慶 Ta-ch'ing 庚申	22,1,1140 [1,2,1139 Synchr.] —
								人慶 Jên-ch'ing 癸亥	18,1,1143 [6,2,1144 Synchr.] –,5/7,1143
								天盛 T'ien-shêng 丁卯	2,2,1147 [10,2,1149 Synchr.] —
								乾祐 Ch'ien-yu 戊子	11,2,1168 [7,2,1171 Synchr.] —

1. Sung shih c.486, 4b.
2. Sung shih c.486, 4b.
3. Liao shih c.115, 4b.
4. Liao shih c.115, 5a. In the same year (1122) Liao was defeated by Chin.
5. Sung shih c.486, 8a, which says, however, aged 57, i.e. born 1083.
6. Sung shih c.486, 8b.
7. Sung shih c.486, 9a: aged 70, reigned 55 years.

1.	2.	3.	4.	5.	6.	7.	8.	9.	10.
H 桓宗 Huan Tsung	昭簡 Chao chien	純祐 Ch'un-yu	—	1st s of G	–,–,1177	–,–,1193[1]	1,3,1206[2]	天慶 T'ien-ch'ing 甲寅	24,1,1194 —
I 襄宗 Hsiang Tsung	敬穆 Ching mu	安全 An-ch'üan	—	s of 仁友 Jên-yu and gds of F	–,–,1170	–,3,1206	13,9,1211[3]	應天 Ying-t'ien 丁卯	30,1,1207 [10,2,1206 Synchr.] —
								皇建 Huang-chien 庚午	27,1,1210 —
J 神宗 Shên Tsung	英文 Ying wên	遵頊 Tsun-hsü	—	s[4] of 彥宗 Yen Tsung	–,–,1163	12,8,1211[3] — –,4,1212 as 夏國王[5] abdicated –,–,1223[6]	–,5/7,1226[6]	光定 Kuang-ting 辛未	17,1,1211 —
K 獻宗 Hsien Tsung	—	德旺 Tê-wang	—	s of J	–,–,1181	–,–,1223[7]	–,8,1226[8]	乾定 Ch'ien-ting 癸未	2,2,1223 —
L —	—	晛(睍) Hsien	—	s of 清平郡王 Ch'ing p'ing Chün wang	–,–,	–,–,1226 deposed –,7/8,1227[9]	–,7/8,1227[10]	寶慶[11] Pao-ch'ing 丙戌	30,1,1226[11]

1. Synchronismes says 9th moon.
2. Sung shih c.486, 9a : ....發遂殂.
3. Sung shih c.486, 9a, though the dates of I's death and J's accession do not agree.
4. Sung shih c.486, 9a.
5. Sung shih c.486, 9a.
6. Sung shih c.486, 9b.
7. Synchronismes says 12th moon.
8. Sung shih c.486, 9b.
9. Yüan shih c.1, 9b: 李晛降; 10a: 平西夏.-"conquered Hsi Hsia."
10. Synchronismes p.389.
11. Synchronismes p.389.

趙 Chao ： 東京 汴 Pien; 南京 應天 Ying-t'ien; 西京 河南 Ho-nan; 北京 大明 Ta-ming ： 宋 Sung

1.	2.	3.	4.	5.	6.	7.	8.	9.	10.
a 僖祖 (960) Hsi Tsu	立道肇基積德起功懿文憲武睿和至孝 (1107) Li tao chao chi chi tê ch'i kung i wên hsien wu jui ho chih hsiao 文獻 (960) Wên hsien 文獻睿和 (1012) Wên hsien jui ho	朓 T'iao							
b 順祖 (960) Shun Tsu	惠元 (960) Hui yüan	珽 T'ing	—	s of a					
c 翼祖 (960) I Tsu	簡恭睿德 (1012) Chien kung jui tê 簡恭 Chien kung (960)	敬 Ching	—	s of b					
d 宣祖 (960) Hsüan Tsu	武昭 (960) Wu chao	弘殷 Hung-yin	—	s of c					
A 太祖 T'ai Tsu	啓運立極英武睿文神德聖功至明大孝 (1012) Ch'i yün li chi ying wu jui wên shên tê shêng kung chih ming ta hsiao 英武聖文神德 (976) Ying wu shêng wên shên tê 啓運立極英武聖文神德玄功大孝 (1008) Ch'i yün li chi ying wu shêng wên shên tê hsüan kung ta hsiao	匡胤 K'uang-yin	—	2nd s of d	21,3,927	3,2,960	14,11,976	建隆 Chien-lung 庚申	31,1,960 4,2,960
								乾德 Ch'ien-tê 癸亥	28,1,963 4,12,963
								開寶 K'ai-pao 戊辰	2,2,968 16,12,968

宋史 Sung shih c. 1—. 宋會要 Sung hui yao (Shy).

1.	2.	3.	4.	5.	6.	7.	8.	9.	10.
B 太宗 T'ai Tsung cc.4,5	至仁應道神功聖德文武睿烈大明廣孝 (1012) Chih jên ying tao shên kung shêng tê wên wu jui lieh ta ming kuang hsiao 神功聖德文武 (997) Shên kung shêng tê wên wu 至仁應道神功聖德文武大明廣孝 (1008) Chih jên ying tao shên kung shêng tê wên wu ta ming kuang hsiao	炅 (976) Kuei originally 匡乂 Kuang-i 光義 (960) Kuang-i	—	3rd S of d	20,11,939[1] [Shy]	14,11,976	8,5,997	太平興國 T'ai-p'ing-hsing-kuo 丙子	3,2,976 14,1,977
								雍熙 Yung-hsi 甲申	5,2,984 6,12,984 [16,12 Shy]
								端拱 Tuan-kung 戊子	22,1,988 8,2,988 [7,2 Shy]
								淳化 Shun-hua 庚寅	30,1,990 30,1,990
								至道 Chih-tao 乙未	3,2,995 3,2,995
C 真宗 Chên Tsung cc.6-8	應[2]符稽古神功讓德文明武定章聖元孝 (1047) Ying fu chi ku shên kung jang tê wên ming wu ting chang shêng yüan hsiao 文明武定章聖元孝 (1024) Wên ming wu ting chang shêng yüan hsiao	恆 (995) Hêng originally 德昌 Tê-ch'ang 元休 (983) Yüan-hsiu 侃 (988) K'an	—	3rd S of B	23,12,968	8,5,997	23,3,1022	1. 咸平 Hsien-p'ing 戊戌	31,1,998 31,1,998
						9	10		
						4. 天禧 T'ien-hsi 丁巳	31,1,1017 31,1,1017	2. 景德 Ching-tê 甲辰	25,1,1004 25,1,1004
						5. 乾興 Ch'ien-hsing 壬戌	4,2,1022 4,2,1022	3. 大中祥符 Ta-chung-hsiang-fu 戊申	10,2,1008 15,2,1008
D 仁宗 Jên Tsung	體天法道極功全德神文聖武睿哲明孝 (1083) T'i t'ien fa tao chi kung ch'üan tê shên wên shêng wu jui chê ming hsiao 神文聖武明孝 (1063) Shên wên shêng wu ming hsiao	禎[3] (1018) Chên originally 受益 Shou-i	—	6th S of C	30,5,1010	23,3,1022	30,4,1063	1. 天聖 T'ien-shêng 癸亥	25,1,1023 25,1,1023
				9	10	9	10		
				8. 至和 Chih-ho 甲午	11,2,1054 26,4,1054 [10,5, Shy]	5. 康定 K'ang-ting 庚辰	15,2,1040 5,4,1040	2. 明道 Ming-tao 壬申	14,2,1032 11,12,1032
				9. 嘉祐 Chia-yu 丙申	20,1,1056 23,10,1056 [24,10 Shy]	6. 慶曆 Ch'ing-li 辛巳	4,2,1041 16,12,1041 [Shy]	3. 景祐 Ching-yu 甲戌	23,1,1034 18,1,1034 [23,1, Shy]
						7. 皇祐 Huang-yu 己丑	5,2,1049 7,1,1049 [5,2, Shy]	4. 寶元 Pao-yüan 戊寅	7,2,1038 16,12,1038

1. Sung shih c.4, 1a has 十月十七日甲辰; Sung hui yao 帝系一之四, 1a, 十月七日. 甲辰 was in fact the 7th day (20,11,939). Sung shih ibid. says the name Kuei was taken in 977 (卽位之二年).
2. Sung shih c.8, 10a, 膺.
3. Li tai ming jên.... piao p.515 misprints 禎 Chêng. Sung hui yao 帝系一之五 (全唐文) 1a has 禎 Chêng.

1.	2.	3.	4.	5.	6.	7.	8.	9.	10.
E 英宗 Ying Tsung c.13	體乾應歷隆功盛德憲文肅武睿聖宣孝 (1083) T'i ch'ien ying li lung kung shêng tê hsien wên su wu jui shêng hsüan hsiao[1] 憲文肅武宣孝 (1067) Hsien wên su wu hsüan hsiao	曙 Shu originally 宗實 Tsung-shih	—	13th s of 允讓 Yüng-jang, s of 元份 Yüan-fên (-pin), 4th s of B	16, 2, 1032	1, 5, 1063	25, 1, 1067	治平 Chih-p'ing 甲辰	21, 1, 1064 21, 1, 1064
F 神宗 Shên Tsung cc.14-16	紹天法古運德建功英文烈武欽仁聖孝 (1095) Shao t'ien fa ku yün tê chien kung ying wên lieh wu ch'in jên shêng hsiao 英文烈武聖孝 (1085) Ying wên lieh wu shêng hsiao	頊 Hsü	—	1st s of E	25, 5, 1048	25, 1, 1067	1, 4, 1085	熙寧 Hsi-ning 戊申 元豐 Yüan-fêng 戊午	6, 2, 1068 6, 2, 1068 17, 1, 1078 23, 12, 1077
G 哲宗 Chê Tsung cc.17, 18	憲元繼道顯德定功欽文睿武齊聖昭孝 (1113) Hsien yüan chi tao hsien tê ting kung ch'in wên jui wu ch'i shêng chao hsiao 欽文睿武昭孝 (1100) Ch'in wên jui wu chao hsiao 憲元繼道世德揚功欽 --- as 1st title above (1104) Hsien yüan chi tao shih tê yang kung ch'in --- etc.	煦 Hsü	—	6th s of F	4, 1, 1077	1, 4, 1085	23, 2, 1100	元祐 Yüan-yu 丙寅 紹聖 Shao-shêng 甲戌 元符 Yüan-fu 戊寅	18, 1, 1086 18, 1, 1086 19, 1, 1094 29, 4, 1094 4, 2, 1098 2, 7, 1098

1. Sung hui yao 帝系一之十一 a has 膺 for 應 and 神 shên for 聖 shêng.

<table>
<tr><th>1.</th><th>2.</th><th>3.</th><th>4.</th><th>5.</th><th>6.</th><th>7.</th><th>8.</th><th>9.</th><th>10.</th></tr>
<tr><td rowspan="4">H
徽宗
Hui Tsung

cc.19-22</td><td rowspan="4">體神合道駿烈遜功聖文仁德憲慈顯孝 (1142)
Tʻi shên ho tao chün lieh hsün kung shêng wên jên tê hsien tzʻŭ hsien hsiao
聖文仁德顯孝 (1137)
Shêng wên jên tê hsien hsiao</td><td rowspan="4">佶
Chi</td><td rowspan="4">—</td><td>11th s of F</td><td>2,11,1082</td><td>23,2,1100
abdicated
18,1,1126[1]</td><td>4,6,1135</td><td rowspan="2">1. 建中靖國
Chien-chung-ching-kuo
辛巳</td><td rowspan="2">31,1,1101
10,12,1100</td></tr>
<tr><td>9</td><td>10</td><td>9</td><td>10</td></tr>
<tr><td rowspan="2">6. 宣和
Hsüan-ho
己亥</td><td rowspan="2">12,2,1119
16,3,1119</td><td>4. 政和
Chêng-ho
辛卯</td><td>10,2,1111
15,12,1110</td><td>2. 崇寧
Chʻung-ning
壬午</td><td>21,1,1102
14,12,1101</td></tr>
<tr><td>5. 重和
Chʻung-ho
戊戌</td><td>24,1,1118
15,12,1118</td><td>3. 大觀
Ta-kuan[2]
丁亥</td><td>26,1,1107
13,8,1106</td></tr>
<tr><td>I
欽宗
Chʻin Tsung

c.23</td><td>恭文順德仁孝 (1161)
Kung wên shun tê jên hsiao</td><td>桓 (17,12,1102)
Huan
originally
亶 Tan
烜 (27,2,1102)
Hsüan</td><td>—</td><td>1st s of H</td><td>23,5,1100[3]</td><td>19,1,1126
deposed
25,3,1127
taken to the North
10,5,1127</td><td>14,6,1161</td><td>靖康
Ching-kʻang
丙午</td><td>25,1,1126</td></tr>
</table>

1. H was taken captive 21,3,1127; removed to the North 10,5,1127. He died at 五國城 Wu-kuo chʻêng. News of his death reached the South 21,9,1137, the coffin reached Lin-an on 16,9,1142, and he was buried near Shao-hsing on 27,10,1142. For the identification of Wu-kuo chʻêng, and for the alleged grave of H outside 延吉 Yen-chi hsien in Kirin, see Chung kuo ku chin ti ming ta tzʻŭ tien pp. 114-5.
2. 太觀 Tai-kuan in Sung hui yao c.1,1a.
3. Synchronismes p.367 (with which Li tai ming jên ....piao p.515 agrees) gives the dates of birth and death as 1096 and 1156 respectively.

趙 Chao [汴 Pien] provisional capital (行在 <u>hsing tsai</u>) 臨安 Lin-an 南宋 Nan Sung

1.	2.	3.	4.	5.	6.	7.	8.	9.	10.
J 高宗 Kao Tsung c.24–32	受命中興全功至德聖神武文昭仁憲孝 (1191) Shou ming chung hsing ch'üan kung chih tê shêng shên wu wên chao jên hsien hsiao 聖神武文憲孝 (1187) Shêng shên wu wên hsien hsiao	構 Kou	德基 Tê-chi	9th s of H	12.6.1107	12.6.1127 — abdicated 24.7.1162	9.11.1187	建炎 Chien-yen 丁未	13.2.1127 12.6.1127
								「明受 Ming-shou[2] 己酉	22.1.1129 1.4.1129」
								紹興 Shao-hsing 辛亥	31.1.1131 31.1.1131
K 孝宗 Hsiao Tsung c.33–35	紹統同道冠德昭功哲文神武明聖成孝 (1197) Shao t'ung t'ung tao kuan tê chao kung chê wên shên wu ming shêng ch'êng hsiao 哲文神武成孝 (1194) Chê wên shên wu ch'êng hsiao	昚 (1162) Shên — originally 伯琮 Po-ts'ung — 瑋 (1160) Wei	元永 (1162) Yüan-yung — 元瓌 (1160) Yüan-kuei	s of 子偁 Tzŭ-ch'êng descended from A (but <u>Shy</u>, 帝系一之七, 1a has: 孝宗高宗之子也 — i.e. K s of J)	27.11.1127	24.7.1162 — abdicated 18.2.1189	28.6.1194	隆興 Lung-hsing 癸未	5.2.1163 23.12.1162
								乾道 Ch'ien-tao 乙酉	13.2.1165 13.2.1165
								淳熙 Shun-hsi 甲午	4.2.1174 —

1. The 南渡 <u>nan tu</u>, or migration of the Court to the south, was a complicated series of wanderings which filled eleven years. Kao Tsung was enthroned at his Southern Capital 應天 Ying-t'ien, the modern 歸德 Kuei-tê in Ho-nan. The beginning of the years 1128, 1129 found him at 揚州 Yang-chou; on 23.2.1129 he crossed the River to 鎮江 Chên-chiang, and on 5.3.1129 reached 杭州 Hang-chow, where the Empress (太后) had arrived on 28.12.1128, and used the Governor's Residence (<u>i.e.</u> the former palace of Ch'ien Ch'iu, see p. 68) as his travelling lodge (以州治為行宮). He left Hang-chou on 11.5.1129, but was there again 21–30.11.1129. He then went to 越州 Yüeh-chou (or 紹興 Shao-hsing) until 6.1.1130. On 11.10.1129 he had already resolved to travel in 浙西 Chê-hsi (which seems to have been the eastern part of modern Chê-chiang and Chiang-su), and on 13.3.1130 had gone as far south as 溫州 Wên-chou. Meantime the enemy had captured Hang-chou on 24.1.1130, defeated the Sung troops north-east of the city, and were pursuing the Emperor toward Yüeh and 明 Ming (or 寧波 Ning-po); but they seem to have retired to the north almost immediately, and so, after wandering by sea and land in south-east Chê-chiang for four or five months, Kao Tsung came back to Yüeh-chou on 20.5.1130, and stayed there till 29.1.1132 when he went on board his boat to sail on the next day and, after waiting for the tide before he could cross the river, reached Hang-chou (now called Lin-an) on 2/3.2.1132, meaning perhaps to go on to 建康 Chien-k'ang. He stayed however at Lin-an till 10.11.1134, when he left by boat reaching 平江 P'ing-chiang (or 蘇州 Su-chou) on 14.11.1134. He left again on 17.2.1135 and came back to Lin-an on 22.2.1135, where he stayed till 28.9.1136. He moved to P'ing-chiang once more on 5.10.1136, left on 20.3.1137, and reached Chien-k'ang (the modern Nanking on the River) on 25.3.1137. Leaving Chien-k'ang on 19.3.1138 he finally arrived at Lin-an on 3.4.1138. The <u>Sung shih</u> c.29, 2a ends with the words: 是歲始定都于杭 "The capital was not fixed at Hang until this year (1138)". These details are taken from the <u>Sung shih</u> cc.25–29, confirmed and slightly amplified by the 宋會要 <u>Sung hui yao</u> (方域二之三). In c.85, 5b it is said that Kao Tsung came to Lin-an from Chien-k'ang in the intercalary 8th moon (16.9–14.10) 1129, a statement which is wholly inconsistent with the annals. The 乾道臨安志 <u>Ch'ien tao lin an chih</u>, c.1170, c.1, 1a, dates the decree, which does not seem to be recorded in the <u>Sung shih</u> cc.29 or 85, for establishing the capital at Lin-an in the 3rd moon (11.4–10.5) 1138. The same book, c.2, 3a, says that Hang was called Lin-an on 15.12.1129, whereas the <u>Sung shih</u> c.25, 7b, gives 1.8.1129. ~~~ After his abdication in 1162 Kao Tsung was known officially as 太上皇帝 T'ai shang Huang Ti and popularly as 德壽宮 Tê shou kung, the name of his palace.

2. After a rebellion of a few weeks the Emperor and the Year Title Chien-yen were restored on 22.4.1129.

1.	2.	3.	4.	5.	6.	7.	8.	9.	10.
L 光宗 Kuang Tsung c. 36	循道憲仁明功茂德温文順武聖哲慈孝 (1203) Hsün tao hsien jên ming kung mao tê wên wên shun wu shêng chê tz'ŭ hsiao 憲仁聖哲慈孝 (1200) Hsien jên shêng chê tz'ŭ hsiao	惇 Tun	—	3rd s of K	30. 9.1147	18. 2.1189 — abdicated 24. 7.1194	17. 9.1200	紹熙 Shao-hsi 庚戌	7. 2.1190 23.12.1189
M 寧宗 Ning Tsung c. 37–40	法天備道純德茂功仁文哲武聖睿恭孝 (1227) Fa t'ien pei tao ch'un tê mao kung jên wên chê wu shêng jui kung hsiao 仁文哲武恭孝 (1225) Jên wên chê wu kung hsiao	擴 K'uo	—	2nd s of L	19.11.1168	24. 7.1194 9. 4 嘉定 Chia-ting 戊辰	17. 9.1224 10. 19. 1.1208 15. 1.1208	1 慶元 Ch'ing-yüan 乙卯 2 嘉泰 Chia-t'ai 辛酉 3 開禧 K'ai-hsi 乙丑	12. 2.1195 9.12.1194 5. 2.1201 27. 1.1201 22. 1.1205 2. 1.1205
N 理宗 Li Tsung c. 41–45	建道備德大功復興烈文仁武聖明安孝 (1266) Chien tao pei tê ta kung fu hsing lieh wên jên wu shêng ming an hsiao	昀 (1224) Yün originally 均 Chün 貴和 Kuei-ho 竑 Hung 貴誠 (1224) Kuei-ch'êng	—	s of 希瓐 Hsi-lu, descended from A 9. 7 開慶 K'ai-ch'ing 己未 8 景定 Ching-ting 庚申	26. 1.1205 10. 25. 1.1259 29.12.1258 19. 2.1260 26. 1.1260	17. 9.1224 9. 5 淳祐 Shun-yu 辛丑 6 寶祐 Pao-yu 癸丑	16.11.1264 10. 13. 2.1241 19.10.1240 31. 1.1253 4.10.1252	1 寶慶 Pao-ch'ing 乙酉 2 紹定 Shao-ting 戊子 3 端平 Tuan-p'ing 甲午 4 嘉熙 Chia-hsi 丁酉	9. 2.1225 5. 1.1225 8. 2.1228 15.12.1227 31. 1.1234 8.12.1233 28. 1.1237 17. 1.1237
O 度宗 Tu Tsung c. 46	端文明武景孝 (1274) Tuan wên ming wu ching hsiao	禥 (1252) Ch'i originally 孟啓 Mêng-ch'i 孜 (1251) Tzŭ	長源 (1260) Ch'ang-yüan	s of 與芮 Yü-jui, br of N	2. 5.1240	16.11.1264	12. 8.1274	咸淳 Hsien-shun 乙丑	19. 1.1265 20.12.1264
P 恭宗 Kung Tsung[1] c. 47	瀛國公 (1276) Ying kuo Kung	顯 Hsien	—	s of O	14.10.1270[2]	12. 8.1274	—	德祐 Tê-yu 乙亥	29. 1.1275 21.11.1274

1. This title, given in Conc. néom., Li tai ming jên..piao, &c., does not seem to be mentioned in c. 47.

2. Sung shih c. 47, 1a, 咸淳六年九月己丑生. As 己丑 chi-ch'ou did not fall in the 9th moon in 1270, chi may be an error for 乙 i; but Li tai ming jên..piao, 515, makes the year of birth 辛未 hsin-wei, 1271, and then chi-ch'ou in the 9th moon was 2.11.1271. The little Emperor was taken captive on 21.2.1276, and did homage to Qubilai on 15.6.1276 at Shang-tu, whither Bayan had brought him the day before. cf. Yüan shih c. 9, 4a; 127, 6b; 錢塘遺事 Ch'ien t'ang i shih c. 9, 14b.

1.	2.	3.	4.	5.	6.	7.	8.	9.	10.
Q 端宗 Tuan Tsung c. 47	建國公 Chien kuo Kung 吉王(1274) Chi Wang 益王(1276) I Wang	昰 Shih	—	s of O	–.–.1268[1]	14. 6.1276[2]	8. 5.1278	景炎 Ching-yen 丙子	18. 1.1276 14. 6.1276
R — c. 47	永國公 Yung kuo Kung 信王(1274) Hsin Wang 廣王(1276) Kuang Wang 衛王(1276) Wei Wang	昺 Ping	—	s of O	–.–.1271	10. 5.1278	19. 3.1279	祥興 Hsiang-hsing 戊寅	25. 1.1278 23. 5.1278

1. The *Li tai ming jên ..piao* (following 張惟驤·季易 Chang Wei-hsiang (Chi-i) 歷代帝王疑年錄 *Li tai ti wang i nien lu*, 1 *chüan*, 1926, and 疑年錄彙編 *I nien lu hui pien* 16 *ch.* 補錄 *Pu lu* 1 *chüan* 分韻人表 *Fên yün jên piao* 1 *chüan*, 1925) supplies the birthdays of Q in 1268 and of R in 1271.
2. Shih was enthroned at 福州 Fu-chou and died at 硐州 Kang-chou.
3. Ping was enthroned at Kang-chou and drowned at 厓山 Ai shan at the mouth of the West River.

遼 Liao

Introduction

The dates of the early Year Titles of this dynasty seem to be uncertain. Mayers, Chinese Reader's Manual, 1874, basing his tables on 齊召南 Chi Chao-nan Li tai ti wang nien piao, 1777, and followed by Giles, Dictionary, 1892, 1912, Mathews, Dictionary, 1931, 1947, makes T'ien-hsien 925, Hui-t'ung 937, Ta-t'ung 946, T'ien-lu 947. Synchronismes, 1905, p. 320 &c. follows the Liao shih with 926, 938, 947, 947; Chung kuo ti hao piao ti i lan, 1939, has 926, 937, 947, 947.

Wu tai shih c.73 fol. 4a has a note by the author, Ou-yang Hsiu (1007–1072), to say: The mistakes in the Ch'i-tan year titles as recorded by various authorities are many, and the dates are quite unreliable. Only those which ever appeared in China can be trusted. I note that the text of the decree of Yeh-lü Tê-kuang establishing Kao Tsu of the Chin says, 'Now in the ninth T'ien-hsien year, ping-shên in the series of years.' This year was the first T'ien-fu year (936) of the Chin, and calculating it upward we obtain the third T'ien-ch'êng year of the T'ang, mou-tzŭ (928), as the first T'ien-hsien year. According to the Ch'i-tan Appendix (Chiu wu tai shih c.137, 3a-b; cf. Wu tai shih c.72, 3b) Tê-kuang was established in the same year as Ming Tsung of the T'ang (926), and in his third year changed the title to T'ien-hsien; and this exactly agrees with the above. And again, relying on the fact that when Tê-kuang destroyed Chin and entered Pien, proclaiming amnesty, in the fourth K'ai-yün year (947), it was called the tenth Hui-t'ung year; if we calculate it back we obtain third T'ien-fu year (938) as the first Hui-t'ung year. Thus T'ien-hsien was completed in ten years and the eleventh year was changed to Hui-t'ung. Only for these two is the evidence very clear; the rest are all untrustworthy.

The next important document is from Ssŭ-ma Kuang (1019–1086) 資治通鑑考異 Tzŭ chih t'ung chien k'ao i c.29, 3a-b. On the entry 契丹阿保機稱帝改元神冊 "The Ch'i-tan A-pao-chi took the title of Emperor and changed the year title to Shên-ts'ê" he comments: The 紀年通譜 Chi nien t'ung p'u (by 宋庠 Sung Hsiang, 996–1086) says, The Chiu [wu tai] shih has no record about the year titles of [A-]pao-chi. Now among the Ch'i-tan there is a kalendar with a consecutive record of 120 years. [Professor Haloun found references to this kalendar, 日曆 jih li, in the Liao shih c.14, 2a (6.4.1003), c.15, 1b (5.6.1011), which seem to show that it was made early in the eleventh century.] In the third Ching-yu year (1036) in the winter a mission was sent north to 幽 Yu and 薊 Chi to obtain this kalendar; and so we may count the series of years and find that it takes 乙亥 i-hai (915) to be the beginning and does not fix the Shên-ts'ê (策) period until the next year (916); & after that there was T'ien-tsan also. I note that the history of the Ch'i-tan in the Wu tai shih begins from Yeh-lü Tê-kuang to record the name of T'ien-hsien and suspect that at that time they had not yet obtained the tradition. Or else the Marauders, ashamed that [A-]pao-chi should have no year titles, made them retrospectively. . . . The 虜庭雜記 Lu t'ing tsa chi (a lost work by 趙志忠 Chao Chih-chung, flor. c. 1045) says, 'When T'ai Tsu had attacked and swallowed up the kingdom of 奚 Hsi, he still appointed a man of Hsi to be Prince of Hsi as of old, ordering the Ch'i-tan to take command of the army. And again, when he extinguished P'o-hai and captured the prince Ta-yin-chuan, he appointed his own eldest son to be Prince of Tung-tan in P'o-hai with the title of Jên-huang Prince, styling himself T'ien-huang Prince, and then first instituted year titles, one called T'ien-tsan and another called Shên-ts'ê, and the dynasty was named Great Liao. . . .' . . . Before A-pao-chi was addressed as Emperor no exact dates are seen in the histories. The Biography of Chuang Tsung &

the Ch'i-tan History (Chiu wu tai shih c. 137, 2a) say that this was after Chuang Tsung ascended the imperial throne (923) and Li Ts'un-shên held Fan-yang. The Han kao tsu shih lu and the T'ang yü lu both say that A-pao-chi issued an order uniting the clans, and then was called Emperor in the Ch'ien-ning period (894–897) before Liu Jên-kung fortified Yu chou (c. 894: Wu tai shih c. 39, 5b-6a). Hsüeh's History puts this at the end of Chuang Tsung T'ien-yu (923: see above). According to the Chi nien t'ung p'u A-pao-chi's first Shên-ts'ê year was ping-tzŭ (916) in the cycle, and that was Chuang Tsung's 13th T'ien-yu year (916) or the 2nd Chêng-ming year (916) of the Liang, and this is not like the end of T'ien-yu and after Chuang Tsung had ascended the throne. The Pien i lu says that in the fifth moon of the 2nd K'ai-p'ing year (908) T'ai Tsu granted A-pao-chi a memorandum in which he still called him a minister and spoke of him as serving our dynasty and looking to the government to send down to confirm his appointment. This must have been before he styled himself Emperor; can that have been before Liu Jên-kung fortified Yu chou? The T'ang yü lu story of Ch'i-tan affairs is wholly taken from the Han kao tsu shih lu and is full of mistakes, so that we do not really know in what year he took the title of Emperor. Now I fix it at this point because of the change of year title. [Ssŭ-ma assumes, apparently, that if the makers of the kalendar fixed its beginning in 915 and the period Shên-ts'ê in 916 it was because they believed that A-pao-chi took the title of Emperor then.]

The essential passage, already quoted by Ou-yang Hsiu (p. above), is in the Chiu wu tai shih c. 75, 4b-5a: In the 11th moon (17.11–16.12.936) the Ch'i-tan Lord met the Emperor (Shih Ching-t'ang, Chin dynasty A, p.) in the camp and said, '... I wish to appoint you Son of Heaven'. The Emperor persistently declined; but the troops exhorted & begged him to comply. So he ordered that an altar should be built south of the walls of Chin-yang (T'ai-yüan in Shan-hsi) and formally appointed the Emperor to be Sovereign Ruler of Great Chin (大晉皇帝). The Ch'i-tan Lord took off his own coat and cap and gave them to him. [Liao shih, Annals of T'ai Tsung 11th year (c. 3, 4b), 'In the winter 10th moon chia-tzŭ he ennobled Ching-t'ang as Prince of Chin; in the 11th moon, ting-yu, he appointed Ching-t'ang to be Sovereign Ruler of Great Chin.'] The text of the decree says, Now in the ninth T'ien-hsien year, ping-shên in the series of years, the eleventh moon, of which the new moon was ping-hsü, the twelfth day ting-yu, the Sovereign Ruler of the Great Ch'i-tan declares: .... When the ceremony was finished the Emperor returned.

From the places quoted above it seems to be clear that something was done about Year Titles early in 926, on the conquest of 渤海 P'o-hai. The date of that conquest is uncertain, but the authorities at my disposal seem to make it 926. The Liao shih, compiled in 1343, more than 400 years after the event, says in c. 2, 3a that P'o-hai finally submitted on the 6 March 926, and that in consequence (以平渤海) A-pao-chi changed the Year Title to T'ien-hsien on 26 March. There seems to be no contemporary evidence that the two earlier Year Titles had any existence, though the Liao shih not only uses them but records the dates on which they were decreed. Ssŭ-ma Kuang suspected that they had been invented and applied retrospectively to the ten or twelve years before Hsien-t'ien; and this seems to be confirmed by the rather obscure passage from the Lu t'ing tsa chi, a book written c. 1050 but probably based on the Liao archives. It says (p. above) that it was on the conquest of Po-hai that A-pao-chi "first instituted year titles", and then names not T'ien-hsien but T'ien-tsan and Shên-ts'ê, in that reversed order. The best evidence for T'ien-hsien, as Ou-yang points out, is the date of the Liao decree recorded by Hsüeh Chü-chêng in 972, where a year which was certainly 936 is called "the ninth T'ien-hsien year". This is supported by the statement that Tê-kuang changed the year title to T'ien-hsien "in his third year" (Chiu wu tai shih c.137,3b; Wu tai shih c.72,3b). Though not enthroned till December 927, he had succeeded his father in 926, and his third year, which he made the first T'ien-hsien year, was 928.

On the whole it may be probable that the Liao had no Year Titles before 926 when, on the conquest of Po-hai, Shên-ts'ê and T'ien-tsan were retrospectively invented. The compilers of the Liao shih, believing that these two titles were genuine and finding a record of the making of some change in 926, may easily have assumed that this must have been the beginning of the T'ien-hsien period, which for them would thus have had twelve years, 926–937. That it really had only ten years is further shown by the chronology of the Ch'i tan kuo chih given below, p. 97.

For Chao Chih-chung and his books the following extracts, owed to the kindness of Professor Haloun, are of interest, and seem to show that he lived in the middle or in the second half of the eleveth century:—

1. "虜廷雜記十卷 Lu t'ing tsa chi ten chüan: The above was written by the Ch'i-tan captive, Chao Chih-chung, and records various matters of the Marauders Court from 阿保謹 A-pao-chin (872–926) to Yeh-lü Tsung-chên (1016–1055). 李清臣 Li Ch'ing-ch'ên (1032–1101) say, Chih-chung served the Marauders as chung shu shê jên. He offended Tsung-chên and came home. He presented this book and the 契丹地圖 Ch'i tan ti t'u, in which he speaks of the affairs of the Marauders in great detail."
(郡齋讀書後志 Chün chai tu shu hou chih by 晁公武 Ch'ao Kung-wu (c. 1144) c. 1, 21b)

2. "陳振孫 Ch'ên Chên-sun in his 直齋書錄解題 Chih chai shu lu chieh t'i says, 陰山雜錄 Yin shan tsa lu sixteen chüan, anonymous; 莆田鄭氏書目 P'u t'ien chêng shih shu mu says that it was written by Chao Chih-chung." (遼史拾遺補 Liao shih shih i pu c.2, 13b)

3. "The 默記 Mo chi by 王銍 Wang Chih (c. 1126) says, The Yü-pu Chao Chih(至)-chung, who to the Court from the north, had been Han lin hsüeh shih and State Historian among the Liao. He wrote the Lu t'ing tsa chi in which he speaks of Shêng Tsung (971–1031), . . . 晁補之 Ch'ao Pu-chih (1053–1110) was Minister of Education at the Northern Capital and so had read this book." (Liao shih shih i c. 19, 3b)

4. "In the 孫公談圃 Sun kung t'an p'u by 劉延世 Liu Yen-shih (c. 1100) 孫升 Sun Shêng (c. 1095) says, When Chao Chih-chung returned to Court from the Ch'i-tan he was promoted to the office of Ch'eng-lang. He asked to be sent as an envoy, but this was not granted. . . . When Chih-chung came back to China he presented a report, and he had obtained a very large number of Ch'i-tan characters; for he had been official Historian for the Ch'i-tan."
(Liao shih shih i pu c. 2, 12b–13a)

耶律 Yeh-lü[1]

上京臨潢 Lin-huang[2] (938) 東京遼陽 Liao-yang (938)
中京鎮州 Chên chou (947), 遼西 Liao-hsi (1007), 大定 Ta-ting[3] (1007)
南京析津 Hsi-ching (?928) 西京大同 Ta-t'ung[4] (1044)

契丹 Ch'i-tan or 遼 Liao[5]

1.	2.	3.	4.	5.	6.	7.	8.	9.	10.
A 太祖 T'ai Tsu[6]	大聖大明神烈天 (1052) Ta shêng ta ming shên lieh t'ien 昇天 (926) Shêng t'ien 大聖 (927) Ta shêng 大聖大明天 (1008) Ta shêng ta ming t'ien	億 I[7]	阿保機[8] A-pao-chi 啜里只 Cho-li-chih	1st s of 德祖 Tê Tsu[9]	–, –, 872	27, 2, 907	6, 9, 926	元年 First year 丁卯	15, 2, 907
								神冊 Shên-ts'ê 丙子	6, 2, 916 17, 3, 916
								天贊[10] T'ien-tsan 壬午	31, 1, 922 23, 3, 922
(c. 1, 2)								天顯 T'ien-hsien 丙戌	15, 2, 926 21, 3, 926

遼史 *Liao shih* cc. 1—30, &c. 舊五代史 *Chiu wu tai shih* cc. 137 五代史 *Wu tai shih* cc. 72, 73.

1. 阿保機…自號天皇王以其所居横帳地名為姓曰世里世里譯者謂之耶律名年曰天贊 (*wts* c. 72, 2a). The same statement (with some corruption of the text) is found in a quotation from *Lu t'ing tsa chi* (in *Tzŭ chih t'ung chien k'ao i* - see p. 91 above) where it is connected with the conquest of P'o-hai in (?) 926, and with the coining of the year-title T'ien-tsan at the same time.

2. 神冊三年(918)城之名曰皇都 (*Ls* c. 37, 1b) - "fortified it and named it 'Imperial Capital'."

3. 升鎮州為中京 (947) - *Ls* c. 4, 7a; 故 王牙帳地二十五年城之 - *Ls* c. 39, 1a.

4. 因建西京 (c. 936)…重熙十三年 (1044) 升為西京 - *Ls* c. 41, 1b.

5. The old national and dynastic title of 契丹 Ch'i-tan (decreed in 916 - *Ch'i tan kuo chih* c. 1, 2a) was changed to Liao on the conquest of P'o-hai, in c. 926, according to *Lu t'ing tsa chi* (see p. 91 above); in 937 according to *Ch'i tan kuo chih* and *Li tai ti wang nien piao*; in 938 according to *Wu tai shih* c. 72, 5a; or on 24.2.947 according to *Liao shih* c. 4, 7a. At any rate Tê-kuang was called 契丹主 'Ch'i-tan Lord', and called himself 大契丹皇帝 'Sovereign Ruler of the Great Ch'i-tan', in December 936. cf. *Chiu wu tai shih* c. 75, 4b and p. 92 above. Ch'i-tan was restored in 983 (*Li tai ti wang nien piao*), or in 1013 (*Ch'i tan kuo chih* (年譜) fol. 2a); and both these books agree that Liao was resumed in 1066. These changes do not appear in the Annals of the *Liao shih* under the years 983, 1012, 1065, or 1066.

6. Title conferred on 25.10.926 - *Liao shih* c. 2, 4a; but not until 947 according to *Wu tai shih* c. 72, 7b.

7. This name seems to have been given with the posthumous titles in February 927 - *Wu tai shih* c. 72, 3b, with which *Wu tai hui yao* agrees. *Li tai ti wang nien piao* gives 907. *Liao shih* c. 1, 1a records the name (諱) without date, and gives A-pao-chi as the 字 *tzŭ*.

8. Ou-yang Hsiu writes in his 歸田錄 *Kuei t'ien lu* (ed. S.P.T.K., 歐陽文忠公集) c. 2, 2a: The Ch'i-tan A-pao-chi was at the height of his power in the last days of the T'ang and in the Wu Tai times. In the K'ai-p'ing period (907—910) he often sent complimentary missions to Liang, and Liang also sent complimentary messages in return. There is a current tradition that in the 金門集 *Chin mên chi* by 李琪 Li Ch'i (c. 935) there was a decree granted to the Ch'i-tan, and the name was written 阿布機 A-pu-chi. The writer of the decree at the time ought not to have made a mistake, but yet, ever since the Wu Tai, when it appears in other writers it is always A-(保)pao-chi, and even now the Ch'i-tan people themselves call it A-pao-chi, and cannot be wrong. Moreover there was Chao Chih-chung, originally a Chinese, who was taken captive in his youth. He was an intelligent man and took the *chin shih* degree among the Marauders, and reached a prominent official position. When at last he escaped & came home he was able to tell of the government, history, geography, and customs of the Marauders in great detail; and he also said that they really called A-pao-chi 阿保謹 A-pao-chin. I do not know which is right. This is where the sage is on his guard against publishing what is uncertain.
[Mongol final -n in the nominative of a noun may, of course, be disregarded, and is usually dropped in the indefinite; but it belongs to the stem. - G.H.] In the edition of the *Histories* here used the

遼 Liao

1.	2.	3.	4.	5.	6.	7.	8.	9.	10.
B 太宗 (947) T'ai Tsung c. 3, 4	孝武惠文 (1052) Hsiao wu hui wên 孝武 (1008) Hsiao wu	德光 Tê-kuang — 濟 Chi (本名)	德謹 Tê-chin — 堯骨 (小字) 耨庫 c.137.3a 屈 c.72.3a Yao-ku (-k'u or -ch'ü)	2nd s of A	–.–.902	11.12.927	15.5.947	會同 Hui-t'ung 戊戌	2.2.938 17.12.938
								大同¹ Ta-t'ung 丁未	25.1.947 24.2.947
C 世宗 Shih Tsung c. 5	孝和莊憲 (1008) Hsiao ho chuang hsien 孝和 (952) Hsiao ho	阮 Juan	兀欲 (小字) Wu-yü	1st s of 倍 Pei, 1st s of A	–.–.918	16.5.947	7.10.951	天祿 T'ien-lu 丁未	25.1.947 1.11.947
D 穆宗 Mu Tsung c. 6, 7	孝安敬正 (1052) Hsiao an ching chêng	璟 Ying	述律 (小字) Chu-lü	1st s of B	–.–.931	11.10.951	12.3.969	應曆 Ying-li 辛亥	9.2.951 11.10.951
E 景宗 Ching Tsung c. 8, 9	孝成康靖 (1052) Hsiao ch'êng k'ang ching 孝成 (983) Hsiao ch'êng	賢 Hsien	賢寧 Hsien-ning 明扆 (小字) Ming-i	2nd s of C	–.–.948	13.3.969	13.10.982	保寧 Pao-ning 己巳	21.1.969 13.3.969
								乾亨 Ch'ien-hêng 己卯	31.1.979 17.12.979
F 聖宗 Shêng Tsung c. 10–17	文武大孝宣 (1031) Wên wu ta hsiao hsüan	隆緒 Lung-hsü	文殊奴 (小字) Wên-shu-nu	1st s of E	–.–.971	14.10.982	25.6.1031	¹統和 T'ung-ho 癸未	16.2.983 22.7.983
						9.	10.		
						³太平 T'ai-p'ing 辛酉	15.2.1021 18.12.1021	²開泰 K'ai-t'ai 壬子	26.1.1012 16.12.1012
G 興宗 Hsing Tsung c. 18–20	神聖孝章 (1101) Shên shêng hsiao chang	宗真 Tsung-chên	夷不董 I-pu-chin 只骨 (小字) Chih-ku	1st s of F	–.–.1016	25.6.1031	28.8.1055	景福 Ching-fu 辛未	26.1.1031 7.7.1031
								重熙 Ch'ung-hsi 壬申	14.2.1032 16.12.1032

(continued from page 94)

Liao shih and Wu tai shih retain A-pao-chi; the Chiu wu tai shih uses the Ch'ien-lung form 安巴堅 An-pa-chien.

9. Lu t'ing tsa chi (in Liao shih c.1 考證) says, 諱斡里 His name was Kuan-li; i.e. Tê Tsu's name.

10. For the problem of the first two Year Titles and for the dates of T'ien-hsien and Hui-t'ung see p. 91. T'ien-hsien (戊子 26.1.928) seems really to have been the first Year Title of T'ai Tsung.

1. Ta-t'ung is omitted in Wu tai shih c.73 and Chiu wu tai shih c.137. In this dynasty the Li tai ti wang nien piao puts each of the dates 926, 938, 947, 969, 979, 1021, 1075, 1111 one year earlier – 925, 937, &c., and has 1083 for 1085, 1119 for 1121, 1092 for 1095, and 1066 for 1065; cf. p. 91 above.

1.	2.	3.	4.	5.	6.	7.	8.	9.	10.
H 道宗 Tao Tsung	孝文 (1101) Hsiao Wên	洪基 Hung-chi	涅鄰 Nieh-lin — 查剌(小字) Ch'a-la	1st s of G	–.–.1032	28. 8.1055	12. 2.1101	[1] 清寧 Ch'ing-ning 乙未	31. 1.1055 9. 9.1055
						9.	10.		
						[4] 大安 Ta-an 乙丑	29. 1.1085 28.[2] 1.1085	[2] 咸雍 Hsien-yung 乙巳	8. 2.1065 8. 2.1065
c.21–26						[5] 壽隆 Shou-lung[3] 乙亥	8. 2.1095 26. 1.1095	[3] 太康 T'ai-k'ang[1] 乙卯	19. 1.1075 7. 1.1075
I —	「天祚 T'ien tso」 豫王 (1141) Yü Wang	延禧 Yen-hsi	延寧 Yen-ning — 阿果(小字) A-kuo	s of 順宗 Shun Tsung, s of H	–.–.1075[4]	12. 2.1101 — deposed 6. 9.1125	6. 9.1125	[1] 乾統 Ch'ien-t'ung 辛巳	31. 1.1101 2. 3.1101
						9.	10.		
c.27–30						[3] 保大 Pao-ta 辛丑	21. 1.1121 21. 1.1121	[2] 天慶 T'ien-ch'ing[5] 辛卯	10. 2.1111 26. 1.1111
J 宣宗 Hsüan Tsung[6] c.30	孝章 Hsiao Chang	淳 Shun	涅里 Nieh-li	gds of G	?–.–.1063	–.–.1122	–.5-7.1122	建福 Chien-fu 壬寅	9. 2.1122 —

1. *Conc. néom.* 525 and *Li tai ti wang nien piao* read 大康 Ta-k'ang.
2. The text, c.24, 3a, only says "this moon" (是月改明年), after mentioning 十二月乙未 (28.1.1085, the last day of the 12th moon), so fixing this date as not later than 28 January.
3. The *Ch'i tan kuo chih* and *Conc. néom.* read 壽昌 Shou-ch'ang; *Synchron.* p.360, Shou-ch'ang, *alias* Shou-lung; Mayers and *Chung kuo jên ming ta tz'ŭ tien*. Shou-lung only. None of these quote any authority, nor has the *Liao shih* any note on the question.
4. This year is given in c.27, 1a, 太康元年; but in c.30, 1a the death of T'ien tso Ti in 1125 at the age of 54 is recorded, and this would put his birth in 1072.
5. *Li tai ti wang nien piao* reads 天度 T'ien-tu, perhaps a misprint.
6. Hsüan Tsung, who was Emperor for a few months during the life of T'ien tso, called his brief usurpation 北遼 Pei Liao, or Northern Liao. The approximate date of his death (夏 summer) is taken from *Li tai ti wang nien piao*. The two following names are also recorded in *Liao shih* c.30 as having been set up, each with a Year Title, at this time: 秦王 Ch'in Wang (with the Empress 德 Tê as Regent), *hui* 定 Ting, — enthroned 1122, † ?1122; 德興 Tê-hsing 壬寅, 9.2.1122; — *hui* 雅里 Ya-li, *tzŭ* 撒鸞 Sa-luan, 2nd s of I, b. 1094, enthroned 1123, † ?1123; 神歷 Shên-li 癸卯, 29.1.1123.

Notes to the following *Ch'i tan kuo chih* Tables:

A. T'ai Tsu, 916: No Year Title is named here, but at the end of this section the total length of the dynasty (oddly made 215 or 229 years) is counted "from *ping-tzŭ* in Shên-ts'ê of T'ai Tsu" (自太祖神冊丙子); and the Annals begin: 神冊元年〔梁均王貞明二年〕是阿保機始自稱皇帝國人謂之天皇王以妻述律氏為皇后置百官建元曰神冊國號契丹.

I. T'ien tso Ti, 1121: Just before the record of Pao-ta the text reads, 戊戌天慶八年 (*i.e.* 1118), giving the equivalents 致和八年 and 天輔元年, but does not say what happened then! The year 1118 was 重和元年, but the change was not made till December, so that 致和 may show the use of contemporary sources.

[九主年譜 <u>Chiu chu nien p'u</u> in <u>Ch'i tan kuo chih</u>, 1.7b] Ch'i-tan (916-936; 1013–1065) : Liao (937-1012; 1066–1124)

1.	2.	3.	4.	5.	6.	7.	8.	9.	10.
A 太祖 T'ai Tsu	大聖 Ta shêng	億 I	阿保机 A-pao-chi (番名)	–	[-884]	. .916 稱帝	, 9.926 六.七	[神冊 Shên-ts'ê 丙子]	6, 2.916
								天贊 T'ien-tsan 辛巳	11, 2,921
B 太宗 T'ai Tsung	嗣聖 Ssŭ shêng	德光 Tê-kuang	耀屈 Yao-ch'ü (元名) [元名耀屈之]	2nd s of A	–	[10/11] 926 即位 [亡]	. ,947 十一.四	天顯 T'ien-hsien 丁亥	5, 2, 927
								會同 Hui-t'ung 丁酉	13, 2,937
C 世宗 Shih Tsung	天授 T'ien shou	阮 Juan	兀欲 Chi-yü (番名)	gds of A s of 東丹王 突欲 T'u-yü	–	, ,947	, ,951 四.九	天祿 T'ien-lu 戊申	13, 2,948
D 穆宗 Mu Tsung	天順 [T'ien shun	景[璟] Ching [後更名明]	述律 Shu-lü	1st s of B	–	, ,951	, ,968 十八.九	應曆 Ying-li 辛亥	9, 2,951
E 景宗 Ching Tsung	孝成 [孝] Hsiao ch'êng	賢 Hsien orig: 明記 Ming-chi		s of C	–	. .968	, ,982 九.十二	保寧 Pao-ning 戊辰	2, 2,968
								乾亨 Ch'ien-hêng 甲戌	26, 1,974
F 聖宗 Shêng Tsung	天輔 T'ien fu	隆緒 Lung-hsü		1st s of E	[-971]	. .983 [年十二即位] [c.7.1a =982]	[25, 6] 1031 十.六[三]	統和 T'ung-ho 癸未	16, 2,983
								開泰 K'ai-t'ai 癸丑	13, 2,1013
								太平 T'ai-p'ing 壬戌	4, 2,1022
G 興宗 Hsing Tsung	文成 Wên ch'êng	宗貞 Tsung-chêng [宗真 I-chên in c.9 7a, & in 世系之圖]	木不孤 Mu-pu-ku	8th s of F	[-1015]	, ,1031	,1055 二十三.八	景福 Ching-fu 壬申	14, 2,1032
								重熙 Ch'ung-hsi 癸酉	3, 2,1033
H 道宗 Tao Tsung	天福 T'ien fu	洪基 Hung-chi	–	s of G	–	, ,1055	, ,1100 六.10.	1 清寧 Ch'ing-ning 乙未	31, 1,1055
						9. 3 壽昌 Shou-ch'ang 乙亥	8. 2.1095	2 咸雍 Hsien-yung 乙巳	8, 2.1065
I –	天祚 T'ien tso	延禧 Yen-hsi	–	gds of H s of 秦王 元吉 Yüan-chi	–	, ,1101 deposed . ,1124	, ,1125 乙巳	乾統 Ch'ien-t'ung 辛巳	31, 1,1101
								天慶 T'ien-ch'ing 辛卯	10, 2,1111
								保大 Pao-ta※ 辛丑	21, 1.1121

完顏 Wan-yen 上京會寧 Hui-ning; 東京遼陽 Liao-yang; 北京大定 Ta-ting 西京大同 Ta-tung; 南京 (938), 燕京 (1012), 中都 (1153) 大興 Ta-hsing 金 Chin (28, 1, 1115)

1	2	3	4	5	6	7	8	9	10
A 太祖 (1125) T'ai Tsu c.2	應乾興運昭德定功仁明莊孝大聖武元 (1145) Ying ch'ien hsing yün chao tê ting kung jên ming chuang hsiao ta shêng wu yüan	旻 (1115) Min originally 阿骨打 (阿古達) A-ku-ta	—	2nd s of g	1, 8, 1068	–, ?12, 1113 — 28, 1, 1115 (as 皇帝)	19, 9, 1123	收國 Shou-kuo 乙未 天輔 T'ien-fu 丁酉	28, 1, 1115 28, 1, 1115 4, 2, 1117[1] 5, 1, 1117
B 太宗 T'ai Tsung c.3	體元應運世德昭功哲惠仁聖文烈 T'i yüan ying yün shih tê chao kung chê hui jên shêng wên lieh	晟 Shêng originally 吳乞買 (烏奇邁) Wu-ch'i-mai	—	4th s of g	–, –, 1075	27, 9, 1123	7, 2, 1135	天會 T'ien-hui 癸卯	29, 1, 1123 7, 10, 1123
C 熙宗 (1187) Hsi Tsung 閔宗 (1161) Min Tsung c.4	弘基纘武莊靖孝成 (1179) Hung chi tsan wu chuang ching hsiao ch'êng	亶 Tan originally 合剌 Ha-la	—	gds of A	–, –, 1119	8, 2, 1135	9, 1, 1150	天眷 T'ien-chüan 戊午 皇統 Huang-t'ung 辛酉	12, 2, 1138 7, 2, 1138 9, 2, 1141 21, 2, 1141
D — c.5	廢帝 Fei Ti 海陵郡王 (1162) Hai ling Chün wang (cancelled later) 煬 (1162) Yang	亮 Liang originally 迪古 Ti-ku	元功 Yüan-kung	2nd s of 遼王宗幹 Liao Wang Tsung-kan	–, –, 1122	9, 1, 1150	15, 12, 1161	天德 T'ien-tê 己巳 貞元 Chêng-yüan 癸酉 正隆 Chêng-lung 丙子	10, 2, 1149 11, 1, 1150 27, 1, 1153 21, 4, 1153 24, 1, 1156 23, 2, 1156
E 世宗 Shih Tsung cc.6-8	光天興運文德武功聖明仁孝 (1189) Kuang t'ien hsing yün wên tê wu kung shêng ming jên hsiao	雍 Yung originally 烏祿 Wu-lu	—	gds of A (s of 睿宗 Jui Tsung c. 69; c. 19, 1a)	–, –, 1123	27, 10, 1161	20, 1, 1189	大定 Ta-ting 辛巳	28, 1, 1161 28, 10, 1161[2]

金史 Chin shih c. 2–

1. 契丹國志 Ch'i tan kuo chih says 天慶八年, i.e. 1118.
2. Chin shih c.5, 10b, 丙午 (27, 10) .... 即皇帝位 .... 丁未 (28, 10) .... 大赦改元大定.

1.	2.	3.	4.	5.	6.	7.	8.	9.	10.
F 章宗 Chang Tsung cc. 9-12	憲天光運仁文義武神聖英孝 (1209) Hsien t'ien kuang yün jên wên i wu shên shêng ying hsiao	璟 Ying	麻達葛 Ma-ta-kê	gds of E (s of 顯宗 Hsien Tsung c.85; c.19,24)	31,8,1168	20,1,1189	29,12,1208	明昌 Ming-ch'ang 庚戌	7,2,1190 7,2,1190
								承安 Ch'êng-an 丙辰	1,2,1196 14,12,1196
								泰和 T'ai-ho 辛酉	5,2,1201 7,1,1201
G _ c.13	衛]紹王 (1216) Wei] Shao Wang	永濟 Yung-chi 允濟 Yün-chi	興勝 (小字) Hsing-shêng	7th s of E	—	29,12,1208	?11,9,1213	大安 Ta-an 己巳	7,2,1209 5,3,1209
								崇慶 Ch'ung-ch'ing 壬申	5,2,1212 5,2,1212
								至寧 Chih-ning 癸酉	24,1,1213 –,5/6,1213
H 宣宗 Hsüan Tsung cc.14-16	繼天興統述道勤仁英武聖孝 (1224) Chi t'ien hsing t'ung shu tao ch'in jên ying wu shêng hsiao	珣 Hsün originally 吾睹補 Wu-tu-pu	—	gds of E (1st s of Hsien Tsung c.85)	–,–,1163	22,9,1213	14,1,1224	貞祐 Chêng-yu 癸酉	24,1,1213 30,9,1213
								興定 Hsing-ting 丁丑	8,2,1217 9,10,1217
								元光 Yüan-kuang 壬午	13,2,1222 15,9,1222
I 哀宗 Ai Tsung cc.17-18	—	守緒 Shou-hsü 守禮 Shou-li 寧甲速 Ning-chia-su	—	3rd s of H	25,9,1198	15,1,1224 abdicated 8,2,1234	9,2,1234	正大 Chêng-ta 甲申	22,1,1224 22,1,1224
								開興 K'ai-hsing 壬辰	24,1,1232 11,2,1232
								天興 T'ien-hsing 壬辰	24,1,1232 5,5,1232
J _ c.18	末帝 Mo Ti	承麟 Ch'êng-lin	—	—	—	9,2,1234	9,2,1234		

1.	2.	3.	4.	5.	6.	7.	8.	9.	10.
K — cc.29,30	治平 (1328) Chih-p'ing 「泰定皇帝 T'ai ting Huang ti」	Yäsun tämur 也孫鐵木兒	—	1st s of Kammala 甘麻剌 (顯宗 Hsien Tsung), 1st s of Činkim	28,11,1293[1]	4,10,1323	15,8,1328	泰定 T'ai-ting 甲子	27,1,1324 3,1,1324
								至和 Chih-ho 戊辰	12,2,1328 7,4,1328
— cc.30,32	—	阿里吉八	—	1st s of K	—	–,10,1328 deposed 14,11,1328	—	天順 T'ien-shun 戊辰	12,2,1328 –,10,1328
L 文宗 Wên Tsung cc.32-36	聖明元孝 (1334) Shêng ming yüan hsiao[2]	Togh tämur 脫鐵木兒 圖帖睦爾	Jijagatu 扎牙篤 扎牙篤	2nd s of H	16,2,1304	16,10,1328 abdicated 26,2,1329	2,9,1332	天歷 T'ien-li 戊辰	12,2,1328 16,10,1328
M 明宗 Ming Tsung c.31	翼獻景孝 (1330) I hsien ching hsiao	Kušala 和世球 和世剌	Qutuγtu 忽都篤 護篤圖	1st s of H	22,12,1300	27,2,1329	30,8,1329		
L 文宗 Wên Tsung (continued)	see above					restored 8,9,1329		至順 Chih-shun 庚午	20,1,1330 25,5,1330
N 寧宗 Ning Tsung c.37	沖聖嗣孝 (1338) Ch'ung shêng ssŭ hsiao	Irinčinbal 懿憐質班 亦憐真班 亦璘真班 亦璘只班 etc.	—	2nd s of M	1,5,1326	23,10,1332	14,12,1332		
O — cc.38-47	順 (1370) Shun	Togh-an tämur 妥懽貼睦爾 妥歡帖睦爾	—	1st s of M	25,5,1320	19,7,1333 fled from Ta-tu 10,9,1368	23,5,1370	元統 Yüan-t'ung 癸酉	17,1,1333 15,11,1333
								[後]至元 [Hou] Chih-yüan 乙亥	25,1,1335 8,12,1335
								至正 Chih-chêng 辛巳	18,1,1341 18,1,1341

1. *Yüan shih* c.29,1a, where 十三年 is a mistake for 三十年; cf. c.30,10a, where the Emperor's age at his death is given as thirty-six.
2. The Tablet of Wên Tsung was removed from the Ancestral Temple in July 1340, – *Yüan shih* c.36,4b.

The Mongol Rulers

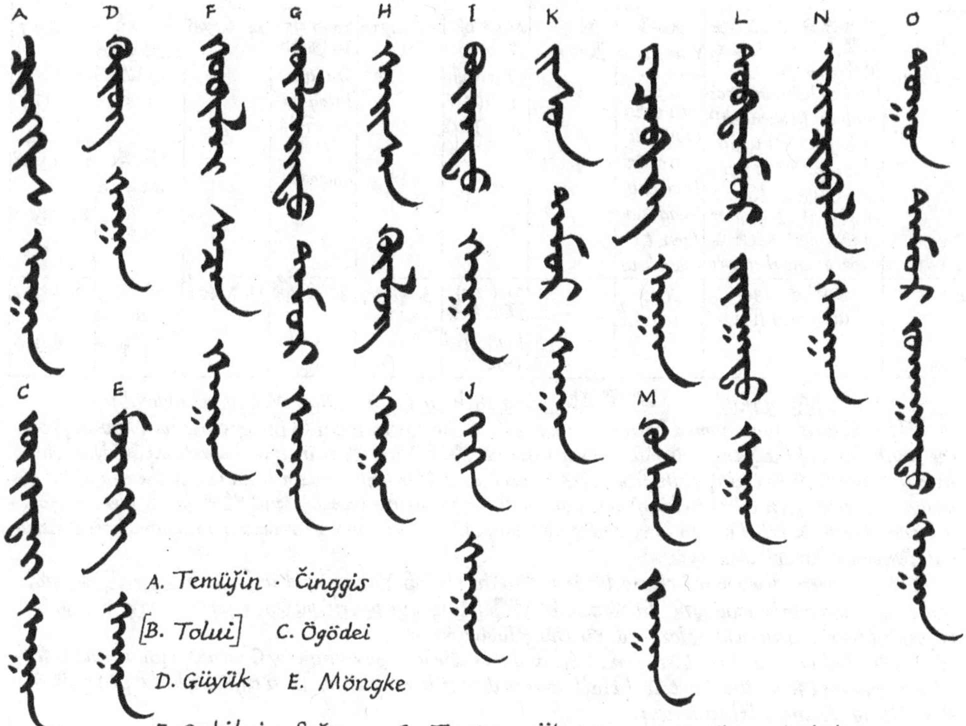

A. Temüǰin · Činggis

[B. Tolui] C. Ögödei

D. Güyük E. Möngke

F. Qubilai · Sečen G. Temür · Ölǰeitü H. Qaišan · Külük

[I. Buyantu J. Gegen] K. Yesün temür L. Tuq temür · J̌iyayatu

M. Qutuqtu N. *Irenǰibal O. Toqon temür

朱 Chu : 南京應天 Nan ching Yïng-t'ien : 北京順天 Pei ching Shun-t'ien[1] : 明 Ming

1.	2.	3.	4.	5.	6.	7.	8.	9.	10.
A 太祖 T'ai Tsu c. 1–3	開天行道肇紀立極大聖至神仁文義武俊德成功高(1538) K'ai t'ien hsing tao chao chi li chi ta shêng chih shên jên wên i wu chün tê ch'êng kung kao : 高(1398) Kao : 聖神文武欽明啓運俊德成功統天大孝高(1403) Shêng shên wên	元璋 Yüan-chang 2. wu ch'in ming ch'i yün chün tê ch'êng kung t'ung t'ien ta hsiao kao	國瑞 Kuo-jui	4th s of 朱世珍 Chu Shih-chên (仁祖 Jên Tsu)	–.–.1328	28. 7.1356 吳國公 Wu kuo kung 23. 1.1368 皇帝 Huang Ti	24. 6.1398	吳元年 First year of Wu 丁未 洪武 Hung-wu 戊申	31. 1.1367 –. 1.1367 20. 1.1368 23. 1.1368
B — c. 4	恭閔惠(1736) Kung min hui	允炆 Yün-wên[2]	—	2nd s of 懿文太子 I wên T'ai tzŭ[3]	5.12.1377	30. 6.1398[4]	13. 7.1402[5]	建文[6] Chien-wên 己卯	6. 2.1399 30. 6.1398

明史 Ming shih 明實錄 Ming shih lu (17th century MS. at Cambridge)

1. The dynasty was named Ming on 23.1.1368. The city (known to Europeans as Nanking) on the south bank of the Yang-tzŭ River was named 應天 Ying-t'ien in 1356, became the 南京 Nan-ching from 1368 to 1378, 京師 Ching-shih from 1378 to 1421, and Nan-ching again from 1421 to the end of the dynasty. The northern city (Peking) was named 北平 Pei-p'ing in 1368, and 順天 Shun-t'ien in 1403. It became the 北京 Pei-ching in 1403 and 京師 Ching-shih in 1421, though remaining nominally 行在 Hsing-tsai (temporary capital) until 1441.

2. 允炆 Yün-wên: the second character is written thus in the Shih lu and in Li tai ming jên..piao, 518, and seems always to be read wên. In 明史本紀補纂 Ming shih pên chi pu tsuan, 1777, ed. 1932, c. 4, 1a, it is printed 炆 p'u, and in the Harvard-Yenching Tables 炇 p'u.

3. I wên T'ai tzŭ was the eldest son of A, and this title was given him by C on 26.7.1402 when his tablet was removed from the Ancestral Hall, where it had been put by B in 1398 with the titles 興宗孝康 Hsing Tsung, Hsiao k'ang.

4. The Shih lu gives the date of accession as 21.6.1398.

5. This was the officially presumed date of death, and the supposed corpse, taken from the ruins of the burnt palace, was buried on 20.7.1402. But there were persistent rumours that B had escaped, perhaps disguised as a monk, and fear that he might re-appear seems to have haunted C to within a year of his own decease. The monk 溥洽 Pu-hsia, who had been imprisoned for more than ten years suspected of having connived at B's escape, was only released at the dying request of 姚廣孝 Yao Kuang-hsiao (+3.5.1418). And 胡濙 Hu Jung was employed for no less than 13 or 14 years (1407–16, 1419–23) in searching China for the fugitive; and it seems that the same fear was at least one of the reasons for the despatch of the missions of Chêng Ho and others to the Indian Ocean. In the story, as it stands in the Life of Hu Jung (Ming shih c. 169, 1b), we are not told what his final report was, but we may infer that he had reason to believe that B was then dead, as we read 至是疑始釋 "[the Emperor's] suspicion was then at last allayed". According to the Shih lu the Emperor left Peking on 29.8.1423 to attack Aruqtai (阿魯台), who had crossed the frontier on 25.8., reaching 宣府 Hsüan fu on 4.9.1423 and leaving again on 10.9. On 16.9. he reached 萬全 Wan-ch'üan in the wide region of Hsüan fu, and it was probably there that Hu Jung came to present his final report on 20.9.1423, and to offer objects of good omen (瑞光圖榔梅靈芝), which may have been his way of expressing that all was well without open allusion to the fugitive.

Another story is that as late as 1440 楊應(行)祥 Yang Ying-hsiang, a monk from Yün-nan, came to

1.	2.	3.	4.	5.	6.	7.	8.	9.	10.
C 成祖(1538) Ch'êng Tsu — 太宗(1424) T'ai Tsung c. 5–7	啓天弘道高明肇運聖武神功純仁至孝文(1538) Ch'i t'ien hung tao kao ming chao yün shêng wu shên kung ch'un jên chih hsiao wên: 體天弘道高明廣運聖武神功純仁至孝文(1424) T'i t'ien hung tao kao	棣 Ti 2. ming kuang yün shêng wu shên kung ch'un jên chih hsiao wên	—	4th s of A	11. 6. 1360	17. 7. 1402	12. 8. 1424	永樂 Yung-lo 癸未	23. 1. 1403 30. 7. 1402
D 仁宗 Jên Tsung c. 8	敬天體道純誠至德弘文欽武章聖達孝昭(1425) Ching t'ien t'i tao ch'un ch'êng chih tê hung wên ch'in wu chang shêng	高熾 Kao-chih 2. ta hsiao chao	—	1st s of C	16. 8. 1378	7. 9. 1424	29. 5. 1425	洪熙 Hung-hsi 乙巳	20. 1. 1425 7. 9. 1424
E 宣宗 Hsüan Tsung c. 9	憲天崇道英明神聖欽文昭武寬仁純孝章(1435) Hsien t'ien ch'ung tao ying ming shên shêng ch'in wên chao wu k'uan jên	瞻基 Chan-chi 2. ch'un hsiao chang	—	1st s of D	16. 3. 1399[1]	27. 6. 1425	31. 1. 1435	宣德 Hsüan-tê 丙午	8. 2. 1426 27. 6. 1425
F 英宗 Ying Tsung c. 10, 12	法天立道仁明誠敬昭文憲武至德廣孝睿(1464) Fa t'ien li tao jên ming ch'êng ching chao wên hsien wu chih tê kuang	祁鎮 Ch'i-chên 2. hsiao jui	—	1st s of E	29. 11. 1427	7. 2. 1435 — deposed 22. 9. 1449	23. 2. 1464	正統 Chêng-t'ung	18. 1. 1436 7. 2. 1435

Kuang-hsi pretending to be "the Chien-wên Emperor" (Ming shih c. 4, 4a). Although his age of more than 90 years proved him to be an impostor he was put in prison and died there four months later. A variant of this story makes B actually return to the palace, where he was identified by 吳亮 Wu Liang, an old eunuch who had always served him in his youth. "When Chien-wên met Wu he asked, 'Are you not Wu Liang?' Wu replied 'I am not'. Then Chien-wên narrated an old story, known only to Wu and himself, to prove his identity. Wu turned aside to weep, and the Emperor was recognized." For the details of this story I am indebted to Mr C. W. Wang the author of 奉天靖難記注 Fêng t'ien ching nan chi chu, 1948, and for references to the special authorities:– 屠叔方 T'u Shu-fang 建文朝野彙編 Chien wên ch'ao yeh hui pien, c. 1600; 趙士喆 Chao Shih-chê 建文年譜 Chien wên nien p'u, c. 1635, recently reprinted; 谷應泰 Ku Ying-t'ai 明史紀事本末 Ming shih chi shih pên mo, 1658, c. 17; 王世貞 Wang Shih-chêng in his 弇山堂別集 Yen shan t'ang pieh chi.

On the whole then it seems to be likely that B died, if not in 1402, at least before September 1423. (cf. P. Pelliot, T'oung-pao, 1935, pp. 303–6; T'ai tsung shih lu c. 9, 9b; 109, 10a, b; 126, 2b–7a;)

6. By a decree of 18. 7. 1402 this title was abolished and 1402 described as the 35th Hung-wu year – 洪武三十五年. Ming shih c. 5, 3b; T'ai tsung shih lu c. 9, 7a.

1. This exact date is found in the Shih lu (Hsüan tsung c. 1, 1a), as are some others also.

1.	2.	3.	4.	5.	6.	7.	8.	9.	10.
G — c. 11	恭仁康定景(9.1.1476) Kung jên kang ting ching 廢帝郕戾王 Fei Ti Ch'êng li Wang[1]	祁鈺 Ch'i-yü	—	2nd s of E	11. 9.1428	22. 9.1449 — deposed 24. 2.1457	14. 3.1457	景泰 Ching-t'ai 庚午	14. 1.1450 22. 9.1449
F ~ c. 12	~	~	~	~	~	restored 11. 2.1457	~	天順 T'ien-shun 丁丑	26. 1.1457 15. 2.1457
H 憲宗 Hsien Tsung c. 13-14	繼天凝道誠明仁敬崇文肅武宏德聖孝純(1487) Chi t'ien ning tao ch'êng ming jên ching ch'ung wên su wu hung tê shêng hsiao ch'un	見深(1457 Chien-shên originally 見濬 Chien-chün	—	1st s of F	9.12.1447	28. 2.1464	9. 9.1487	成化 Ch'êng-hua 乙酉	27. 1.1465 28. 2.1464
I 孝宗 Hsiao Tsung c. 15	達天明道純誠中正聖文神武至仁大德敬(1505) Ta t'ien ming tao ch'un ch'êng chung chêng shêng wên shên wu chih jên ta tê ching	祐樘 Yu-têng	—	3rd s of H	30. 7.1470	22. 9.1487	8. 6.1505	弘治 Hung-chih 戊申	14. 1.1488 22. 9.1487
J 武宗 Wu Tsung c. 16	承天達道英肅睿哲昭德顯功弘文思孝毅(1521) Ch'êng t'ien ta tao ying su jui chê chao tê hsien kung hung wên ssŭ hsiao i	厚照 Hou-chao	—	1st s of I	14.11.1491[2]	19. 6.1505	20. 4.1521	正德 Chêng-tê 丙寅	24. 1.1506 19. 6.1505
K 世宗 Shih Tsung c. 17-18	欽天履道英毅聖神宣文廣武洪仁大孝肅(1567) Ch'in t'ien lü tao ying i shêng shên hsüan wên kuang wu hung	厚熜 Hou-tsung 2. jên ta hsiao su	—	1st s of 祐杬 Yu-yüan, 2nd s of H	16. 9.1507	27. 5.1521	23. 1.1567	嘉靖 Chia-ching 壬午	28. 1.1522 27. 5.1521
L 穆宗 Mu Tsung c. 19	契天隆道淵懿寬仁顯大光武純德弘孝莊(1572) Ch'i t'ien lung tao yüan i kuan jên hsien wên kuang wu ch'un tê hung hsiao	載垕 Tsai-hou 2. chuang	—	3rd s of K	4. 3.1537	4. 2.1567	5. 7.1572	隆慶 Lung-ch'ing 丁卯	9. 2.1567 4. 2.1567

1. G had been Ch'êng Wang before and after his reign; Li was the posthumous title given in 1457.
2. Ming shih c.15,2a. But in Wu tsung shih lu c.1,1a, the day is 26.10.1491 (Hung-chih 4.9.24).

明 Ming

1.	2.	3.	4.	5.	6.	7.	8.	9.	10.
M 神宗 Shên Tsung c.20-21	範天合道哲肅敦簡光文章武安仁止孝顯(1620) Fan t'ien ho tao chê su tun chien kuang wên chang wu an jên chih hsiao hsien	翊鈞 I-chün	—	3rd s of L	4. 9.1563	19. 7.1572	12. 8.1620	萬曆 Wan-li 癸酉	2. 2.1573 19. 7.1572
N 光宗 Kuang Tsung c. 21	崇天契道英睿恭純憲文景武淵仁懿孝貞(1620) Ch'ung t'ien ch'i tao ying jui kung ch'un hsien wên ching wu yüan jên i hsiao chêng	常洛 Ch'ang-lo	—	1st s of M	.8/9.1582	28. 8.1620	26. 9.1620	泰昌 T'ai-ch'ang 庚申	?28. 8.1620[1] 10.10.1620
O 熹宗 Hsi Tsung c. 22.	達天闡道敦孝篤友章文襄武靖穆莊勤悊(1627) Ta t'ien shan tao tun hsiao tu yu chang wên hsiang wu ching mu chuang ch'in chê	由校 Yu-chiao	—	1st s of N	. .1605	1.10.1620	30. 9.1627	天啓 T'ien-ch'i 辛酉	22. 1.1621 1.10.1620
P — c.23-24	莊烈愍(1644) Chuang lieh min	由檢 Yu-chien	—	5th s of N	.1/2.1611	2.10.1627	25. 4.1644	崇楨 Ch'ung-chêng 戊辰	5. 2.1628 2.10.1627
q —	福王 Fu Wang	由崧 Yu-sung	—	? s of N	—	.10.1644	.1/1.1645	弘光 Hung-kuang 乙酉	28. 1.1645 —
r —	唐王 T'ang Wang	聿鍵 Yü-chien	—		—	.6/7.1645	.9/10.1646	隆武 Lung-wu 乙酉	28. 1.1645 .6/7.1645
s —	唐王 T'ang Wang	聿鐭 Yü-yü	—		—	.12.1646	. 1.1647	紹武 Shao-wu 丙戌	16. 2.1646 .12.1646
t —	永明王, or 桂王 Yung ming, Kuei Wang	—	—		—	.12.1646	.5/6.1662	永曆 Yung-li 丁亥	5. 2.1647 —

1. On 28.8.1620 it was decreed that T'ai-ch'ang should be the title of "the next year" (辛酉 1621). The Emperor died on 26.9.1620, and on 10.10.1620 his successor decreed that T'ai-ch'ang should be used for "this year after the eighth moon" (是年八月以後), perhaps including the 8th moon (28.8.—25.9.)—Ming shih c. 21, 6a; 22, 1a.

2. r was enthroned at 福州 Fu-chou, s at 廣州 Kuang-chou, t at 肇慶 Chao-ch'ing. The dynasty is commonly regarded as finally extinguished in 1662; but an Almanack dated 1676 (大明永曆三十年丙辰) is preserved in St Johns College at Cambridge. Synchronismes p. 456, from which q—t are taken, adds 淮王 Huai Wang (東武 Tung-wu 戊子) 1648, and 魯王 Lu Wang 1650, without further note. Conc. néom. p. 526, from which the names of r and s are also taken, omits Huai Wang and has "1645–1663 Lou Wang 魯王 (1.6.9 [=2.7.1645])".

愛新覺羅 Ai-hsin-chüeh-lo : 遼陽 Liao-yang 盛京(1625) Shêng-ching : 清 Ch'ing

1.	2.	3.	4.	5.	6.	7.	8.	9.	10.
a 肇祖 Chao Tsu	原 Yüan	都督孟特穆 Tu-tu-mêng-tê-mu	—	—	—	—	—	ᠠᡳᠰᡳᠨ ᡤᡳᠣᡵᠣ	Family Name Aisin gioro
b 興祖 Hsing Tsu	直 Chih	都督福滿 Tu-tu-fu-man	—	gt-gds of a	—	—	—		
c 景祖 Ching Tsu	翼 I	覺昌安 Chüeh-ch'ang-an	—	4th s of b	—	—	‥3.1583		
d 顯祖 Hsien Tsu	宣 Hsüan	塔克世 T'a-k'o-shih	—	4th s of c	—	—	‥3.1583		
e 太祖 T'ai Tsu	承天廣運聖德神功肇紀立極仁孝睿武端毅欽安弘文定業高 (1736) Chêng t'ien kuang yün shêng tê shên kung chao chi li chi jên hsiao jui wu tuan i ch'in an hung wên ting yeh kao:	努爾哈赤 Nu-êrh-ha-ch'ih [1]. 承——孝武 (1636): omit 端‥安 (1662): omit 欽安 (1723):	—	1st s of d	‥‥1559[2]	‥1583 17.2.1616	30.9.1626	天命 T'ien-ming 丙辰	17.2.1616
f 太宗 T'ai Tsung	應天興國弘德彰武寬溫仁聖睿孝敬敏昭定隆道顯功文 (1736) Ying t'ien hsing kuo hung tê chang wu k'uan wên jên shêng jui hsiao ching ming chao ting lung tao hsien kung wên: omit 敬……功 (1643): omit 敬‥定 (1662): omit 昭定 (1723):	皇太極 Huang-t'ai-chi originally 黃台吉 Huang-t'ai-chi	—	8th s of e	28.11.1592	20.10.1626	21.9.1643	天聰 T'ien-ts'ung 丁卯	16.2.1627
								崇德 Ch'ung-tê 丙子	7.2.1636 15.5.1636

P. Hoang, Tableau chronologique de la Dynastie de la Grande Pureté Ta-ts'ing 大清 in JNCBRAS Vol. 33, 1901, pp. 185–235. 清史稿 Ch'ing shih kao cc. 1–25.

1. The earlier titles are the same as the final one except for the parts omitted as indicated.
2. 東華錄 Tung hua lu c. 1, 19b gives this date as 13.11.1592 (an obvious mistake for 1559) and says he was 35 (= 25) when he was enthroned and 68 at his death.

愛新覺羅 Ai-hsin-chüeh-lo 順天(北京) Shun-t'ien (1644) 江寧(南京) Chiang-ning 清 Ch'ing (15,5,1636)

1.	2.	3.	4.	5.	6.	7.	8.	9.	10.
A 世祖 Shih Tsu	體天隆運定統建極英睿欽文顯武大德弘功至仁純孝章 (1736) T'i t'ien lung yün ting t'ung chien chi ying jui ch'in wên hsien wu ta tê hung kung chih jên ch'un hsiao chang:	福臨 Fu-lin 2 omit 定.. 極 and 顯武 (1661); omit 顯武 (1723):	—	9th s of f	15, 3, 1638	8, 10, 1643	5, 2, 1661	順治 Shun-chih 甲申	8, 2, 1644 7, 10, 1643
B 聖祖 Shêng Tsu	合天弘運文武睿哲恭儉寬裕孝敬誠信中和功德大成仁 (1736) Ho t'ien hung yün wên wu jui chê kung chien k'uan yü hsiao ching ch'êng hsin chung ho kung tê ta ch'êng jên:	玄燁 Hsüan-yeh 2 omit 中和 (24, 1, 1723):	—	3rd s of A	4, 5, 1654	7, 2, 1661	20, 12, 1722	康熙 K'ang-hsi 壬寅	18, 2, 1662 7, 2, 1661
C 世宗 Shih Tsung	敬天昌運建中表正文武英明寬仁信毅睿聖大孝至誠憲 (1799) Ching t'ien ch'ang yün chien chung piao chêng wên wu ying ming k'uan jên hsin i jui shêng ta hsiao chih ch'êng hsien:	胤禎 Yin-chêng 2 omit 睿聖 (1735):	–	4th s of B	13, 12, 1678	27, 12, 1722	8, 10, 1735	雍正 Yung-chêng 癸卯	5, 2, 1723
D 高宗 Kao Tsung	法天隆運至誠先覺體元立極敷文奮武孝慈神聖純 (1799) Fa t'ien lung yün chih ch'êng hsien chüeh t'i yüan li chi fu wên fên wu hsiao tz'ŭ shên shêng ch'un.	弘曆 Hung-li	—	4th s of C	25, 9, 1711	18, 10, 1735 abdicated 9, 2, 1796	7, 2, 1799	乾隆 Ch'ien-lung 丙辰	12, 2, 1736
E 仁宗 Jên Tsung	受天興運敷化綏猷崇文經武孝恭勤儉端敏英哲睿 (1820) Shou t'ien hsing yün fu hua sui yu ch'ung wên ching wu hsiao kung ch'in chien tuan ming ying chê jui.	顒琰 Yung-yen	—	15th s of D	13, 11, 1760	9, 2, 1796	2, 9, 1820	嘉慶 Chia-ch'ing 丙辰	9, 2, 1796 15, 9, 1795

清 Ch'ing

1.	2.	3.	4.	5.	6.	7.	8.	9.	10.
F 宣宗 Hsüan Tsung	效天符運立中體正至文聖武智勇仁慈儉勤孝敏成 (1850) Hsiao t'ien fu yün li chung t'i chêng chih wên shêng wu chih yung jên tz'ŭ chien ch'in hsiao ming ch'êng	旻寧 Min-ning	—	2nd s of E	16,9,1782	3,10,1820	25,2,1850	道光 Tao-kuang 辛巳	3,2,1821
G 文宗 Wên Tsung	協天翊運執中垂謨懋德振武聖孝淵恭端仁寬敏顯 (1862) Hsieh t'ien i yün chih chung ch'ui mu mou tê chên wu shêng hsiao yüan kung tuan jên k'uan ming hsien.	奕詝 I-chu	—	4th s of F	17[1],7,1831	9,3,1850	22,8,1861	咸豐 Hsien-fêng 辛亥	1,2,1851
H 穆宗 Mu Tsung	繼天開運受中居正保大定功聖智誠孝信敏恭寬毅 (1875) Chi t'ien k'ai yün shou chung chü chêng pao ta ting kung shêng chih ch'eng hsiao hsin ming kung k'uan i.	載淳 Tsai-ch'un	—	1st s of G	27,4,1856	11,11,1861	12,1,1875	同治 Tung-chih 壬戌	30,1,1862
I 德宗 Tê Tsung	同天崇運大中至正經文緯武仁孝睿智端儉寬勤景 (1909) T'ung t'ien ch'ung yün ta chung chih chêng ching wên wei wu jên hsiao jui chih tuan chien k'uan ch'in ching	載湉 Tsai-t'ien	—	2nd s of 奕譞 I-huan (醇王 Ch'un Wang, 7th s of F	14,8,1871	25,2,1875 The Empress Dowager 慈禧 Tz'ŭ-hsi was Regent except from 4,3,1889 till 19,9,1898	14[2],11,1908	光緒 Kuang-hsü 乙亥	6,2,1875
J —	—	溥儀 Pu-i	—	1st s of 載灃 Tsai-li, br of I	7,2,1906	2,12,1908 abdicated 12,2,1912		宣統 Hsüan-t'ung 己酉	22,1,1909

1. Ch'ing shih kao c. 20, 1a.
2. Bland and Backhouse, Annals and Memoirs of the Court of Peking, 1914, give the day as 13 (p. 439), 14 (p. 493), or 22 (p. 165), but 14 is the correct date according to Ch'ing shih kao c. 24, 30b.

北平 Pei-p'ing(1912), 南京 Nan-ching(1932), 重慶 Ch'ung-ch'ing(1938) : 中華民國 Chung hua min kuo

1. office	2. 姓 hsing	3. 名 ming	4. 字 tzŭ	5. birth	6. election	7. retirement	8. death
臨時大總統 lin shih Ta tsung t'ung	孫 Sun	文 Wên	逸仙 I-hsien 中山 Chung-shan	12.11.1866	1.1.1912	1.4.1912	12.3.1925
大總統 Ta tsung t'ung	袁 Yüan	世凱 Shih-Kai	慰亭 Wei-t'ing	. .1858	10.3.1912[1]	5.6.1916	5.6.1916
" " " " " "	黎 Li	元洪 Yüan-hung	宋卿 Sung-ch'ing	. .1864	7.6.1916	30.7.1917	. .1928
" " " " " "	馮 Fêng	國璋 Kuo-chang	華符 Hua-fu	. .1858	1.8.1917	30.9.1918	. .1919
" " " " " "	徐 Hsü	世昌 Shih-ch'ang		. .1858	10.10.1918[2]	2.6.1922	. .1936
" " " " " "	黎 Li	元洪 Yüan-hung	宋卿 Sung-ch'ing	. .1864	3.6.1922	30.9.1923	. .1928
" " " " " "	曹 Ts'ao	錕 K'un	仲珊 Chung-shan	. .1862	1.10.1923	2.11.1924	. .1938
臨時執政 Chih chêng	段 Tuan	祺瑞 Ch'i-jui	芝泉 Chih-ch'üan	. .1864	24.11.1924	20.4.1926	. .1936
國民政府主席 Kuo min chêng fu chu hsi	汪 Wang[3]	兆銘 Chao-ming	精衛 Ching-wei	. .1885	1.7.1926	30.9.1928	. .1944
國民政府主席 Kuo min chêng fu chu hsi	蔣 Chiang[4]	中正 Chung-chêng	界石 Chieh-shih 仃石 Ting-shih	31.10.1887	1.10.1928	30.1.1932	
ditto	林 Lin	森 Sên	子超 Tzŭ-ch'ao	11.2.1867	30.1.1932	1.8.1943	1.8.1943[5]
ditto	蔣 Chiang	as above	as above	as above	13.9.1943[6]		

1. *The Western kalendar was adopted as from 1.1.1912. The dates on this page, kindly supplied by Mr F. Y. Chai of the Chinese Embassy in London, are not always easily to be reconciled with the Historical Supplement to the 辭海 Tzŭ hai, 1937. This states on p. 48 that, on the abdication of the Hsüan-t'ung Emperor on 12.2.1912, Sun declined the office of Provisional President and that Yüan accepted it, and was elected President in 1913. In 1915 Yüan was elected Emperor and planned to be enthroned on 9.1.1916, and the year 1916 was to have the Year Title 洪憲 Hung-hsien. But after one or two postponements the project was abandoned on 22.3.1916, and Yüan seems to have been President until his death.*

2. *Tzŭ hai Suppl. p. 49 says that Hsü was elected in the North in 1918, while Sun became 大元帥 Ta yüan shuai in the South in 1917; and that Hsü declined to be President in 1919; and that Sun was elected President in 1921, taking office on 5.5.1921; but it adds, in agreement with the dates here given, that Hsü retired in 1922 and was succeeded by Li. It was a time of civil war and great confusion.*

3. *Tzŭ hai Suppl. does not mention Wang, who in 1942 was "usurping (偽 wei) President of the State Council" (Kuo min chêng fu chu hsi) at Nan-ching under the Japanese.*

4. *蔣介石先生 Chiang chieh shih hsien shêng, 1937, c. 1, 1a, says, "his first name (ming) was 周泰 Chou-t'ai, his school name 志清 Chih-ch'ing, his style (tzŭ) 瑞元 Jui-yüan; later he took his present names." On fol. 2b it says he was born on 15.9.1887 (meaning 31 October) by the lunar kalendar. The date 13.9.1943 is taken from "The Times" of 14.9.1943.*

5. *"The Times" of 3.8.1943 supplies Lin's dates. Tzŭ hai Suppl. p. 53 puts his election in 1931.*

6. *The Communists under 毛澤東 Mao Tsê-tung ended the Min kuo in October 1949, but Chiang still maintained independence in Formosa in November 1955.*

INDEXES

1. Temple Titles

2. Memorial Titles

When the Title consists of two words of which the first is 孝, the 孝 is omitted.
When the Title consists of more than eight words, the first two and last two are entered and the number of intervening words is noted.

MEMORIAL TITLES

MEMORIAL TITLES

3. Names (Hui)

4. Styles

STYLES

5. Family Names

6. Year Titles

YEAR TITLES

YEAR TITLES